The Mahābhārata

AN ENGLISH VERSION BASED ON SELECTED VERSES

The Mahābhārata

AN ENGLISH VERSION BASED ON SELECTED VERSES

CHAKRAVARTHI V. NARASIMHAN

Columbia University Press
NEW YORK

Prepared for the Columbia College Program
of Translations from the Oriental Classics
Wm. Theodore de Bary, Editor

The addition to the "Records of Civilization: Sources and Studies" of a group of translations of Oriental historical materials, of which this volume is one, was made possible by funds granted by Carnegie Corporation of New York. That Corporation is not, however, the author, owner, publisher, or proprietor of this publication, and is not to be understood as approving by virtue of its grant any of the statements made or views expressed therein.

Clothbound editions of Columbia University Press
books are Smyth-sewn and printed on permanent
and durable acid-free paper.

ORIGINALLY PUBLISHED AS
NUMBER LXXI OF THE
RECORDS OF CIVILIZATION: SOURCES AND STUDIES
EDITED UNDER THE AUSPICES OF THE
DEPARTMENT OF HISTORY, COLUMBIA UNIVERSITY

PUBLISHED IN INDIA, BURMA, CEYLON, NEPAL, SIKKIM,
BHUTAN, TIBET, AFGHANISTAN, AND EAST PAKISTAN BY
OXFORD BOOK & STATIONERY CO.

ISBN 0-231-02624-2 *Cloth*
ISBN 0-231-08321-1 *Paperback*

PRINTED IN THE UNITED STATES OF AMERICA
LIBRARY OF CONGRESS CATALOG CARD NUMBER: 64-10347

10 9 8 7

To My Father

Records of Civilization: Sources and Studies

Preface

The *Mahābhārata* was translated in a continuous narrative form by K. M. Ganguli and published by P. C. Roy towards the end of the last century. (This translation is now being reissued.) It was also translated, verse by verse, by M. N. Dutt between 1895 and 1901. There is a free translation, in verse, of selected episodes relating to the main theme of the epic (along with a similar work on the *Rāmāyaṇa*) by R. C. Dutt, first published in an Everyman's Library edition in 1910. The story of the *Mahābhārata* in free narrative form, written in English by C. Rajagopalachari, was published by the Bharatiya Vidya Bhavan in 1951.

The purpose of the present work is to give a straightforward narrative account of the main theme of the epic: the rivalry between the Pāṇḍavas and the Kauravas. To some extent Rajagopalachari's book has the same purpose; its secondary purpose may have been perhaps to remind the average Indian of the glories of his country's classical heritage, of which the most colossal literary work is the *Mahābhārata*. At any rate it had such an effect on me. I also found the book very useful in helping me to decide which episodes were relevant to the main theme of the epic.

The *Mahābhārata* is the longest epic in any language, consisting as it does of some 88,000 verses in its shortest recension. For the purpose which I had in mind, I have selected only those verses which relate to the main theme, and which help to provide a more or less continuous narrative. This process of selection reduced the total number of verses translated to some 4,000. These have been listed at the end of the book. The verses themselves have been translated so as to approximate closely to the meaning of the original Sanskrit, but they have not been translated literally or word for word. A literal translation, verse by verse, was attempted in the first instance, but it was found to be repetitive in many places, besides being somewhat discontinuous and difficult to read. For this reason, wherever such repetition occurs, it has been omitted; and many epithets of a repetitive nature have also been left out, e.g., "mighty-armed," "chastiser of enemies." Vocatives such as "O bull among men," or "O mighty king," have also been omitted.

In addition to the vocatives, I have also had to omit all reference to the narrator. As scholars are aware, there are three narrators mainly involved in the *Mahābhārata*. The first is the sage Sauti or Suta who related the story of the Mahābhārata (as narrated by Vaiśaṁpāyana at the court of King Janamejaya) to the sages assembled at the Naimiśa forest. Then there is Vaiśaṁpāyana himself, who is the narrator of the greater part of the work. Finally there is Sañjaya, the courtier and constant attendant of King Dhṛtarāṣṭra, who was given celestial sight by the sage Vyāsa in order that he might give the blind king a complete account of the fighting. Thus the main narrators are as follows: Sauti or Suta for the early chapters of Ādi Parva, Sañjaya for Bhīṣma, Droṇa, Karṇa, and Śalya Parvas, and Vaiśaṁpāyana for the rest.

It is well known that the *Mahābhārata* contains many episodes unconnected with the main theme, as well as extensive sections which are concerned mainly with teachings on ethics, polity, or philosophy. Under the scheme adopted for the present work, all these have had to be excluded. As a result I have regretfully had to leave out practically the whole of Śānti Parva and Anuśāsana Parva, which are most important from the didactic point of view.

Although the book has been arranged in chapters and paragraphs, each paragraph is a translation mainly of a group of connected verses. At the end of the book the chapters are correlated to the original Sanskrit so that the reader who wishes to refer to the original may be able to trace readily the relevant text.

Throughout I have, in general, referred to the principal characters by only one name, although they are referred to by a variety of names in different places in the original. At the end of the book will be found a list of these names, as well as certain Sanskrit words and phrases which it would have been tedious to translate repeatedly in the body of the book. Explanatory footnotes have thus been kept to the minimum.

A guide to the pronunciation of Sanskrit names, words, and phrases follows this Preface.

I believe that this is the first translation based mainly on the new Poona edition of the *Mahābhārata*, which is considered to be the most scholarly and authoritative of all. While the use of this text has the advantage of authority, it has certain disadvantages. For example, certain episodes in the *Mahābhārata* (which are well known in India) are not to be found in this edition.

Thus, in Chapter XXIII, there is a reference in other editions to a silent prayer that Draupadi addressed to Lord Kṛṣṇa when the wicked Duḥśāsana attempted to disrobe her in public. This reference is not to be found in the Poona edition (see footnote to Chapter XXIII).

Again, in Chapter XXV, there is a reference in other editions to the fact that the Sun-god gave Yudhiṣṭhira a copper vessel which would be inexhaustible. This episode is not mentioned in the Poona edition (see footnote to Chapter XXV).

In Chapter XXVI there is a reference in other editions to a curse pronounced on Arjuna by the heavenly nymph Ūrvaśī because he would not respond to her overtures while learning dancing from her in heaven. The curse made Arjuna a eunuch for a specified period, and as a result he spent a whole year in the court of Virāṭa as Bṛhannaḍā, the dancing master of Princess Uttarā. This episode too is not to be found in the Poona edition.

In Chapter LXIV there is a reference in other editions to Lord Kṛṣṇa's artificially causing darkness before the actual time of sunset in order to give a false sense of confidence to Jayadratha, thus facilitating his killing by Arjuna. This incident is also not referred to in the Poona edition.

I have used the Poona edition for the following Parvas which have already been published: Ādi, Sabhā, Āraṇyaka, Virāṭa, Udyoga, Bhīṣma, Droṇa, Karṇa, and Śānti. For the other Parvas, I have used the P. C. Roy edition.

This version is essentially a condensation of the main story of the epic, and not a literal translation. Even so, my work was greatly facilitated by the earlier translation of the epic, by K. M. Ganguli, in the form of a continuous narrative, and by M. N. Dutt's verse-by-verse rendering. Specifically, I have used the M. N. Dutt version as a stand-by for the entire epic with the exception of Bhīṣma Parva and Droṇa Parva, for which I have used the Ganguli translation. These earlier translations have made my work, especially the selection of verses for translation, much easier, and I wish to acknowledge my indebtedness to them.

My daughter Kanakalatha (now Mrs. J. Mukund) was of great help to me in compiling the glossary and entering diacritical marks throughout the text.

I would also like to acknowledge my gratitude to Miss Elisabeth L. Shoemaker of Columbia University Press, who went over the text at every stage of the publication of this book.

C. V. NARASIMHAN

Guide to Pronunciation

The examples for the pronunciation of such sounds as ṭ, ṭh, ḍ, ḍh, and ṛ are only approximate, as there are no exact equivalents in English.

a	as in *a*bate
ā	as in f*a*ther
ai	as in *ai*sle
au	as in h*ow*
b	as in *b*ear
bh	same sound aspirated
c	as in *ch*urch
ch	same sound aspirated
d	as in a*d*here
dh	same sound aspirated
ḍ	as in *d*umb
ḍh	same sound aspirated
e	as in pr*ey*
g	as in *g*un
gh	same sound aspirated
h	as in *h*um
ḥ	a symbol called visarga, pronounced like the h in *h*um
i	as in f*i*ll
ī	as in pol*i*ce
j	as in *j*ug
jh	same sound aspirated
k	as in *k*ill
kh	same sound aspirated
l	as in *l*ead
m	as in *m*ap
ṁ	stands for a nasal sound, in assonance with the consonant that follows
n	as in *n*udge
ṅ	as in si*ng*
ñ	as in si*n*ge
ṇ	as in mor*n*ing
ṅ	stands for a nasal sound, in assonance with the consonant that follows
o	as in *o*pen
p	as in *p*ear
ph	same sound aspirated
r	as in *r*ear
ṛ	as in *rhy*thm
s	as in *s*tand
ṣ	as in bu*sh*
ś	as in *s*ugar
t	as in en*t*rée (French)

th	same sound aspirated
ṭ	as in *t*ear
ṭh	same sound aspirated
u	as in f*u*ll
ū	as in r*u*de
v	as in i*v*y
y	as in *y*ellow

This system of transliteration, while following that generally used in scholarly works, differs somewhat from the conventional spelling of Sanskrit words in English. Its advantage is that it permits a much more exact pronunciation. Examples of some words in the more conventional transliteration, especially those that have found their way into English usage, are given in the list below for comparison with their transliteration here.

Conventional transliteration	*System adopted in text*
Achyuta	Acyuta
Ashvamedha	Aśvamedha
Bhishma	Bhīṣma
Chakra	Cakra
Dakshina	Dakṣiṇā
Dhritarashtra	Dhṛtarāṣṭra
Kashi	Kāśī
Krishna	Kṛṣṇa
Kshatriya	Kṣatriya
Lakshmi	Lakṣmī
Rishi	Ṛṣi
Shakti	Śakti
Shankara	Śaṅkara
Shiva	Śiva
Shringi	Śṛṅgī
Upanishad	Upaniṣad
Vaishya	Vaiśya
Vishnu	Viṣṇu
Vritra	Vṛtra
Yudhishthira	Yudhiṣṭhira

Table of Contents

Introduction

I

The *Mahābhārata* is admittedly the longest, and perhaps the greatest, epic poem in any language. According to its reputed author, the sage Vyāsa, it was intended to be a treatise on life itself, including religion and ethics (dharma śāstra), polity and government (artha śāstra), philosophy and the pursuit of salvation (mokṣa śāstra). In fact two of the longest books in the epic (Śānti Parva and Anuśāsana Parva) deal with these subjects.

The main theme of the epic, however, is the rivalry between the cousins, the Pāṇḍavas and the Kauravas, which culminates in the great battle of Kurukṣetra. (Their relationship is set out in the genealogical tables.) Apart from this, there are a number of episodes, fables, and myths either unconnected or indirectly connected with the main theme. These episodes contribute to the great length of the epic, which in its shortest recension consists of some 88,000 verses.

The story opens with the great snake sacrifice of King Janamejaya, great-grandson of Arjuna. At the conclusion of the snake sacrifice the sage Vyāsa, who is in a sense the grandfather of Arjuna, arrives, and Janamejaya wants to hear from him the history of the great battle between his ancestors and the Kauravas. The sage commands one of his disciples to narrate the history of the Pāṇḍavas and the Kauravas.

This history starts with King Śantanu of the Kuru race. The king rules at Hāstinapura and he has a son Devavrata by the river goddess Gaṅgā. The king falls in love with a maiden of the fishing community, Satyavatī, and pines for her. Devavrata comes to know of this and goes to the father of the maiden to seek her hand in marriage for his father. The father makes the condition that such issue as his daughter might bear to the king should succeed to the throne. Devavrata accepts this condition and, besides abdicating all his rights to the throne, takes a vow of celibacy for life so that no offspring of his might claim the throne and start a war of succession with the progeny of the fishergirl. The vow is so terrible that from that time Devavrata is known as Bhīṣma (the terrible).

Śantanu has two sons by Satyavatī, Citrāñgada and Vicitravīrya. Citrāñgada dies young and Vicitravīrya succeeds to the throne. Bhīṣma captures by force of arms the three daughters of the king of Kāśī to become the brides of Vicitravīrya. The first daughter, Ambā, declares her love for Śālva, the king of Saubha, and is therefore set free. Ambā however is rejected by Śālva, and from then on her only passion in life is to take revenge on Bhīṣma. She is reborn in the family of King Drupada as Śikhaṇḍī and is the instrument of Bhīṣma's downfall.

The other two princesses, Aṁbikā and Aṁbālikā, are wedded to Vicitravīrya, who however dies before having any issue by them. Thereupon, for the perpetuation of the dynasty, Satyavatī invokes the assistance of the sage Vyāsa. Through his grace the two princes, Dhṛtarāṣṭra and Pāṇḍu, are born.

In due course, Dhṛtarāṣṭra marries Gāṅdhārī, the daughter of the king of Gāndhāra. Since he was born blind, Gāndhārī perpetually goes about blindfolded in order that she may not excel her husband in any way. She gives birth to a hundred sons, the Kauravas, of whom the eldest is Duryodhana and the second Duḥśāsana. Her brother Śakuni is the evil genius of Duryodhana.

Pāṇḍu takes two wives, Kuṅtī and Mādrī. Kuṅtī, who is the aunt of Lord Kṛṣṇa, has been taught by the sage Durvāsa to invoke the gods to obtain offspring. She takes advantage of this advice even before her marriage and has a son, Karṇa, whose father is the sun god. To conceal her transgression, Kuṅtī abandons him at birth, and he is brought up by a charioteer. After Kuṅtī's marriage to Pāṇḍu, her husband is placed under a curse which restrains him from begetting children, and Kuṅtī's gift enables her to produce three sons,

Yudhiṣṭhira, Bhīma, and Arjuna, and to aid Mādri who has twin sons, Nakula and Sahadeva. The five brothers become known as the Pāṇḍavas. Pāṇḍu dies relatively young and Mādrī joins him on the funeral pyre, leaving her sons to the care of Kuṅtī.

The wise Vidura, a brother of Dhṛtarāṣṭra and Pāṇḍu, looks after the Pāṇḍavas and is the trusted counsellor of Dhṛtarāṣṭra. Bhīsma, too, is interested in the education of his grand-nephews and engages as their teacher the great archer Droṇa. Droṇa is anxious to take revenge on King Drupada, who was a classmate of his but subsequently disowned him, and Arjuna becomes his favourite pupil. In due course Droṇa conquers the kingdom of Drupada with the help of his pupils, especially Arjuna. In his turn Drupada craves vengeance against Droṇa, and prays for and obtains a son, Dhṛṣṭadyumna, who is destined to be the slayer of Droṇa.

When the heroes have completed their education there is a display of their skill and strength. In the course of the display Karṇa enters the lists and challenges Arjuna to a duel. He emulates every one of the feats of Arjuna. Duryodhana is so pleased with him that he makes him king of Aṅga and thus secures a valuable ally against the Pāṇḍavas.

Meanwhile, on account of his uncontrollable jealousy, Duryodhana attempts to kill the Pāṇḍavas in a fire, from which they escape with Vidura's help. After various adventures they reach the court of Drupada, who is looking for a suitable match for his daughter Draupadī. His son Dhṛṣṭadyumna announces his readiness to give away his sister to anyone who can perform a prescribed feat with a mighty bow. All the kings try their hands at this feat and fail, but Arjuna, who is pretending to be a Brāhmaṇa, is successful and wins the princess Draupadī. By the command of his mother, all five Pāṇḍavas marry the princess.

Thereafter Vidura advises Dhṛtarāṣṭra to seek a reconciliation with the Pāṇḍavas and the old king bestows on them a portion of the kingdom with the capital at Iṅdraprastha. After a while Arjuna goes on a pilgrimage, in the course of which he meets and falls in love with Lord Kṛṣṇa's sister Subhadrā. Encouraged by Kṛṣṇa, Arjuna takes her away from the city of Dvārakā and marries her.

After some years the Pāṇḍavas erect a magnificent palace at Indraprastha and perform a great sacrifice in connection with the coronation of Yudhiṣṭhira. This splendid event inflames the jealousy of Duryodhana, whose uncle Śakuni gives him the idea of challenging the Pāṇḍavas to a game of dice, in which he is adept. He knows of Yudhiṣṭhira's weakness for gambling and is confident that he can play upon it to Duryodhana's advantage. In the game which follows, Yudhiṣṭhira first loses all his wealth and then pledges his brothers and himself as stakes. After losing all, he stakes the princess Draupadī, who is also lost. Draupadī is insulted by Duḥśāsana, who attempts to disrobe her in the presence of the entire court. The effort fails because of a miracle and the abashed King Dhṛtarāṣṭra restores their kingdom to the Pāṇḍavas. Again they are challenged to a gambling match with the provision that the losers should spend twelve years in exile in the forest and the thirteenth year incognito. In due course Yudhiṣṭhira loses this match and goes with his brothers and Draupadī to the forest.

Somehow the Pāṇḍavas eke out twelve years of miserable life in the forest. In the course of these twelve years Arjuna, who is the offspring of Indra, the king of the celestials, visits Indra in heaven and acquires from him and from the other gods many wonderful weapons. There is also an episode in which Duryodhana is worsted in battle by the Gandharvas and is made a captive by them. The Pāṇḍavas rescue him from this plight.

The Pāṇḍavas then spend the last year of their exile incognito in the court of Virāṭa. The king's commander in chief, Kīcaka, conceives an uncontrollable passion for Draupadī and pursues her with such determination that Draupadī has to seek the protection of Bhīma, who kills Kīcaka in a hand-to-hand fight. At the end of the year the Pāṇḍavas are able to save the kingdom of Virāṭa from invasion by the Kauravas and others and the grateful king bestows his daughter, the princess Uttarā, on Abhimanyu, Arjuna's son by Subhadrā.

Thereafter, having spent the stipulated period of thirteen years in exile, the Pāṇḍavas are anxious to claim back their kingdom. At the same time they prepare for war in case they should not be able to regain their kingdom by peaceful means. Emissaries are exchanged.

In the first place Drupada's priest calls on Dhṛtarāṣṭra, who sends back as his emissary Sañjaya, not only to plead for reconciliation but also to ascertain the strength of the Pāṇḍavas. Sañjaya's mission is followed by an effort on the part of Lord Kṛṣṇa himself to secure the restoration of the Pāṇḍava kingdom by peaceful means. This effort fails because of Duryodhana's obstinacy, and both sides have to resort to war.

The fighting takes place on the historic plain of Kurukṣetra and lasts eighteen days. During the first ten days Bhīṣma is the supreme commander of the Kaurava forces, but on the tenth day he allows himself to be mortally wounded and for the next five days the preceptor Droṇa becomes the supreme commander. He is made to give up the fight by an untruth uttered by Yudhiṣṭhira to the effect that Aśvatthāmā (which is the name of Droṇa's son) has been slain. For the next two days Karṇa is the supreme commander, until he is slain by Arjuna. On the last day Śalya leads the Kuru host and is killed by Yudhiṣṭhira. During these eighteen days Abhimanyu, on the Pāṇḍava side, and all the Kauravas with the exception of Duryodhana are also killed.

Then Duryodhana takes refuge in a lake to which he is traced by the Pāṇḍavas and challenged to single combat. In the mace duel that follows between Duryodhana and Bhīma, Duryodhana is mortally wounded by a blow below the belt. That night three of Duryodhana's supporters, led by Droṇa's son Aśvatthāmā, slay the Pāṇḍava forces while they are fast asleep. The only survivors of this wholesale massacre are the five Pāṇḍavas themselves, Lord Kṛṣṇa, and Sātyaki.

Thus the Pāṇḍavas succeed to a devastated kingdom, over which Yudhiṣṭhira rules for fifteen years while Dhṛtarāṣṭra continues as the nominal king. Thereafter Dhṛtarāṣṭra retires to the forest, followed by Gāndhārī and Kuntī. While he is in the forest the sage Vyāsa contrives a wonderful reconciliation between the Pāṇḍavas and the Kauravas. Shortly afterwards the old king and the two queens are consumed in a forest fire.

Some twenty-one years later Lord Kṛṣṇa himself chooses to leave the world after all his kinsmen have been killed during a drunken orgy, and thereafter the Pāṇḍavas also decide to conclude their earthly existence. They proceed to the Himālaya mountains and one by one they all fall by the wayside, except for Yudhiṣṭhira. He is finally welcomed to Heaven by Indra but does not find his brothers and Draupadī there. At the same time he finds Duryodhana occupying an honourable place in Heaven. He then chooses to leave Heaven to look for his brothers and his queen "since Heaven is where my brothers and Draupadī are." By an illusion he is shown a view of them in hell along with Karṇa, but the illusion is soon lifted and he is reunited with them in Heaven. Since Heaven is a place where there is no room for malice, jealousy, or anger, the Pāṇḍavas and the Kauravas are finally reconciled.

II

The perennial appeal of the *Mahābhārata* consists, I believe, mainly in the fact that, although it is an epic of the exploits of heroes, it also reveals a very human story. The human beings who pass through its pages display frailty as well as greatness. Even Lord Kṛṣṇa, who is believed to be one of the incarnations of Viṣṇu himself, behaves as a human being. In fact, in Chapter LXXXVI he has explained why he must behave in this way.

The human failings of many of the characters are revealed in various situations. Thus the same Bhīṣma who relinquished his right of succession to a throne and took a vow of celibacy for life, in order that his father might be able to marry the woman of his choice, shows a strange indifference at the time of the gambling match, when Draupadī is insulted by Duḥśāsana. He rises again to his true stature when, after having fought the Pāṇḍavas for nine days, he reveals to them the means by which his own destruction can be brought about.

The old and blind King Dhṛtarāṣṭra is full of decent instincts, but extremely weak when dealing with his own son. He is ready to endow the Pāṇḍavas with a kingdom with its capital at Khāṇḍavaprastha after their marriage with Draupadī. Again, after the gambling match, in response to Draupadī's appeal, he restores to the Pāṇḍavas their freedom as well as their lost kingdom. When Duryodhana shows his obstinacy after the Pāṇḍavas have spent their thirteen years of exile, he pleads with him repeatedly but he cannot overrule his son because of his inherent weakness.

As his trusted counsellor, Vidura always speaks the truth as he sees it and is a true friend and well-wisher of the Pāṇḍavas. It is Vidura who saves the Pāṇḍavas from death in the prearranged fire at Vāraṇāvata. He is in fact the only one who has the courage to protest the insult to Draupadī when Duḥśāsana attempts to disrobe her. When the Pāṇḍavas are exiled to the forest he looks after their mother Kuṅtī, and when they have concluded their stipulated period of exile he tries very hard to see that justice is done to them. It is a great pity that his advice is not heeded by the old king or by his obstinate and jealous son.

Duryodhana, too, has courage and strength and the capacity to make friends and hold their loyalty. His generosity towards Karṇa at the beginning of the story makes him a friend for life. Repeatedly he shows his courage. At the same time he is short-sighted, stubborn, and unrelenting in his jealousy of the Pāṇḍavas, and completely regardless of any standard of justice or fairness in his dealings with them. When the Pāṇḍavas say they would be contented with five villages, he says that he will not give them even as much land as could be covered by the point of a pin. Badly advised as he is by his uncle Śakuni and by Karṇa, he makes inevitable the great fight with the Pāṇḍavas and thus brings about the extinction of his whole race.

Karṇa's generosity is legendary and his charity knows no bounds. He feels so indebted to Duryodhana for making him the king of Aṅga that thereafter all attempts by his own mother Kuṅtī and by Lord Kṛṣṇa to wean him away from his loyalty to Duryodhana prove futile. When Iṅdra comes to beg of him the earrings and armour with which he was born and which confer immortality on him, he is ready to give them away even though he is warned of the consequences by his own progenitor, Sūrya the Sun-god. However, he is not only generous to a fault, but also excessively proud, and in the end he facilitates his own downfall by refusing to heed the advice of his charioteer Śalya.

On the Pāṇḍava side Yudhiṣṭhira is supposed to be the embodiment of virtue and truth, although he is not without his share of human frailty. He shows immense fortitude in the face of adversity and demonstrates his freedom from malice and anger against even his worst enemies. Thus, for example, when Duryodhana and his followers are made captives by the Gaṅdharvas, Yudhiṣṭhira sends his brothers to free them. Again, towards the very end of the epic he shows his utter disregard for the pleasures of Heaven if they involve separation from his brothers and from Draupadī. At the same time, in spite of his devotion to truth he is persuaded to tell a falsehood in order to bring about the defeat and death of Droṇa. His weakness for gambling is so great that he not only throws away his kingdom but even stakes his brothers and his own queen, subjecting them to insults besides delivering them into bondage.

Bhīma is, relatively, a simpleton. Possessed of immense physical strength, he is also quick to take offence. When Duḥśāsana molests Draupadī he takes a terrible vow that he will drink the blood from his breast. Draupadī knows how easy it is to play upon him and it is to him she turns when she is pursued by the lustful Kīcaka, and again when all her sons are killed by Aśvatthāmā. His own preceptor, Balarāma, cries "Shame!" when he finally fells Duryodhana by a blow below the belt.

Arjuna is a great warrior and the greatest archer of them all. In episode after episode he reveals his skill, and is applauded most when he provides his grandsire, the dying Bhīṣma, with a pillow of arrows and a drink of spring water. At the same time his fickleness is shown in many episodes, of which his marriage with Subhadrā is only one instance. In spite of strength and skill as a warrior, he is given to self-doubt and introspection from which he has to be aroused again and again by Lord Kṛṣṇa, who is literally the pivot around whom the whole story revolves.

Kṛṣṇa is the trusted guide, philosopher, and friend of the Pāṇḍavas. It is to him that Yudhiṣṭhira turns for advice when he wishes to perform the great sacrifice. It is he who visits the Pāṇḍavas during their exile in the forest and consoles them. From the beginning of the 'Udyoga Parva' he dominates the story. First he goes on a mission to bring about peace and reconciliation between the Pāṇḍavas and Kauravas. When this mission is defeated by Duryodhana's obduracy, he helps the Pāṇḍavas in all possible ways to gather their forces. As Arjuna's charioteer he rouses him from the mood of despondency and introspection and his teachings on this occasion are enshrined in the Bhagavad-Gīta. It is he who neutralizes the irresistible Śakti weapon of Karṇa by sacrificing Ghaṭotkaca. He is responsible for persuading Yudhiṣṭhira to tell a lie which has the effect of so discouraging Droṇa that he gives up the fight. Again it is Kṛṣṇa who suggests to Bhīma that the only way to defeat Duryodhana in the duel between the two is by a blow on the thigh. In the end he is cursed by Gāṅdhārī and is killed by a hunter after all his kinsmen have been killed in a drunken orgy.

Ruskin said of Shakespeare that he has no heroes but only heroines. In the *Mahābhārata* there are many heroes: they may have their failings but they also rise to great heights. It is, however, very difficult to find a true heroine in these pages. Satyavatī is just a scheming mother who is anxious to secure the kingdom for her progeny at all costs. Kuṅtī is a weak character who experiments with the power which the sage Durvāsa bestows on her to invoke the gods for the purpose of having offspring even before she is married. Thereafter she gives up her own first-born son Karṇa rather than let her transgression become known. Only towards the very end of the epic does she show some strength of character when she decides to retire into the forest along with Dhṛtarāṣṭra and Gāṅdhārī.

Unlike Kuṅtī, Gāṅdhārī emerges as a strong character who makes hardly one false gesture or one unworthy remark throughout the epic. She lives through life blindfolded in order that her husband, who is born blind, may not feel a sense of inferiority. She repeatedly urges her son Duryodhana to make peace with the Pāṇḍavas. Even when all her hundred sons have been killed, she is willing to forgive the Pāṇḍavas who were responsible for their death. However, she cannot forgive Kṛṣṇa because she believes that but for his indifference the lives of her sons could have been saved.

In a sense the heroine of the epic is Draupadī, but from the beginning she is subjected to misfortunes which make her character seem somewhat harsh because of her continuous cries for vengeance. She is the victim of the bully Duḥśāsana when in his weakness Yudhiṣṭhira gambles her away. There is a tradition (to which the Poona edition of the epic does not give support) that she refused to tie in a knot her long tresses, by which Duḥśāsana dragged her to the middle of the court, until he was killed. Because of her beauty she becomes the victim of the sinful Kīcaka and, when he insults her in public in the court of King Virāta, she cannot rest until she succeeds in having him killed by Bhīma. Again, when Aśvatthāmā kills her five sons in the course of one terrible night, she appeals to Bhīma who takes off after the fleeing Aśvatthāmā to satisfy her desire for revenge. When the Pāṇḍavas in the end begin their long journey to the other world she is the first to fall because she is the frailest of them all.

Apart from these characters, it is noteworthy that the great battle at Kurukṣetra starts with good intentions and the adoption of a code of fair fighting. As the fighting progresses and increases in its intensity this code is slowly forgotten, and in the end hardly any of it is left. In fact, Duryodhana's charge sheet against Lord Kṛṣṇa in Chapter LXXIV is difficult to answer and Kṛṣṇa himself admits that he resorted to unfair means in order to gain a fair objective.

Throughout the epic there are episodes of unnecessary violence, not only violence in the physical sense but also violence to all human feelings as, for example, when Bhīma fulfils his terrible vow of drinking the blood of Duḥśāsana. At the same time it can be maintained that while there is so much preoccupation with violence and revenge, the essential theme of the epic is really peace and reconciliation. Three missions are exchanged and every effort is made to avert war between the Pāṇḍavas and the Kauravas. It is only when all such efforts have been exhausted that there is the ultimate resort to force.

As for reconciliation, the central episode from this point of view is Chapter LXXXIX in which, by the grace of the holy Vyāsa, the dead heroes emerge from the sacred Gaṅgā "free from all animosity and pride, anger and jealousy." . . . "Son met with father or mother, wife with husband, brother with brother, and friend with friend." At last "they renounced all enmity and became established in friendship." The same element of reconciliation is repeated in Chapter XCVII, when the warriors meet in Heaven where there is no rancour or malice.

This emphasis on the theme of peace and reconciliation is natural and understandable, because it is only a reflection of the hallowed Indian benediction: "Peace, peace, peace!" (Oṁ, Śāntiḥ, śāntiḥ, śāntiḥ!). It may also be said to have a special application to our troubled times, when (like the Pāṇḍavas and the Kauravas) great nations vie with each other in lining up alliances and mastering the science of missilery. But, as the Pāṇḍavas realized even before the fighting began, there is a universal lesson for all to read, which is spelt out by Yudhiṣṭhira in Chapter XL: "In all cases, war is evil. Who that strikes is not struck in return? Victory and defeat, O Kṛṣṇa, are the same to one who is killed. Defeat is not very much better than death, I think; but he whose side gains victory also surely suffers some loss."

The Mahābhārata

As the sacred ocean and the snow-clad mountains are both regarded as mines of precious gems, so is this *Mahābhārata*.

Svarga-Ārohaṇika Parva, V, 62

Ādi Parva

I

At one time there lived a king, named Parikṣit, born in the race of the Kauravas.[1] Like his great-grandfather, Pāṇḍu, he was immensely strong, a splendid archer, and fond of hunting. While engaged in hunting one day, he shot a deer with an arrow, and went in pursuit of the wounded animal. The deer led the king deep into the forest where, tired and thirsty, he came upon an ascetic. Hastening toward him, the king said, "O Brāhman, I am King Parikṣit, the son of Abhimanyu. Did you see where the deer I wounded went?"

The sage, whose name was Śamīka, was observing the vow of silence, and did not reply. Angered by his silence, the king took up a dead snake with the end of his bow and placed it around his neck. The sage did not attempt to stop the king from doing so, nor did he protest. Thereupon the king's anger vanished, and he went away to his capital, leaving the sage as he was.

The sage had a young and bright son named Śṛṅgī, who was very austere and a great observer of vows, but short of temper and difficult to please. As he was coming home one day, his companion Kṛśa teased him about the dead snake on his father's body. On hearing this, Śṛṅgī was overcome by anger, and he pronounced a curse: "Whoever has placed a dead snake on the shoulder of my lean old father, even if he be a king, has committed a crime. He has insulted the Brāhmaṇas and tarnished the fame of the Kuru race. Within

[1] Actually, Parikṣit was a descendant of the Pāṇḍavas. The expression "Kuru race" or "Kauravas" is used here and elsewhere in a generic sense, to include the Pāṇḍavas.

seven days he shall die. Bound by my words, Takṣaka, the king of the serpents, shall cause his death."

Having thus cursed the king, Śṛṅgī went to his father, and saw him with the dead snake still on his body. The sight aroused his anger once again. Weeping with grief, he told his father, "Angered by the insult to you, I have cursed the miscreant, King Parikṣit. That unworthy Kuru richly deserves my curse. Within seven days the serpent-king, Takṣaka, will kill the sinner."

Śamīka said to his irate son, "My child, I do not approve of your act. We live in the king's domains. He is our rightful protector, and therefore we should not mind his faults. O my son, being a man of peace, I shall do what lies in my power to redress the situation. I shall send a message to the king, to tell him, 'O king, my son, who is a mere child and of immature intellect, was angered by your act of disrespect to me, and has cursed you.' "

Accordingly that strict observer of vows, the great sage Śamīka, moved by pity, sent a disciple named Gauramukha, a young man of good manners, to King Parikṣit, with instructions to inquire first about the king's welfare and then to give him the message, which he did.

When he heard of the terrible curse, the king recalled his own sinful act, and felt extremely penitent. However, he grieved not so much over his impending fate as over his act of disrespect to the sage. Giving leave to Gauramukha to depart, he said, "Let the holy one again be gracious to me!"

As soon as Gauramukha had left, the king anxiously consulted all his ministers. Then, aware as he was of all truths, he caused a palace to be erected on a pillar,[2] which could be properly guarded. As an additional precaution the palace was surrounded by physicians with medicines and by Brāhmaṇas well versed in charms. Thus protected, the king discharged all his royal duties, surrounded by his ministers.

Meanwhile, impelled by Śṛṅgī's curse, the snake Takṣaka started on his errand. On his way to Parikṣit, he heard that the king was well

[2] Presumably a raised platform, to facilitate security and protection.

guarded, protected by charms, and provided with medicines which were antidotes to all poisons. Having concluded that the king should be deceived by Māyā and considered what device should be used for this purpose, Takṣaka sent some snakes in the guise of hermits with offerings of fruit, leaves, and water. The king received the hermits, accepted their offerings, and then gave them leave to depart.

When the snakes in hermit guise had left, the king said to his counsellors, "Let us together eat these excellent fruits brought by the hermits." Then from the fruit that the king was holding emerged an ugly copper-coloured insect with black eyes. Holding the insect, the king said to his ministers, "The sun is setting, and I no longer fear the poison. Let this insect, becoming Takṣaka, sting me, so that the curse of the sage may come true and I may expiate my sinful act." So saying, the king smiled and placed the insect on his neck, soon lost consciousness, and passed away.

When the king had been killed by the poison of Takṣaka, the ministers performed his last rites, with the help of the royal priest and the holy Brāhmaṇas. All the residents of the capital met and placed Janamejaya, the young son of the deceased king, on the throne. Although Prince Janamejaya was only a boy, he was intelligent and wise beyond his years. With the help of his ministers and priests, he ruled his kingdom wisely and well, like his great-grandfather [Yudhiṣṭhira].

II

Janamejaya said to his ministers, "You all know what happened to my illustrious father, and how he met his death. When I have heard his story from you, I shall do what is proper." Responding to his request, the virtuous and wise ministers narrated the story of Śṛṅgī's curse and Parikṣit's end.

In great sorrow, Janamejaya said, "I have heard from you the account of my father's journey to heaven. I am now determined to wreak vengeance on his tormentor the wretch Takṣaka." When the illustrious king said this, the ministers expressed their approval. Janamejaya then carried out his determination to perform a snake sacrifice.

The snake sacrifice was duly begun by sacrificial priests who were experts in their respective duties and knew all the rites to be performed. Clad in black, their eyes red from the smoke, they poured offerings in the sacrificial flame, uttering incantations. Then they began to invoke the names of the snakes whose hearts trembled in fear as they were irresistibly impelled to fall into the fire. While they fell, as though paralysed, into the flames, the snakes called piteously to one another.

At this stage, the sage Āstīka,[1] who was the son of Takṣaka's sister, was persuaded to intervene. Finally, when the serpent king Takṣaka himself was about to fall into the sacrificial fire, Āstīka said: "O Janamejaya, grant me a boon. Stop this sacrifice, and let no more snakes fall into the fire." Janamejaya, unhappy at this request, replied, "O illustrious sage, I offer you gold or silver or kine, or anything else you may wish. But let my sacrifice go on." Āstīka said, "O king, I do not ask you for gold, silver, or kine. I only ask that this sacrifice be stopped, so that my maternal relatives may live."

Thereupon, all those assembled, men learned in the scriptures, advised the king with one voice, "Let the Brāhmaṇa receive the boon." Accordingly the king granted Āstīka's request, whereupon loud acclamations of joy rent the sky. The snake sacrifice of Janamejaya came to an end, and the king too was well pleased.

When he heard that Janamejaya had begun the snake sacrifice, the learned sage Kṛṣṇa Dvaipāyana [Vyāsa] went to him. Accompanied by his disciples who were learned in the scriptures, the illustrious man entered the area where the royal sage Janamejaya was performing the sacrifice. There he saw the king seated, with his numerous courtiers around him, like Indra among the celestials.

With hands joined in prayer, amid all those assembled in court, Janamejaya addressed Vyāsa, the best of the Brāhmaṇas, thus, "O Brāhman, with your own eyes you saw the acts of the Kurus and the Pāṇḍavas. I desire to hear their history from you, to learn the cause

[1] How Āstīka came to be related to Vāsuki, Takṣaka, and the snake family is told in detail in another section, the 'Āstīka Parva,' which has not been translated here.

of the quarrel between them, and to know why my ancestors, whose sense was surely clouded by fate, engaged in that great battle. O best of Brāhmaṇas, tell me."

Vyāsa said to his disciple Vaiśampāyana, who was sitting beside him, "Pray repeat, exactly as I have told it to you, the story of the ancient quarrel between the Kauravas and the Pāṇḍavas." Commanded thus by his preceptor, that best of Brāhmaṇas recited in full detail to the king, and to all the warriors and courtiers assembled, the story of the quarrel between the Kauravas and the Pāṇḍavas, which destroyed the kingdom.

III

Pratīpa was a king who did good to all creatures. He reached the source of the river Gaṅgā and spent many years there in penance, along with his wife, so that they might be given a son. At last a son was born to them in their old age, and his name was Mahābhiṣa. He was also called Śaṅtanu, because he was born after his father had controlled his passions.

Śaṅtanu knew that one could conquer the world only by one's own virtuous deeds, and accordingly devoted himself to virtue. When he came of age, his father Pratīpa told him, "O Śaṅtanu, some time ago a girl came to see me, intent on your well-being. If that beautiful and celestial damsel should meet you secretly and ask you to marry her, do not turn her down. Nor should you judge the propriety of anything she does. Do not ask her who she is or to whom she belongs, but take her as your consort. Such is my wish." Having thus instructed his son Śaṅtanu and crowned him as his successor, King Pratīpa entered the forest.

Śaṅtanu, most intelligent of kings, famous on earth as a bowman, was fond of hunting and passed much of his time in the forest. There one day he met a lovely girl, with a figure as radiant as Lakṣmī's. The king was astonished, delighted, and enchanted by her. He gazed steadily at her in rapture as though to drink her charms, but was not satisfied. The maiden too, seeing that brilliant king walking towards her, felt love for him welling up in her heart, and yearned to look at him.

Then the king gently spoke these sweet words to her: "O dazzling, slender-waisted girl, whether you are a lady of the Devas or Dānavas, of the Gaṅdharvas or the Apsaras, of the Yakṣas or the Nāgas, whether you be human or celestial, I ask you to be my wife." When she heard these sweet words of the smiling king, that flawless maiden remembered her promise to the Vasus.

She replied to the king, evoking a thrill of pleasure: "O lord of the earth, I shall marry you in obedience to your wish, but on one condition. Whatever I may do, whether it pleases you or not, you shall leave me alone, and you must not speak harshly to me. As long as you observe this rule, I shall stay with you. But I shall leave you the moment you interfere with me, or reproach me with harsh words." The king said to her, "So be it!" and the maiden was overjoyed.

Having married her, King Śaṅtanu lived happily with her in love and joy. True to his promise, he asked her no questions. He was immensely pleased with her beauty, magnanimity of conduct, and attention to his comforts.

That celestial lady was Gaṅgā, river of the three courses,[1] who had assumed a human form of exceeding fairness and beauty and now lived happily as the wife of Śaṅtanu. Because of her virtues, she had been rewarded with that lion among kings, brilliant as Iṅdra. For his part, the king was so captivated by her goodness and her ardour for him that months, seasons, and years rolled by without his even being conscious of the passage of time.

While he thus sported with her as he wished, she bore him seven sons, all looking like celestials. As soon as each child was born, she threw him into the waters of the Gaṅgā, saying, as she did so, "This is my wish." The king naturally could not approve of such conduct, but he did not speak a word of reproof to her for fear of her leaving him. When the eighth son was born, the king wished to keep his child, and said sorrowfully to the smiling Gaṅgā, "Do not kill this child. Who are you and to whom do you belong? Why do you thus

[1] Celestial, terrestrial, and subterranean.

torture your own sons and kill them? Do not incur the greatest of sins and stand condemned for it."

Gaṅgā said: "As you wish to have a son, I shall not kill this child. You have become the most illustrious of fathers. But the time has come for me to end my stay with you according to our past compact. I am Gaṅgā, the daughter of Jahnu, worshipped by all the great sages. I have lived with you so long to accomplish the design of the celestials. These eight sons I bore you were the illustrious and radiant Vasus, who were forced to assume human form because of the curse of the sage Vasiṣṭha. There was no one on earth who wished to be their progenitor, nor was there any among women who could be their mother. Hence I assumed human form and gave birth to them. You have conquered the whole world by becoming the father of the eight Vasus. My compact with the celestial Vasus was that I would release them from their human birth as soon as they were born. Thus the Vasus have got rid of the curse of the illustrious sage Vasiṣṭha. Bless you! I leave you now. I have kept my promise to the Vasus by living with you this long. I wish this child of mine to be known by the name of Gaṅgādatta."

Thereafter the river goddess disappeared, taking her son with her. That son of Śaṅtanu came to be known as Gāṅgeya, also as Devavrata. He excelled even his father in his many qualities. Handsome like his father, and like him too in conduct, habits, and learning, he became expert in the use of all weapons, celestial as well as ordinary, and was very strong and active, a great hero and car-warrior.

IV

Once Śaṅtanu wounded a deer in the forest and pursued it along the river Gaṅgā. When he saw that there was very little water flowing in the river, he pondered, "Why is the river not flowing freely today as in the past?" Looking for the cause, the king came across a well-built youth of pleasing appearance and great strength, who had checked the free flow of the river Gaṅgā by a barrage of sharp arrows, as Iṅdra might have done with his celestial weapons. The king, who was astonished to see the superhuman feat of the youth, had seen his son only once, a few minutes after his birth; he could not therefore recollect his features so as to identify the lad as his son. As soon as he saw his father, the youth resorted to Māyā and vanished before his very eyes.

Seeing this miracle, the king believed the boy to be his own son, and said to the river Gaṅgā, "Show me the child." Assuming a supremely beautiful form, Gaṅgā emerged with the youth, holding him by his right hand. Though he had seen her before, Śaṅtanu could not recognize that beautiful lady, adorned with ornaments and dressed in fine robes. Gaṅgā then said, "O king, this is the eighth son I bore you. Take him home with you. This hero has studied all the scriptures under Vasiṣṭha; he is expert in the use of all weapons, and the equal of Iṅdra himself in battle; he knows all the weapons that were known to the famous and invincible Paraśurāma. Take home with you this heroic son I bore you; he is a great archer and well versed in the kingly duties."

Thus adjured by her, Śaṅtanu took his son, brilliant as the sun, and proceeded to his own capital, which was like the city of Iṅdra. Having reached the city, Śaṅtanu felt very pleased that all his wishes had been fulfilled. He then crowned and anointed his son as heir apparent. The illustrious Devavrata pleased his father, the other members of the royal family, and all the king's subjects by his exemplary conduct. Thus the mighty king lived happily with his son for four years.

One day the king went to a forest on the banks of the river Yamunā. There he smelt a sweet odour, emanating from somewhere among the trees. Anxious to trace its source, he roamed in the forest until he saw a girl of divine beauty, belonging to the fishing community. He asked that dark-eyed maiden, "Who are you? What are you doing here? What are you afraid of?" She said, "Prosperity be with you: I am a girl of the fishing community. At the command of my father, the king of the fishermen, I row this boat as a ferry across this river for religious merit."

Enchanted by her celestial form, beauty, and fragrance, the king desired to marry the fishergirl. He went to her father and sought her hand. The chief of the fishermen replied to the king, "Even when that fair girl was born, I knew that one day she should be given away in marriage to someone. But, O king, you should know my heart's desire. You are sinless and truthful. If you desire to marry her lawfully, promise me truly that you will do what I ask of you. O king, if you give me the promise, I shall then give you my daughter's hand, for I have no other hope of obtaining for her a husband like you."

"O fisherman," said Śaṅtanu, "only after hearing your request can I say whether I will be able to grant it or not. If it is something which can be granted, I shall certainly do so." The fisherman said, "O king, my wish is that the son born of this girl, and none else, should succeed you as king." But Śaṅtanu was not willing to grant the request of the fisherman, though his body was burning with the flames of desire. He returned to Hāstinapura, with his mind afflicted by grief and his thoughts constantly returning to the fishermaiden.

One day, when Śaṅtanu was thus grieving over the girl of whom he was always thinking, his son Devavrata came to him and said, "All around you is prosperity; all the chiefs obey you. Why then do you grieve thus? O king, why are you so absorbed in your own thoughts, and why do you not confide in me?" Śaṅtanu replied, "Truly my mind is elsewhere. You are my only son, and the sole scion of an illustrious race. Therefore I am sad when I consider the uncertainties of this world. If anything should happen to you, I shall be left with no descendants, though verily you alone are equal to a hundred sons. I do not wish to marry again for this reason. All that I desire is the perpetuation of our dynasty, so that prosperity may always attend you. The men of religion say that he who has only one son has no son at all. My son! you are brave, quick tempered, and ever engaged in the practice of arms, and your end will come only on the battlefield. Hence my doubt: What will happen in the event of your death? This is the only reason for my anxiety!"

Having learnt the cause of the king's grief, the intelligent Devavrata pondered for a while. He then went to see the old minister, who was devoted to his father's welfare, and asked him about the cause of his father's sorrow. From him he learnt about the fishermaiden, and the pledge demanded by the girl's father.

Thereupon Devavrata, accompanied by many elderly Kṣatriya chiefs, went to the chief of the fishermen and asked for his daughter's hand on behalf of his father. The fisherman received him with due respect. After the prince had taken his seat, he spoke to him thus in that assembly of kings: "O best of the Bharata race, you are a lord of great might; you are the son of Śaṅtanu who is the greatest of fathers. What can I tell you? If I were Iṅdra himself, I would still regret having to reject such an attractive proposal. But, as the father of this girl, I have this to say: the only disadvantage I perceive is the existence of a son by a former queen."

To this Devavrata, having his father's interests at heart, replied in the hearing of all the chiefs: "O foremost of truthful men, bear witness to the vow I am about to take. There is none born or to be born who will dare take such a vow." Turning to the chief of the fishermen he said, "I shall do as you have requested. The son that will be born of your daughter shall be our king."

The chief of the fishermen, wishing to be certain that he should secure the kingdom for his daughter's progeny, replied: "O you who are devoted to truth, the pledge that you have taken in the presence of these chiefs for the sake of [my daughter] Satyavatī is worthy of you. I have no doubt whatever that it will never be broken by you. But I have great doubt in respect of any issue you may have."

The truthful Devavrata, knowing what was in the fisherman's mind, and anxious to do good to his father, then said, "O chief of the fishermen, listen to the vow I now take for the sake of my father before all these chiefs. O chiefs, I gave up my right to the throne only a few moments ago. I shall now settle the question that has arisen in respect of my issue. O fisherman, from this day I adopt the vow of celibacy. Even if I am without issue, I shall still attain the everlasting regions."

Hearing these words, the fisherman was delighted and thrilled. He said, "I bestow her." Thereupon in the heavens the apsaras, the celestials, and the various sages began to rain flowers upon Devavrata's head, while they exclaimed: "This man is Bhīṣma [the terrible]."

Bhīṣma then said to the illustrious lady, "O mother, mount this chariot, and let us go home." Helping the beautiful maiden to get into his car, Bhīṣma hastened to Hāstinapura, and told Śaṅtanu all that had taken place. All the assembled chiefs and kings applauded him together and individually for his great feat, exclaiming, "He is truly Bhīṣma." In recognition of his son's great sacrifice, which pleased him immensely, Śaṅtanu gave Bhīṣma the boon of dying at will.

V

After the marriage celebrations were over, King Śaṅtanu installed his beautiful bride in his palace. In due course, Satyavatī bore Śaṅtanu a son, a mighty hero, named Citrāṅgada, and another prince, named Vicitravīrya, who became a great bowman. While Vicitravīrya was still a boy the wise King Śaṅtanu passed away. After Śaṅtanu's death, in accordance with Satyavatī's wishes, Bhīṣma installed Citrāṅgada on the throne.

Citrāṅgada was peerless among men and defeated all rival kings by his strength of arms. Witnessing the defeat of even the celestials, besides ordinary human beings and asuras, at his hands, the mighty king of the Gaṅdharvas, who was his namesake, challenged him to a fight. The battle between those two powerful men, the chief of the Kauravas and the king of the Gaṅdharvas, took place at Kurukṣetra and raged for three long years on the banks of the river Hiraṇvatī. During that fierce battle, which was marked by showers of arrows, the Gaṅdharva took advantage of his greater power of Māyā to kill the heroic Kuru king. Having killed Citrāṅgada, the Gaṅdharva, master of many strange weapons, returned to heaven.

When that mighty prince, a tiger even among kings, was killed, Bhīṣma performed all his funeral rites. Thereafter, the mighty Bhīṣma arranged for the coronation of his brother Vicitravīrya and installed him on the Kuru throne. Because his brother was still a minor, Bhīṣma ruled over the kingdom, as desired by Satyavatī.

When in the course of time his brother had attained manhood,

Bhīṣma thought of getting Vicitravīrya married. Coming to know that the king of Kāśī was holding a svayaṁvara for the three princesses, his daughters, who matched the apsaras in beauty, Bhīṣma, greatest of car-warriors, mounted a chariot and proceeded, with the permission of his mother, to the city of Vārāṇasī [Kāśī].

There Bhīṣma saw the many kings who had come from every direction, and also the princesses. While the various kings present were being called one by one by name, Bhīṣma himself chose those maidens for his brother. Taking the princesses on his chariot, the best of warriors, Bhīṣma, addressed the assembled kings in a thunderous voice. He said, "The svayaṁvara form of marriage is highly spoken of by kings. But the wise men have said that a wife taken by force is to be highly prized. Therefore, O kings, I am taking away these maidens by force. You may strive, with all your might, to defeat me or be defeated. O kings! I stand here, ready to fight." Having said this to the assembled kings and the king of Kāśī, the heroic Bhīṣma placed the maidens on his chariot and rode away.

With drivers ready and splendid horses harnessed to their chariots, the assembled kings, armed to the teeth, gave chase to the retreating Bhīṣma. A thrilling battle between the many kings on one side and Bhīṣma on the other then took place. The kings discharged tens of thousands of arrows at Bhīṣma at the same time. Bhīṣma, however, destroyed them in the air, even before they could strike him. Adept as he was in the use of all arms, he defeated them all in battle, and proceeded towards his capital, accompanied by the princesses.

Next the great car-warrior, King Śālva, challenged Bhīṣma to a duel. Countering Śālva's weapons with his own, Bhīṣma killed first the driver and then the horses of his opponent. Having defeated Śālva, Bhīṣma let him escape with his life, for the sake of the princesses. Thereafter Śālva returned to his own capital.

His triumph complete, Bhīṣma, foremost of warriors, returned to Hāstinapura, where he bestowed on his younger brother Vicitravīrya the virtuous maidens whom he had won by his own might. Then, according to royal custom, Bhīṣma began to make arrangements for his brother's marriage, in consultation with Satyavatī. While he was thus engaged, the eldest princess of Kāśī approached him and said, "I had long ago set my heart on marrying Śālva, the king of Saubha. He too wished to marry me, and this was also my father's wish. I would have chosen Śālva if the svayaṁvara had taken place. In the light of all this, you who know the precepts of virtue may do what you think proper." When the princess had told him all this in the conclave of Brāhmaṇas, the heroic Bhīṣma began to ponder what should be done. After discussion with the Brāhmaṇas learned in the scriptures, the virtuous Bhīṣma gave leave to Aṁbā, the eldest daughter of the king of Kāśī, to depart.

Bhīṣma then gave the other two princesses, Aṁbikā and Aṁbālikā, in marriage to his younger brother Vicitravīrya according to the prescribed rites. Vicitravīrya, ruler of the earth, lived with his wives in uninterrupted enjoyment of married bliss for seven years after which, while still young, he was attacked by consumption. Despite the best efforts of his friends and well-wishers and the attention of physicians, the Kuru prince went down like the setting sun, and passed away.

VI

Plunged in grief by the death of her son, the unfortunate and unhappy Satyavatī performed, along with her daughters-in-law, his last rites. Then turning her mind to virtue and the importance of the perpetuation of the dynasty, the illustrious lady said to Bhīṣma, "O best of men, my son and your dear brother, though possessed of great strength, has gone to heaven while still so young. O mighty hero, I therefore request you, for the continuance of our royal line, to beget offspring on these queens of your brother, the Kāśī princesses, who are young and beautiful and who also desire to have children. It behoves you to perform this virtuous task at my request."

Thus urged by his mother, and by friends, the worthy Bhīṣma replied in accordance with the essence of virtue: "O mother, what you request is certainly authorised by religion. But you know I have taken a vow of celibacy. O queen, I shall however disclose to you the long-sanctioned practice of the Kṣatriyas, which may be resorted to for saving the line of Śantanu from extinction."

"In olden days," Bhīṣma continued, "the great Paraśurāma exterminated the Kṣatriya race from the face of the earth twenty-one times over by his swift arrows. Thereupon the Kṣatriya women raised children with the help of the usually continent Brāhmaṇas. In accordance with this precedent, let a Brāhmaṇa of good character be invited, and offered much wealth; let him enable the wives of Vicitravīrya to conceive offspring."

Then Satyavatī said, "O Bhīṣma, what you say is true. Since I trust you implicitly, I shall now explain the means of perpetuating our line. My father was a pious man, and as an act of religious merit he kept a boat for ferrying passengers across the river. It so happened one day that the great sage Parāśara, wise and virtuous among men, boarded my boat for crossing the river Yamunā. As I was taking him across the river, that sage became full of desire for me and spoke to me in soft and sweet words. On the one hand I was afraid of my father, but I also greatly feared the sage's curse. Therefore, having got from him great boons, I could not resist his desire. Thus, while we were still on the boat he covered the region in a thick fog, and prevailed over me—a mere girl—by his great lustre. Till then my body had emitted a revolting odour of fish, but the sage dispelled it and endowed me with the fragrance that I now have. The sage told me, 'Even after bearing my child on an island in this river, you shall remain a virgin.' "

Satyavatī continued: "The son of Parāśara, thus born of me in my maidenhood, has become a great sage, named Dvaipāyana. That illustrious man, who by his ascetic power divided the scriptures into four parts, has become known on earth as Vyāsa, and also as Kṛṣṇa on account of his dark complexion. At my request, as well as yours, in your incomparable radiance, he will surely enable the wives of your brother to conceive auspicious sons."

When the name of the great sage was thus mentioned, Bhīṣma said, with joined hands, "Your suggestion is most acceptable to me. It is indeed desirable, virtuous, and beneficial." Thereupon Satyavatī mentally invoked the sage Kṛṣṇa Dvaipāyana. As soon as he knew that his mother had thought of him, the sage, who was then interpreting the scriptures, came at once to her in all secrecy.

Satyavatī, seeing her son after such a long time, formally welcomed him, embraced him with her arms, and bathed him with her tears. She then said, "O holy one, Vicitravīrya was my youngest son, as you are my eldest born. As Bhīṣma was his brother on the father's side, so are you on the mother's side. Because of his vow of celibacy Bhīṣma, who is devoted to truth, does not wish to beget children or to rule the kingdom. For the sake of the kindness you bear for all creatures, and for the protection of all, it behoves you to do as I say. Vicitravīrya has left two widows, fair as the daughters of the celestials. They are young and beautiful, and they wish to have sons in accordance with Dharma. O my son, help them conceive sons worthy of our dynasty, so that our line may continue."

Vyāsa said, "O Satyavatī, you know what is consistent with virtue, both in this world and the next. You are also a lady of great wisdom. Therefore, motivated by virtue, I shall obey your command and do what you desire, seeing that this practice is in conformity with precedent. But if I am to beget a son so quickly and so unseasonably then the princesses should tolerate my ugliness. If Kausalyā [Aṁbikā] will not mind my body, my appearance, my garb, and my odour, may she become with child even today!" So saying, the sage disappeared.

Satyavatī then went to see her daughter-in-law, and spoke to her privately. In amiable words, designed to promote both temporal and spiritual welfare, she said, "The wise Bhīṣma, seeing that his father's race is faced with extinction, has made a proposal to me which is designed to promote virtue. But, O my daughter, its fulfilment depends on you. Accomplish it, and bring back to life the lost line of the Bhāratas." Thus Satyavatī succeeded in persuading the virtuous princess to agree to her proposal which was in accordance with virtue. She then invited the Brāhmaṇas, sages, and other guests to a feast.

Then, as promised, the truthful sage, Vyāsa, visited Aṁbikā first, entering her bedroom while the lamp was burning. Seeing his dark face, his matted locks of the colour of copper, his blazing eyes, and his grim beard, the princess closed her eyes in fear. In order to fulfil his mother's desire, he spent that night with her. But the princess of Kāśī was overcome by fright and could not bear to look at him.

When he emerged, Satyavatī asked her son Vyāsa, "Will she have an accomplished son?" The self-controlled and greatly wise Vyāsa replied, "The son will be like an elephant in strength; he will be learned and a great royal sage; he will be very fortunate, powerful, and intelligent; and he will beget one hundred mighty sons. But on account of his mother's fault, he will be born blind."

Hearing these words, Satyavatī said to her son, "O great ascetic, how can one who is blind be a worthy king of the Kuru line? To protect his kith and kin and continue the dynasty of his forbears it behoves you to give another king to the Kuru race." The great sage said, "So be it!" and went away. In due time Kausalyā [Aṁbikā] gave birth to a blind son, who was named Dhṛtarāṣṭra.

The blameless Satyavatī then obtained the consent of her second daughter-in-law, and invoked Vyāsa as before. Vyāsa came according to his promise and went to the second wife. But Aṁbālikā became pale with fear on seeing the sage. Seeing her pale with fright and afflicted with sorrow, Vyāsa said to her, "As you have become pale by seeing my ugliness, so will your son be pale in complexion. O beautiful lady, your son shall also be named Pāṇḍu [pale]!" Having said this, the illustrious sage went away.

Seeing him come out, Satyavatī asked him about the child. He told her that the child would be born pale. Hearing this, his mother begged the sage again for another son, and the sage replied, "So be it!" In due course the lady Aṁbālikā gave birth to a son. He was of pale complexion, though brilliant and endowed with all auspicious marks. This son Pāṇḍu afterwards begot those mighty bowmen, the five Pāṇḍavas.

Some time afterwards Satyavatī sent her eldest daughter-in-law again to Vyāsa. But the princess, beautiful as a daughter of the celestials, remembered the ugly visage and repellent odour of the great sage, and was afraid; in consequence she did not act according to Satyavatī's wishes. Instead, the princess of Kāśī decked a maidservant with her own ornaments and sent her to Vyāsa. The maidservant rose and saluted the sage as he came in and waited upon him respectfully. Greatly pleased with her, the sage blissfully spent the night with her. When he rose to leave, he said, "O amiable girl, you shall no longer be a maidservant. Your son will be very fortunate and virtuous, and the foremost of all intelligent men." Thus was born the brother of Dhṛtarāṣṭra and Pāṇḍu, the supremely wise son of Kṛṣṇa Dvaipāyana, who was known by the name of Vidura.

VII

From their birth, Bhīṣma brought up Dhṛtarāṣṭra and Pāṇḍu and the wise Vidura as if they were his own sons. In accordance with the usual rites of their order, they engaged themselves in study and the observance of vows; by the time they had grown to young manhood, they were expert in athletic feats, adept in archery, learned in the scriptures, and skilful in fighting with club, sword, and shield. They were skilled in horsemanship and in the management of elephants; they were learned in the science of morality. They shone equally in history, mythology, and many other branches of learning, and mastered the inner meaning of the scriptures. In all these activities they became proficient with practice. Pāṇḍu excelled all men in the science of archery, and Dhṛtarāṣṭra in personal strength. There was none in the three worlds to equal Vidura in his devotion to religion and virtue, and in his knowledge of the science of morality.

Bhīṣma heard from the Brāhmaṇas that Gāndhārī, daughter of Subala, had been worshipping the bountiful deity Śiva, and obtained the boon that she would bear one hundred sons. He then sent emissaries to the king of Gāndhāra, seeking her hand on behalf of Dhṛtarāṣṭra. Subala hesitated on account of the blindness of the bridegroom. But taking into consideration his noble blood and the fame of the Kurus, he bestowed the virtuous Gāndhārī on Dhṛtarāṣṭra.

Gāndhārī was informed of the blindness of Dhṛtarāṣṭra, and of her parents' wish notwithstanding to bestow her upon him. Devoted to her husband, Gāndhārī bandaged her own eyes with a cloth, gathered into many folds, out of her desire not to excel her husband in any way.

In due course Śakuni, the son of the king of Gāndhāra, brought his sister, endowed with great wealth, to the Kurus, and gave her away in the proper manner to Dhṛtarāṣṭra. He then returned to his own capital. The beautiful Gāndhārī pleased all the Kurus by her exemplary conduct and respectful attentions.

One day Gāndhārī pleased Vyāsa, who had arrived at the palace hungry and fatigued. He granted her a boon, and she expressed her desire to have one hundred sons like her husband. Some time afterwards, she became pregnant, but bore the burden in her womb for two years without being delivered, and was therefore much afflicted with grief.

Meanwhile she heard that Pāṇḍu's queen Kuntī had borne a son, bright as the morning sun. She could not help feeling that in her case the time of bearing the child in the womb was too long. Deprived of reason by her grief, she struck her womb with force, without the knowledge of Dhṛtarāṣṭra. Thereupon she brought forth a hard mass of flesh like an iron ball which had been in her womb for two years. On learning this, Vyāsa, best of ascetics, soon came to her and saw that mass of flesh. He asked Gāndhārī, "What have you done?" She revealed the truth to him, saying "Having heard that Kuntī had first given birth to a prince, bright as the sun, I struck at my womb in grief. You gave me the boon that I should bear one hundred sons. But only this ball of flesh has emerged instead."

Vyāsa said, "O Gāndhārī, it shall be as I said. I have never uttered a lie even in jest. Let one hundred jars, filled with ghee, be brought quickly and let cool water be sprinkled on this ball of flesh." The ball of flesh, being thus cooled with water, split into parts, each about the size of a thumb. These were then placed in the jars, which were stationed in a concealed spot and carefully watched. The holy one bade Gāndhārī open the lids of the jars only after two years. Having given these instructions and made these arrangements, the holy and wise Vyāsa went to the Himālaya mountains to perform penance.

It was thus that Prince Duryodhana was born. According to the order of birth, however, Yudhiṣṭhira, the eldest son of Pāṇḍu, was senior to him. As soon as a son had been born to him, Dhṛtarāṣṭra said: "Summon the Brāhmaṇas, as well as Bhīṣma and Vidura. The prince Yudhiṣṭhira is the eldest of our line. There is no doubt that he should succeed to the kingdom in his own right."

At that time beasts of prey, jackals, and crows made ominous noises everywhere. Seeing these frightful portents, the assembled Brāhmaṇas and the wise Vidura said to Dhṛtarāṣṭra, "It is clear that your son will be the exterminator of your race. The peace of the family depends upon his being abandoned. There will be great calamity in keeping him." Though he was thus adjured by Vidura and by all those learned Brāhmaṇas, the king did not heed their advice, because of his natural love for his son. There were born within a month one hundred sons to Dhṛtarāṣṭra, and also a daughter, Duḥśalā.

VIII

The chief of the Yadus, named Śūra, had a son, Vasudeva, and a daughter, Pṛthā, whose beauty was matchless on earth. As had been promised, Śūra gave Pṛthā in adoption to his childless cousin and close friend, the high-souled Kuṅtibhoja. Hence she also came to be known as Kuṅtī. In her adopted father's house Kuṅtī's duties were to worship the family deities and look after the guests.

One day, by her solicitude, she pleased the terrible and notoriously short-tempered sage Durvāsa, who was learned in the mysteries. Through his foresight, Durvāsa could see that Kuṅtī would have difficulty in conceiving sons. He therefore taught her an invocatory spell, saying to her, "Through the radiance of those celestials whom you invoke by this spell, you will obtain progeny."

After a while the virtuous Kuṅtī out of curiosity tried the spell and invoked the sun god. That brilliant deity the Sun, who sees everything in the world, immediately appeared before her, and the beautiful Kuṅtī was overcome by astonishment at this wondrous sight. The light of the universe, the Sun, got her with child. Thus was born the hero of divine ancestry, known all over the world by the name of Karṇa, the foremost of warriors. He was born wearing armour and earrings.

Thereafter the Sun restored Kuṅtī's maidenhood and returned to heaven.

Afraid of her friends and relatives, Kuṅtī resolved to hide her transgression. She accordingly threw her handsome son into the river, from which he was rescued by a charioteer. He and his wife Rādhā brought up the infant as their own son, giving him the name of Vasuṣeṇa, because he was endowed with wealth even at birth, namely armour and earrings. Vasuṣeṇa grew up to be very strong and energetic, and adept in the use of all weapons. He used to worship the Sun until the afternoon sun scorched his back. When he was thus engaged in worship, the heroic, truthful, and high-souled Vasuṣeṇa would give away to the Brāhmaṇas anything on earth which they requested of him.

Once Iṅdra, the protector of all living things, came to him for alms, adopting the guise of a Brāhmaṇa, and asked him for his armour and the earrings. Perplexed though he was at Iṅdra's request, he cut off the armour from his body, and also his earrings from his ears, and gave them, dripping with blood, to Iṅdra with joined hands. Greatly surprised at his generosity, Iṅdra gave him the Śakti weapon, saying, "Be your foe a celestial, asura, human being, Gaṅdharva, Nāga, or Rākṣasa, if you hurl this missile at him, it will certainly kill him." The son of Sūrya, who till then was known by the name of Vasuṣeṇa, came to be called Karṇa [the cutter] after this act of unequalled generosity.

IX

Kuṅtibhoja held a svayaṁvara for his beautiful and virtuous daughter. There she saw that tamer of lions and elephants, the mighty Pāṇḍu, in the midst of all the kings present. She chose him for her husband, even as Paulomī chose Iṅdra.

Bhīṣma also obtained for Pāṇḍu, in exchange for much wealth, the daughter of the king of Madra, Mādrī, who was famous for her beauty in all the three worlds, after which he solemnized the marriage of the high-souled Pāṇḍu.

One day, while roaming in the forest, Pāṇḍu saw two deer in the act of mating, and hit both of them with five sharp and swift arrows, embellished with golden feathers. They were an ascetic, the son of a sage, and his wife, with whom he was thus disporting in the form of a deer. "I am the sage Kiṅdama, without equal in austerity," said the deer. "You have killed me in the act of mating in the form of a deer, a form I have assumed out of modesty. Though you will not be visited with the sin of killing a Brāhmaṇa, since you did not know who I was, you shall however be punished similarly: when you are overcome by desire in the company of your wife, you shall also die!"

Thus cursed, Pāṇḍu returned to his capital, and explained his predicament to his queens, after which he said to Kuṅtī: "At my request, you should have children endowed with all good qualities by the grace of a Brāhmaṇa who is a great sage; if you do so, I shall go the same way as those with sons." To this request, Kuṅtī, ever interested in her husband's welfare, replied to Pāṇḍu, "O king, since you so desire, I shall invoke a god as taught me by Durvāsa, so that we may have issue." Pāṇḍu said: "Among the gods Dharma is the one who bestows spiritual merit. Hence I request you to invoke the god Dharma this very day."

Gāṅdhārī had been pregnant for a year when Kuṅtī invoked the eternal Dharma for progeny, worshipping him and repeating in the proper form the invocation which Durvāsa had taught her. She was then united with Dharma in his spiritual form and, in time, gave birth to a fine boy. As soon as the child was born, a voice with no visible source said: "This child will certainly be virtuous. He will be known as Yudhiṣṭhira; he will be famous over the three worlds. He will be splendid, determined, and renowned."

Having been blessed with this virtuous son, Pāṇḍu bade Kuṅtī ask for a son of great physical strength, since the Kṣatriyas were the foremost in strength. In response to her husband's request, Kuṅtī invoked Vāyu, who begot the mighty Bhīma, of great strength. On his birth, the supernatural voice said: "This child will be the greatest of all strong men." Duryodhana was born on the very day on which Bhīma was born.

Thereafter the illustrious Pāṇḍu consulted with the great sages and asked Kuṅtī to observe certain vows for one full year. At the end of the period Pāṇḍu said, "O beautiful one, Iṅdra the king of the celestials is pleased. Invoke him and conceive a son." In response, the illustrious Kuṅtī invoked Iṅdra, the lord of the celestials, who came to her and begot Arjuna. As soon as the prince was born, a supernatural voice boomed over the whole sky with a loud and deep roar, saying: "O Kuṅtī, this child will be as strong as Kārtavīrya and Śibi, invincible in battle as Iṅdra himself. He will spread your fame everywhere, and will acquire many celestial weapons."

After the birth of Kuṅtī's sons, and those of Dhṛtarāṣṭra, Mādrī privately spoke to Pāṇḍu thus, "It is my great grief that, though we are of equal rank, my husband should have sons by Kuṅtī alone. If the princess Kuṅtī will arrange that I may have sons, she will do me a great kindness, and it will also be of benefit to you."

Thereupon Pāṇḍu again spoke to Kuṅtī privately. He said, "O blessed lady, give me some more sons, and ensure the funeral oblations for myself and my ancestors. O blameless one, aid Mādrī, as though with a raft across the river, by helping her to obtain progeny. Thus you will obtain great renown."

Kuṅtī then said to Mādrī, "Think of some celestial by whose grace you may obtain worthy offspring." Thereupon Mādrī reflected a little and invoked the twin Aśvins. Both of them came to her and sired twin sons, namely Nakula and Sahadeva, unmatched for beauty on earth. On their birth, the supernatural voice said: "The twins will be handsome and good, and will excel all men in beauty, energy, and wealth. They will glow with splendour."

The sages living in Śataśṛṅga[1] invoked blessings on the princes and performed their birth rites with devotion. They named the eldest of Kuṅtī's sons Yudhiṣṭhira, the second Bhīmasena, and the third Arjuna. Mādrī's twin sons they named Nakula and Sahadeva. The five sons of Pāṇḍu and the hundred sons of Dhṛtarāṣṭra, the ornaments of the Kuru race, bloomed like lotuses in a lake.

One day Pāṇḍu saw Mādrī adorned with jewels, and his desire was

[1] Name of a mountain, meaning literally "a hundred peaks."

aroused. But as soon as he touched her, he died. Thereupon Mādrī ascended Pāṇḍu's funeral pyre, asking Kuntī to bring up her children with kindness and love. Then Vidura, King Dhṛtarāṣṭra, Bhīṣma, and other relatives performed the last rites of Pāṇḍu and Mādrī and offered the funeral oblations.

Thereafter the sons of Pāṇḍu were brought by the citizens to Hāstinapura. There the Pāṇḍavas performed all the purifying rites prescribed in the scriptures. They grew up in royal style in their father's house, sporting with the sons of Dhṛtarāṣṭra, whom they excelled in all the boyish games. Bhīma vanquished all the sons of Dhṛtarāṣṭra in various feats. Seeing his extraordinary strength, Duryodhana, the mighty son of Dhṛtarāṣṭra, conceived a lasting enmity towards him.

X

Once the great sage Bharadvāja happened to see the beautiful nymph Dhṛtācī in the sacrificial place, when her dress was accidentally blown aside by the wind. Aroused by this sight, the sage dropped his seed in a vessel [droṇa], in which the wise Droṇa was born. He read all the Scriptures.

Bharadvāja had a royal friend, named Pṛṣata, who had a son named Drupada. Prince Drupada went every day to Bharadvāja's hermitage, where he played and studied with Droṇa. When Pṛṣata died, the mighty Drupada succeeded to the kingdom of the Northern Pāñcālas.

At about the same time the illustrious Bharadvāja also passed away; thereupon, in accordance with his late father's wishes, and being desirous of offspring, Droṇa married Kṛpī, the daughter of Śaradvata. Ever engaged in sacrifices and penance, the pious Kṛpī bore Droṇa a son, named Aśvatthāmā. As soon as he was born, he neighed like a horse. Thereupon a voice from the skies said, "As this child neighed like a horse and could be heard over a great distance, he will be known by the name of Aśvatthāmā [the horse-voiced]."

Droṇa, who was extremely pleased at having a son, then became deeply interested in the study of archery. He heard that the great-souled Paraśurāma was giving away all his wealth to Brāhmaṇas.

Seeing Paraśurāma as he was leaving for the forest, Droṇa said, "Know me to be Droṇa, best of Brāhmaṇas, who has come to you seeking wealth."

Paraśurāma said, "O treasury of penance! I have already given away to the Brāhmaṇas my gold and whatever wealth I had." "O Paraśurāma," said Droṇa, "give me then all your arms and weapons, and teach me the secrets of launching and withdrawing them." Paraśurāma said: "So be it!" He gave away all his weapons to Droṇa and taught him the science of arms and all its secrets. Droṇa, considering himself amply rewarded and feeling well pleased, went to see his dear friend Drupada.

In due course approaching Drupada, the son of Pṛṣata, Droṇa said, "Know me as your friend." Drupada said: "Our former friendship was based on the bonds of skill; but time, that erodes everything, wears out friendship too." Thus rebuffed by Drupada, the mighty Droṇa was filled with wrath. He reflected for a moment, while he made up his mind as to his course of action, and then went to Hāstinapura, the city of the foremost of the Kurus.

XI

Anxious to give his grandsons a superior education, Bhīṣma inquired about tutors who were brave and well skilled in the science of arms. He decided that the preceptor of the Kurus should be strong, intelligent, and illustrious, and complete master of the science of arms.

When he heard that a stranger had arrived [in Hāstinapura], Bhīṣma knew that this must be Droṇa and decided that he was the right tutor for his grandsons. Welcoming Droṇa, he asked him why he had come to Hāstinapura. Droṇa told him everything. Bhīṣma then appointed Droṇa as the preceptor and gave him various gifts. He presented his grandsons, including the sons of Pāṇḍu, according to custom, and handed them over to Droṇa, who accepted them all as his pupils.

Droṇa called them aside when they saluted him, and said privately to them: "O princes, in my heart I have one special yearning; promise me that you will fulfil it when you have become proficient in arms." To these words the Kuru princes made no reply. Arjuna, however, gave his promise.

Thereupon Droṇa taught Arjuna how to fight from the back of a horse, on an elephant, on a chariot or on the ground, in single combat or in a crowd. He taught him how to fight with the club, the sword, the spear, and the dart. Two of Droṇa's pupils, Duryodhana and Bhīma, became highly proficient in club fighting; Aśvatthāmā surpassed the others in the mysteries of the science of arms; the twins Nakula and Sahadeva outshone everybody in swordsmanship; Yudhiṣṭhira was first among car-warriors.

Arjuna reigned supreme in every field; he excelled all in intelligence, in concentration, in strength, and in zest, and was famous unto the limits of the ocean as the foremost of car-warriors. He was unequalled not only in the use of arms but also in his love and regard for his preceptor. Though all the royal pupils received the same instruction, yet the mighty Arjuna by his excellence became the only Atiratha among all the princes. The wicked sons of Dhṛtarāṣṭra became jealous of Bhīma's strength and Arjuna's many accomplishments.

When the sons of Dhṛtarāṣṭra and Pāṇḍu had thus become proficient in arms, Droṇa said to King Dhṛtarāṣṭra, "O king, your sons have completed their studies. Permit them to display their skill." The king replied, with joy in his heart: "O Droṇa, O best of Brāhmaṇas, great is your achievement!" By order of the king, the masons built a huge arena according to the rules, with a grandstand for the king and the royal ladies. Then, with Yudhiṣṭhira at their head, the heroic princes followed each other in the order of their age and began to display their wonderful skill in arms.

At the command of the preceptor, the youthful Arjuna, equipped with leather protector for the finger, his quiver full of arrows, bow in hand, and wearing golden armour, performed the initial rites of propitiation and entered the arena like the evening cloud reflecting the rays of the setting sun. His very entrance caused a stir among the spectators. When they had calmed down a little, Arjuna displayed before his preceptor his easy mastery of arms and his great skill in the use of the sword, the bow, and the club.

While the spectators were watching Arjuna's feats in wide-eyed wonder, that conqueror of hostile cities, Karṇa, entered the spacious arena. The entire assembly of people remained motionless staring at the newcomer. Curious to know his name, they asked one another in agitation, "Who is he?" Then, in a voice deep as thunder, Karṇa, foremost of eloquent men, said to Arjuna, whom he did not know to be his brother: "O Arjuna, I shall repeat before these spectators all that you have just done. Do not be surprised." Thus challenged, Arjuna was abashed and angry, but Duryodhana was touched with affection for the challenger. With the permission of Droṇa, the powerful Karṇa, ever fond of battle, duplicated all the feats that Arjuna had displayed a little earlier.

Thereupon Duryodhana with his brothers embraced Karṇa with joy and spoke to him thus: "O mighty hero, welcome to you! Your arrival is our good fortune. The entire Kuru kingdom and I myself are at your service." Karṇa replied, "I desire only your friendship."

Karṇa then challenged Arjuna to a duel. When the two heroes were ready with their great bows, Kṛpa, the son of Śaradvata, who knew all the rules governing such duels, said: "O mighty hero, tell us of your father and mother, of your family, and of the royal line which you adorn. It is only after knowing your lineage that Arjuna can decide whether or not to fight with you." Duryodhana announced, "O preceptor, it is said that royalty may be claimed by three classes of men, namely, by a person of noble birth, by a hero, and by a leader of soldiers. If Arjuna is unwilling to engage in a duel with one who is not a king, I shall install Karṇa at once as the king of Aṅga."

Without delay the mighty car-warrior Karṇa was seated on a golden seat, and crowned as the king of Aṅga by those learned in the rites, with unhusked rice, flowers, waterpots, gold, and much wealth. When the cheers subsided, Karṇa said to the Kaurava king, Duryodhana, "What can I give you compared with your gift of a kingdom? O great king, I shall do your bidding." Duryodhana replied, "I seek only your friendship." Then Karṇa said, "So be it!" They thereupon joyfully embraced each other and felt very happy.

Having obtained Karṇa, Duryodhana forgot his fears aroused by Arjuna's skill in arms. The heroic Karṇa, accomplished in arms, spoke words of comfort to Duryodhana. Yudhiṣṭhira too was impressed with the conviction that there was no bowman on earth like Karṇa.

XII

One day the preceptor Droṇa called his pupils together and asked for his dakṣiṇā[1] from them all. He said, "I want you to capture the king of Pāñcāla, Drupada, in battle and bring him securely to me. That will be the most precious dakṣiṇā you can give me." Saying "So be it!" and armed with quivers of arrows, the princes mounted their cars and went with Droṇa to win wealth for their preceptor. They attacked the Pāñcālas and killed them, and then besieged the capital of the famous Drupada. Successful in capturing Drupada, along with his ministers, they brought him to Droṇa.

Droṇa, remembering his former enmity towards Drupada, now humiliated, bereft of wealth, and completely subdued, spoke thus to him, "I have quickly laid waste your kingdom and your capital. Do you wish to renew our old friendship and to receive your life at my hands?" Smiling, he added, "O king, be not afraid for your life. We Brāhmaṇas are lenient. I seek your friendship again. I shall grant you one half of your kingdom. You may rule the territory lying to the south of the Gāngā, and I shall rule the northern part. O king of Pāñcāla, if it pleases you, know that I am your friend from now on." Drupada said, "O Brāhman, such generosity is not surprising in men of noble soul and great strength. I am pleased to accept your friendly offer and I desire your eternal friendship."

Then Droṇa released Drupada, and with a pleased heart he bestowed upon him half the kingdom. Drupada, however, was unable to recover his peace of mind, being obsessed by his hatred of Droṇa. He knew

[1] Guru-dakṣiṇā is the offering that pupils make to their preceptor on the successful conclusion of their studies.

he could not hope to avenge his defeat by superior force, nor by spiritual power, in which too he was aware of being weak. Hence King Drupada desired the birth of a son, who would be the instrument of his revenge.

XIII

Meanwhile the wicked-minded Duryodhana continued to nurse his jealousy of Bhīma's superior strength and Arjuna's many accomplishments, and Karṇa, Śakuni, and many other followers of Duryodhana plotted to kill the Pāṇḍavas. The Pāṇḍavas came to know all this, being in the confidence of Vidura, and were able to protect themselves.

One day, on the instructions of Dhṛtarāṣṭra, some clever courtiers depicted the charms of the city of Vāraṇāvata. They referred to the festival of Paśupati [Śiva] which had begun in that city of Vāraṇāvata and described the concourse of people gathered there as the most splendid in the world. The king, noticing that the Pāṇḍavas' interest had been aroused, said to them, "O my sons, if you wish to attend the festival of Vāraṇāvata, go there with your friends and followers, and enjoy yourselves for some time. You may then return to Hāstinapura."

When the king thus spoke to the high-minded Pāṇḍavas, the wicked Duryodhana became very happy. Summoning Purocana, one of the ministers, privately, he said, "On the suggestion of Dhṛtarāṣṭra the Pāṇḍavas are going to Vāraṇāvata, where they will participate in the festival for some time. Go there before them, and erect a splendid quadrangular palace similar to an armoury. In erecting that house, use hemp, resin, and any other inflammable material that is available; but do it in such a way that the Pāṇḍavas and others may not suspect you or examine the structure and find out that it is made of inflammable stuff. After completing the house, invite the Pāṇḍavas with a great show of respect to live in it with Kuṅtī and all their friends. When they have relaxed and begun to enjoy themselves in the city of Vāraṇāvata, and when they are sleeping in that house without suspicion or fear, set fire to its gateway." Purocana, who was ever in

Duryodhana's confidence, repaired speedily to Vāraṇāvata and carried out the prince's instructions faithfully.

Meanwhile the Pāṇḍavas got ready to depart for Vāraṇāvata. They got into their cars, yoked with fine horses fleet as the wind. When ascending their chariots, they felt uneasy and touched the feet of Bhīṣma, of King Dhṛtarāṣṭra, of the high-souled Droṇa, Kṛpa, and Vidura, and of all the other elders. When everyone else had left, the learned Vidura, conversant with all aspects of virtue, privately warned Yudhiṣṭhira and made him aware of the dangers ahead, after which he bade them farewell and returned to his house. The Pāṇḍavas then left for Vāraṇāvata, and were greeted by the people of the town on their arrival.

Welcomed by the citizens and greeting them in return, the Pāṇḍavas entered the populous and decorated city. When they had lived there for ten days, Purocana spoke to them about the house, called "Śiva" [blessed], though it was in truth the very opposite. Visiting that house, and smelling the odour of fat mixed with ghee and lac products, Yudhiṣṭhira observed to Bhīma that the building was made of inflammable materials. "If this house is known to be a fire-trap" said Bhīma, " then let us return to the safe place where we lived first." Yudhiṣṭhira said, "I think we should live here, without showing any suspicion; but we must seek some sure means of escape. Let us excavate in all secrecy, this very day, an underground exit. If we can keep it secret, then the fire will not consume us."

Just then a friend of Vidura, well skilled in excavation work, came and spoke thus to the Pāṇḍavas in private. "I have been sent by Vidura; I am an expert in excavation. Tell me what work you desire me to perform." Yudhiṣṭhira replied: "O friend, I know you to be a dear friend of Vidura, pure, true, and ever devoted to him. There is no predicament of ours which the learned Vidura does not know. The danger anticipated by Vidura is now very near. Deliver us from this without Purocana's knowledge." The miner replied, "So be it!" He began carefully and secretly the work of excavation, and soon he had made a big underground passage leading out of the house.

A full year came and went. Seeing them living cheerfully and without suspicion, Purocana was very pleased, and thought the time had come. Observing Purocana in such a frame of mind, Yudhiṣṭhira said to Bhīma, Arjuna, and the twins Nakula and Sahadeva, "The pitiless and sinful Purocana thinks that we are unsuspecting, and he has thus been completely taken in. I think that now is the time for our escape."

One night, on the occasion of an almsgiving, Kuṅtī invited a large number of Brāhmaṇas and also a number of ladies to dinner. They ate and drank and enjoyed themselves to their heart's content. And late in the night they all returned home with Kuṅtī's leave. The same night, impelled by fate, a Niṣāda woman with her five sons came for food, and she too enjoyed herself thoroughly. Then she went to sleep there along with her five sons.

When all the citizens had gone to bed and a strong breeze was blowing, Bhīma set fire to the house, in which Purocana too was sleeping. Thereupon the fire began to blaze with intensity and with a mighty roar which awoke the people of the city. Suspecting what was afoot, the people said, "The wicked Purocana built this house under the directions of Duryodhana, and he has now set fire to it. That evil man has burnt those best of men, the innocent and unsuspecting Pāṇḍavas, and has himself been burnt to death, as decreed by fate." Meanwhile the sorrowful Pāṇḍavas emerged with their mother out of the underground passage and left unnoticed. Bhīma, endued as he was with great speed and strength, carried his mother and all his brothers.

In the morning all the people of the city came to the spot to see what had happened to the Pāṇḍavas. When they put out the fire they saw that the house was made of lac and that the minister Purocana had been burnt to death. They then began to look for the Pāṇḍavas. Seeing the innocent Niṣāda woman who had been burnt to death with her five sons, and taking them to be Kuṅtī and the five Pāṇḍavas, the citizens then informed Dhṛtarāṣṭra that the Pāṇḍavas as well as the minister Purocana had been burnt to death.

When he heard the very unpleasant news of the death of the

Pāṇḍavas, King Dhṛtarāṣṭra displayed great sorrow. The other Kauravas also loudly bemoaned the fate of the Pāṇḍavas. Only Vidura showed little grief, for he knew the truth. Meanwhile, leaving the city of Vāraṇāvata, the Pāṇḍavas proceeded speedily in a southern direction. Guiding themselves in the dark by the stars, they soon reached a dense forest where they slept that night.

XIV

Close to the place where the Pāṇḍavas slept, a rākṣasa named Hidiṁba lived in a śāla tree. Scenting the presence of human beings, that huge man-eating monster spoke thus to his sister: "It is a long time since my favourite food has come my way. My mouth waters in anticipation. I shall overpower the man, cut his throat, and drink my fill of hot, fresh, and frothy blood. Go and find out who is lying asleep in this forest."

The rākṣasī, whose name was also Hidiṁbā, went as her brother had bidden her to the place where the Pāṇḍavas were resting. There she saw the Pāṇḍavas and Kuṅtī fast asleep, while the invincible Bhīma sat awake, keeping watch. Seeing him who resembled a śāla tree and who was uniquely handsome, the rākṣasī was filled with desire. As she was capable of taking on any form, she assumed an excellent human shape and slowly approached the mighty Bhīma.

She said: "O divine creature, I have been sent here on a scouting expedition by my brother of evil disposition, the rākṣasa, who has the intention of eating your flesh. I tell you truly, however, after seeing you, radiant as a celestial, I do not desire anybody else but you as my husband. O mighty-armed hero, let me save you from the rākṣasa, my brother, who eats human flesh. O sinless one, become my husband, and let us live in mountain caves."

Bhīma replied: "O rākṣasī, I desist from fighting your wicked brother only because I am afraid of awakening my mother and brothers who are fast asleep. O you with beautiful eyes, know that no one, be he rākṣasa or yakṣa, Gaṅdharva or human, is capable of overpowering me."

As his sister had been away for a long time, the king of the rākṣasas, Hidiṁba, got down from his tree and came to the spot where the Pāṇḍavas were sleeping. He saw his sister in human form, her head adorned with garlands of flowers and her face radiant as the full moon. The man-eater, guessing why she had assumed that charming human form, became very angry. He said to her, "I shall even now kill you along with all those on whose behalf you are trying to betray me."

Seeing that the rākṣasa was so annoyed with his sister, Bhīma smiled and said, "O Hidiṁba, why do you disturb these people who are sleeping peacefully? O wicked rākṣasa, fight me first, without loss of time. When I have killed you, men frequenting this forest will no longer be bothered by you, and can walk here in peace."

Hidiṁba readily accepted Bhīma's challenge. Fighting like two large and full-grown elephants mad with rage, they pulled down the trees and tore off the creepers that grew around. The clash between the two awakened the sleeping Pāṇḍavas. Rising from sleep, those best of men and their mother Kuntī were amazed on seeing the extraordinary beauty of the rākṣasī Hidiṁbā. They also saw Bhīma and the rākṣasa Hidiṁba already engaged in combat, dragging each other to and fro, and eager to overwhelm each other, like two strong lions. Arjuna said, "O Bhīma, let me finish off the rākṣasa since you are tired and may need some rest." When Arjuna said these words, Bhīma was overcome by anger. He dashed Hidiṁba to the ground with all his might and killed him like a beast.

Thereafter Bhīma said to the rākṣasī Hidiṁbā, "I know that rākṣasas avenge themselves on their foes by alluring deceptions. Therefore, O Hidiṁbā, begone!" Thereupon, respectfully saluting Kuntī and Yudhiṣṭhira with joined hands, the rākṣasī Hidiṁbā said to them, "O respected lady, you are aware of the pangs that the god of love makes women suffer. O blessed lady, I am suffering them on account of Bhīma. Think of me as a fool or a devotee or a follower, but let me have your son as my husband. Let me go away at will, taking this handsome hero with me. Trust me, O blessed lady. I promise to bring him back."

Yudhiṣṭhira said, "O lady with the speed of fancy! You two may sport as you will during the day, but you must always bring him back every night." Having promised this by saying, "So be it!", the rākṣasī Hidiṁbā took Bhīma with her and went away. Assuming a most beautiful form, and wearing many ornaments, she sported with Bhīma.

In course of time, the rākṣasī Hidiṁbā bore Bhīma a mighty son with terrible eyes, large mouth, pointed ears, copper-like lips, sharp teeth, and fearful appearance. His mother remarked that his head was bald, like a pot, and accordingly they gave him the name of Ghaṭotkaca. He was deeply devoted to the Pāṇḍavas, and became a great favourite of theirs—almost one of them. In time it was to be seen that Ghaṭotkaca had been created by the illustrious Iṅdra for the destruction of the matchless Karṇa, and in order to counteract the Śakti weapon that Iṅdra had given him.

XV

The heroic Pāṇḍavas resumed their wanderings and moved from forest to forest, continuing to study the scriptures, namely the Vedas, the Vedāṅgas, and all other moral sciences. At last they saw their grandsire Vyāsa. Respectfully greeting the illustrious Vyāsa, they stood, along with their mother, with joined hands before him. Vyāsa said, "Not far from here is a beautiful city, where you will be safe. There you may live in concealment until my return." Vyāsa then comforted them and Kuṅtī too, and took them to the city of Ekacakra, where they lived for a while in the house of a Brāhmaṇa.

After many days had passed, a Brāhmaṇa of great austerity came to live in the house of the Pāṇḍavas' host. Kuṅtī and her sons asked the Brāmaṇa if he would tell them about his experiences. Toward the end of his narrative, he spoke to them of the wonderful svayaṁvara of Draupadī, the Pāñcāla princess. He also spoke of the birth of Dhṛṣṭadyumna, of Śikhaṇḍī, and of Draupadī, who was born of no woman, but emerged from the fire in the great sacrifice of Drupada.

Questioned further, the Brāhmaṇa related in detail the circumstances of the birth of Draupadī, as follows:

Unable to forget his defeat at Droṇa's hands, King Drupada wandered among the hermitages of many Brāhmaṇas in search of experts in sacrificial rites. He was dissatisfied with the children and relatives that he already had and was always despondent; his only thought was of revenging himself on Droṇa,

When he met two sages named Yaja and Upayaja, who were studious and self controlled, Drupada requested Yaja to perform a sacrifice by which he could obtain an invincible son able to kill Droṇa in battle. As a reward, he offered Yaja ten million kine. Yaja agreed to perform the sacrifice for the destruction of Droṇa, and began to collect the various ingredients for the sacrifice. In view of the importance of the sacrifice he sought the assistance of Upayaja, who coveted nothing for himself.

King Drupada set about making the preparations needed to ensure the success of the sacrifice, which was begun in due course. When Yaja poured the sanctified libation on the fire, there emerged from the flame a boy who looked like a celestial, and was as bright as the fire from which he had arisen. He wore a crown and excellent armour, and was armed with a sword and a bow and arrows; and he roared frequently.

From the same sacrificial fire emerged a daughter, blessed with good fortune, who was called Pāñcālī. Though her complexion was dark, she was captivating and beautiful, with eyes like lotus petals and curly blue hair. She appeared like a veritable celestial damsel in human form, and her body was redolent with the sweet fragrance of the blue lotus. In sum, no maiden on earth could compare with her in appearance.

The Brāhmaṇas said, "As this son of Drupada possesses confidence and courage, and as he was so brilliant at birth, let him be called Dhṛṣṭadyumna. Since this daughter is dark in complexion, let her be called Kṛṣṇā."[1] Thus were born in the great sacrifice the son and daughter of Drupada.

[1] To avoid confusion with the Lord Kṛṣṇa, she will be invariably referred to hereafter as Draupadī.

After hearing the Brāhmaṇa's narrative, Kuṁtī became restless. She said, "O Yudhiṣṭhira, we have spent many nights in the Brāhmaṇa's house and passed our lives very pleasantly in this beautiful city, living on charity. We have now heard that alms are to be had easily in Pāñcāla and that King Drupada is devoted to the Brāhmaṇas. It is my view that one should not stay too long in one place. Therefore, O son, if you agree, we may now move to Pāñcāla." She spoke similarly to Bhīma, Arjuna, and the twins Nakula and Sahadeva, and they all said, "So be it!" Then Kuṁtī and the Pāṇḍavas saluted and thanked the Brāhmaṇa who had been their host at Ekacakra and started for the beautiful city of the high-souled Drupada.

XVI

The Pāṇḍavas at last arrived in the Pāñcāla country. After seeing the city, they took up their residence in a potter's shed. King Drupada had always cherished a secret desire to give his daughter Draupadī in marriage to Arjuna, the son of Pāṇḍu, but he never spoke of it. Having Arjuna in mind, the Pāñcāla king caused a very rigid bow to be made. He then erected a device in the sky and set up above it a golden target.

King Drupada made the following announcement: "Whoever is able to string this bow and then with these arrows to shoot the mark above the device will obtain my daughter." This proclamation of Drupada's was published far and wide, and in response to it all the kings came there, including Duryodhana and the Kurus, accompanied by Karṇa. There came also many illustrious sages desirous of seeing the svayaṁvara.

Seated in the arena along with the Brāhmaṇas, the Pāṇḍavas observed the unequalled prosperity of the Pāñcāla king. When the arena became absolutely quiet, Dhṛṣṭadyumna stood in the centre of the stage and said in a majestic voice, "Hearken, O ye assembled kings—here is the bow, these are the arrows, and there is the target. You have to shoot the target through the aperture in the device with these fine and sharp arrows. Truly I say, whosoever, being of noble birth, handsome, and strong, performs this difficult feat shall obtain today for his bride my sister Draupadī; I do not speak falsely." After giving this pledge to the assembled kings, Dhṛṣṭadyumna turned to his sister, and informed her of the names, the lineage, and the accomplishments of the assembled kings.

"O blessed girl!" said Dhṛṣṭadyumna. "All the Kṣatriyas celebrated in the world have gathered here on your account. These heroes will try to shoot the target for you. Among them, O fortunate girl, you shall take as your husband him who is able to shoot the target."

Meanwhile the young princes present, decked with earrings, bragged to one another; and each of them, believing himself to be the most skilled in arms, stood up arrogantly flaunting his weapons. But when they tried to perform the prescribed feat, those mighty princes were unable to bend that rigid bow and were all tossed to the ground where they lay motionless. Their bracelets shattered and their earrings crushed, they gave vent to exclamations of woe, having lost their hope of obtaining Draupadī.

When all the kings had failed in their attempts to string the bow, the large-hearted Arjuna rose from the midst of the Brāhmaṇas. While the assembled Brāhmaṇas were talking among themselves, Arjuna came to the bow and stood there like a mountain. He first walked round the bow in due form. Then, bowing his head, he lifted the bow and strung it in an instant. He took up the five arrows, shot the target through the aperture, and felled it to the ground. Thereupon a great tumult rose in the sky and also a great clamour in the arena, while the celestials showered divine flowers on Arjuna's head.

King Drupada was delighted at the feat of the unknown Brāhmaṇa, and desired to assist him with his army. When he announced his wish and intention of bestowing his daughter on that high-souled Brāhmaṇa, the assembled kings, all filled with rage, exchanged glances. Those powerful princes, with arms like iron maces, rose in a body and rushed upon Drupada with their weapons to kill him. Seeing all those princes surging towards him in anger and armed with bows and arrows, Drupada sought refuge with the Brāhmaṇas. Bhīma and Arjuna at once arose to resist the kings advancing upon Drupada like mad elephants, and fought them fearlessly. In the course of the fight Bhīma overcame Śalya in single combat. Seeing that feat of Bhīma, the Lord Kṛṣṇa surmised that both of them were the sons of Kuṅtī. He persuaded the princes to desist, saying, "She has been won fairly." Those heroes among men, Bhīma and Arjuna, who had been severely injured by their enemies, at last emerged from the crowd, looking resplendent, and followed by Draupadī.

Meanwhile, at home, Kuṅtī began to fear various evils that might have befallen her sons, since they did not return even though it was past the time for alms. Out of her love for her sons, Kuṅtī thought that something terrible must have happened to them.

It was late in the afternoon when Arjuna, attended by many Brāhmaṇas and with a Brāhmaṇa preceding him, entered the humble potter's shed, like the sun emerging from the clouds. Those best of men, Bhīma and Arjuna, then came to their mother, and represented Draupadī to her as the "alms" they had obtained that day. Kuṅtī, who was inside the room, did not see her sons or Draupadī. She therefore replied from within, "Share equally, all of you, whatever you have got." A moment later she came out, saw the maiden, and exclaimed, "Alas! what have I said?"

XVII

Kṛṣṇa and Balarāma, who had a shrewd suspicion that the heroes of the svayaṁvara were the Pāṇḍavas, now came to the potter's shed where the Pāṇḍavas were living. Yudhiṣṭhira, foremost of the Kuru race, made kind inquiries about Kṛṣṇa's welfare, and said, "O Vāsudeva, how were you able to trace us, living as we are in hiding?" Kṛṣṇa smilingly replied, "O king, even if a fire is hidden, it can be traced. Who else among men, save the Pāṇḍavas, can perform such feats?" He then blessed them, took leave of them, and went away, accompanied by Balarāma.

Meanwhile Drupada had sent his priest with a message to the Pāṇḍavas. The priest said, "A goodly feast has been prepared for the bridegroom's party by King Drupada to celebrate his daughter's wedding. After completing your daily observances, please join him without delay, along with Draupadī. These splendid cars, adorned with golden lotuses and drawn by swift horses, are truly fit for kings and are at your disposal. I request you all kindly to mount them and drive to the palace of King Drupada." The Pāṇḍavas accepted the invitation of the king. They sent away the priest and, having seated Kuṁtī and Draupadī on one of the cars, they ascended those splendid vehicles and drove to the palace. As befitted a royal banquet, well-dressed waiters and waitresses and accomplished cooks served excellent dishes on plates made of gold and silver.

After dinner King Drupada addressed Prince Yudhiṣṭhira as if he were a Brāhmaṇa. Cheerfully he asked that illustrious son of Kuṁtī, "How should we treat you, as Kṣatriyas or Brāhmaṇas?" Yudhiṣṭhira replied: "O king, we are Kṣatriyas, sons of the famous Pāṇḍu. I am the eldest of the sons of Kuṁtī and these two are Bhīma and Arjuna, who won your daughter in the svayaṁvara. The twins Nakula and Sahadeva are standing near Draupadī. So banish the sorrow weighing on your mind, for we too are Kṣatriyas. This your daughter is like a lotus which has been transplanted from one lake to another." On hearing this, King Drupada was filled with delight. His eyes showed his pleasure and for some time he could not answer Yudhiṣṭhira.

Drupada said, after a while, "O hero, take the hand of my daughter in holy wedlock with all due rites, or give her hand to whomsoever you think best." Yudhiṣṭhira replied: "O king, Draupadī shall be the queen of us all, as ordained by our mother." Drupada then said, "O descendant of Kuru, I know it is permissible for a husband to have many wives, but a wife has never been allowed to have more than one husband. Pure as you are, and acquainted with the moral code, do not commit a sinful act that is against both the scriptures and usage."

Yudhiṣṭhira replied: "O great king, morality is subtle and we do not know its ways. Let us therefore tread the path of our illustrious predecessors." Thereupon they all discussed this matter; and at that very time Vyāsa came there by chance. King Drupada welcomed the great sage with due rites, after which he sought the views of that illustrious man on the subject of the marriage of Draupadī.

Vyāsa replied: "Once upon a time, there lived in a hermitage the daughter of an illustrious sage. She was beautiful and chaste, but she did not get a husband. She propitiated the god Śiva by her strict penance. The Lord appeared before her and said, 'Ask of me whatever you wish.' In reply, she repeatedly said to the Lord, the giver of boons, 'I desire to have a husband endowed with all good qualities.' Śiva gave her the boon with a joyful heart and said, 'You shall have five husbands.'

"She said again, 'O Śiva, I desire to have only one accomplished husband.' The god of gods, well pleased with her, then replied in these auspicious words, 'You have asked me five times, "Give me a husband." O blessed one, it shall therefore be as you have asked. All this will come to pass in one of your future incarnations.'

Vyāsa continued, "O Drupada! That maiden of celestial grace was reborn as your daughter. The faultless Draupadī of the Pṛṣata family was predestined to be the wife of five men. After severe penances, the divine Lakṣmī herself emerged from the great sacrifice as your daughter, for the benefit of the Pāṇḍavas. O king, that beautiful goddess, on whom all the celestials attend, becomes the wife of five husbands, impelled by her own destiny. She was created by Brahmā for this very purpose. Now, knowing all this, do as you desire."

Drupada then said, "I now understand that in her former life Draupadī asked the Lord five times, 'Give me a husband.' The Lord granted her boon accordingly, and he himself knows the propriety of this." Thereupon King Drupada and his son Dhṛṣṭadyumna made preparations for the marriage. The king gave away his daughter Draupadī, duly bathed and adorned with many gems. Then those mighty car-warriors, the ornaments of the Kuru race, took Draupadī's hand day by day in succession. When the wedding celebrations were over, the Pāṇḍavas passed their days happily in the capital of the Pāñcāla king Drupada.

XVIII

Vidura came to know that Draupadī had married the Pāṇḍavas and that the sons of Dhṛtarāṣṭra had returned shamefaced and humiliated. Well pleased at this, he went to Dhṛtarāṣṭra, and told him, "The Kurus are enjoying their good fortune and flourishing." He went on to tell Dhṛtarāṣṭra that the Pāṇḍavas were alive and well, had been well received by Drupada, and had also obtained many powerful allies.

Then Duryodhana and Karṇa came to Dhṛtarāṣṭra and said to him, "It is high time that we consult together, so that the Pāṇḍavas may not devour us all, including our sons, forces, and relatives." In the course of their consultations, Duryodhana suggested: "Let us secretly set up factions amongst the Pāṇḍavas, between the sons of Kuṅtī and those of Mādrī, with the help of trusted and artful Brāhmaṇas."

Karṇa said: "O Duryodhana, in my opinion your thinking is not logical. I do not believe the Pāṇḍavas can be overcome by subterfuge. I feel that it is advisable for us to attack the Pāṇḍavas right now when they are unprepared and exterminate them. O king! I pray you approve of this." Dhṛtarāṣṭra said: "Please take counsel with Bhīṣma, Droṇa, and Vidura: you may then adopt whatever policy may lead to our good." Thereupon the illustrious King Dhṛtarāṣṭra called in all those advisers and consulted them.

Bhīṣma said, "O Dhṛtarāṣṭra, I can never agree to a fight with the sons of Pāṇḍu. Pāṇḍu was as dear to me as you are. The sons of Gāndhārī and the sons of Kuṅtī are equally dear to me. O Dhṛtarāṣṭra, you have as much a duty to protect them as I have. I do not like the prospect of a quarrel with them. Be reconciled with those heroes and give them some territory today, since this is the hereditary kingdom of the Pāṇḍavas too."

Droṇa said: "Sire, I share the views of the illustrious Bhīṣma. Let the sons of Kuṅtī have a portion of the kingdom. This is eternal virtue." Vidura said: "O king, wash yourself of the taint which has stained you, on account of the act of Purocana, by treating the Pāṇḍavas fairly and kindly now." Dhṛtarāṣṭra said to Vidura: "The learned

Bhīṣma, the holy Droṇa, and you yourself have spoken the truth and advised what is good for me. O Vidura, go and bring hither those good people, the Pāṇḍavas, along with their mother, as well as Draupadī of heavenly beauty." Thus, at the bidding of Dhṛtarāṣṭra, Vidura went to Drupada's capital to bring back the Pāṇḍavas.

The illustrious Drupada gave the Pāṇḍavas, as well as his daughter and the wise Vidura, leave to depart. Taking with them Draupadī and the venerable Kuntī, they travelled in pleasurable anticipation to Hāstinapura. On arrival, those illustrious and mighty heroes rested for some time. They were then summoned by King Dhṛtarāṣṭra and Bhīṣma. Dhṛtarāṣṭra said: "O Yudhiṣṭhira, listen with your brothers to these my words. Let no disagreement arise again between us. Take half the kingdom and settle at Khāṇḍavaprastha, protected by Arjuna as are the celestials by Indra. If you reside there, no one will be able to harm you."

The Pāṇḍavas then moved to Khāṇḍavaprastha, led by Lord Kṛṣṇa. Those heroes of unfading splendour beautified the place, turned it into a veritable heaven, and renamed it Indraprastha. On a delightful and auspicious site was erected the palace of the Pāṇḍavas, filled with every kind of luxury, like the palace of the celestial treasurer Kubera himself. There the ever truthful Yudhiṣṭhira virtuously ruled his kingdom along with his brothers.

XIX

Meanwhile Arjuna decided to go on a pilgrimage for twelve years. Toward the end of his journey he visited one after the other all the sacred waters and other holy places that were situated on the shores of the western ocean, and at last came to Prabhāsa. Kṛṣṇa, hearing of Arjuna's pilgrimage and of his arrival in Prabhāsa went to see his friend, the son of Kuntī.

When Kṛṣṇa and Arjuna met, they embraced each other and enquired after each other's health. Those two friends, who were none other than the ancient sages Nārāyaṇa and Nara, then sat down together and had a long talk. Next morning, after he had performed the daily rites, Arjuna was greeted by Kṛṣṇa. Then, riding on a golden chariot, the two friends proceeded to Kṛṣṇa's home in Dvārakā. Arjuna passed many nights in the charming palace of Kṛṣṇa, adorned with gems and filled with every means of enjoyment.

One day the Vṛṣṇis and the Aṅdhakas celebrated a great festival on the Raivataka hill. Kṛṣṇa and Arjuna went together to that splendid and delightful festival. While they were walking around, they saw Bhadrā, the beautiful daughter of Vasudeva, wearing many ornaments and surrounded by her companions. The moment Arjuna saw her, he was smitten with love for her. Kṛṣṇa observed that Arjuna was looking at her with undivided attention. The lotus-eyed one said, smiling, to that best of men, "How is it that the mind of one who wanders in the woods is thus disturbed by desire?"

Having teased Arjuna thus, Kṛṣṇa went on to say, "O Arjuna, she is the sister of Balarāma and myself, and her name is Subhadrā. If in your mind you are bent upon her, I shall then speak to my father." "O Kṛṣṇa," said Arjuna, "tell me how I may obtain her. I shall do anything that is humanly possible in order to have her." Kṛṣṇa said, "Men learned in the precepts of morality say that, in the case of heroic Kṣatriyas, the kidnapping of a girl for the purpose of matrimony is also laudable. O Arjuna, I advise you to take away my sister Subhadrā by force, for who knows what she may do in a svayamvara?"

Meanwhile Subhadrā completed her worship and, having been blessed by all the Brāhmaṇas, made a circuit of the hill and returned towards Dvārakā. Arjuna, suddenly dashing towards her, made her mount his chariot, and having abducted that lady of sweet smiles, he drove towards his own city on his birdlike car.

Seeing Subhadrā thus taken away by force, her armed attendants all ran crying to the city of Dvārakā. Then Balarāma said to Kṛṣṇa, "O Kṛṣṇa, why are you silent? It was because of you that Arjuna was welcomed by us. It seems that the evil-minded befouler of his own race did not deserve such honour. I shall today single-handed rid the earth of all the descendants of Kuru. Never shall I forgive this trespass of Arjuna!"

Kṛṣṇa replied, "Arjuna has not affronted our family by his action; on the contrary, there is no doubt that he has raised our prestige. This match is indeed very proper. Arjuna is as renowned as Subhadrā is illustrious. With this in mind, he has carried her away by force. Who is there that would not be honoured by an alliance with Arjuna, born in the race of Bharata and the great Śaṅtanu, who is also the grandson of Kuṅtibhoja? If Arjuna returns to Iṅdraprastha after defeating us, our good name will suffer. On the other hand, there is no dishonour in conciliation."

Kṛṣṇa's calm counsel prevailed over Balarāma's indignation, and Arjuna went back to Dvārakā, where he was married to Subhadrā. He passed the last days of his pilgrimage at Puṣkara, and returned to Iṅdraprastha after twelve years had been completed. Then Kṛṣṇa's beloved sister Subhadrā gave birth to an illustrious son. That son was Abhimanyu, who had long arms, a broad chest, and beautiful eyes; he was destined to be a hero. The child, waxing like the moon, became from his childhood a favourite of Kṛṣṇa, and also of his father and uncles, and indeed of all the people. He learnt from Arjuna, his father, the science of arms, both human and celestial, with its four branches and ten divisions.

The blessed Pāñcāla princess Draupadī also bore, to her five husbands, five heroic and excellent sons. Prativiṅdhya was born to Yudhiṣṭhira, Sutasoma to Bhima, Śrutakarmā to Arjuna, Śatānīka to Nakula, and Śrutasena to Sahadeva; they were all great car-warriors. Having been blessed with sons, all of whom were like celestials, broad-chested and powerful, the Pāṇḍavas became very happy.

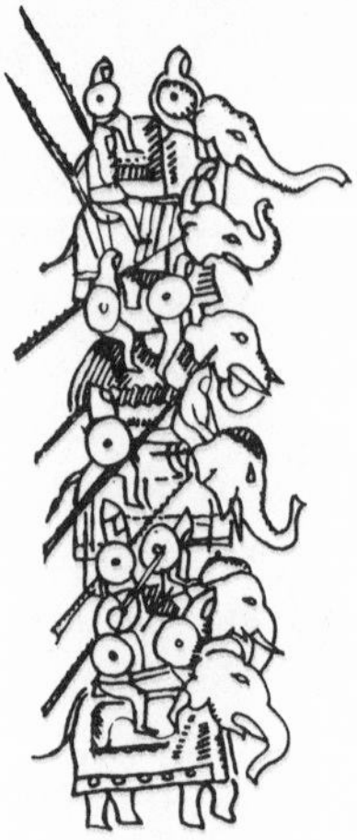

Sabhā Parva

XX

When the Pāṇḍavas decided to erect a splendid hall in Iṅdraprastha, Maya, the chief architect of the Dānavas, volunteered his services. Lord Kṛṣṇa said to Maya, "Build a hall which will be unique in the whole world, and will astound all men who see it." Maya happily accepted this command and designed for the Pāṇḍavas a hall in the form of an aerial car. He then marked out a site ten thousand cubits square, well suited to all the seasons and very picturesque, on which he constructed the hall.

The assembly hall, which covered the entire area of the site, had golden pillars. It was very graceful, radiant as fire, so bright as to dim even the rays of the sun, and sparkled with a heavenly light, like the moon. In that hall Maya built a magnificent tank embellished with lotuses that had leaves made of vaiḍurya and stalks of brilliant gems. It was redolent with the fragrance of lotuses and was stocked with different birds, as well as with tortoises and fish. Having completed the construction of this unique assembly hall in fourteen months, Maya informed Yudhiṣṭhira that the work was done.

When the high-souled Pāṇḍavas were holding court in the assembly hall, the illustrious sage Nārada visited them, accompanied by other sages, in the course of his peregrinations all over the world. Nārada said: "O king! monarchs who perform the rājasūya sacrifice rejoice with Iṅdra. It is said that this sacrifice is full of hurdles. The Brahmarākṣasas like to hinder it. Any small incident may start a war that will destroy the whole world. O king of kings, ponder all this, and do what is beneficial. Be determined in protecting the four castes. Be happy and please the Brāhmaṇas with gifts." After thus advising Yudhiṣṭhira, Nārada departed. Thereupon Yudhiṣṭhira began to consult with his brothers regarding the performance of that most illustrious and difficult of sacrifices, the rājasūya.

After much reflection, Yudhiṣṭhira decided to make preparations for the performance. Thinking that Kṛṣṇa would be the best person to decide the question, he mentally communed with him. Kṛṣṇa immediately came to Yudhiṣṭhira, who received him affectionately, like a brother. Kṛṣṇa was also happy to see his aunt[1] Kuntī, as well as Bhīma.

"O Kṛṣṇa," said Yudhiṣṭhira, "I would like to perform the rājasūya sacrifice; but it cannot be accomplished by a mere wish. You know well how it can be done. My friends suggest that I should perform the rājasūya, but your advice on this matter will be final."

"O best of the Bharatas," Kṛṣṇa replied, "you are endowed with the attributes of an emperor. It is fitting that you should establish your dominion over all the Kṣatriyas. At the same time, I do not believe that you will be able to perform the rājasūya sacrifice as long as the powerful Jarāsandha remains alive. He cannot be defeated in battle by all the asuras and all the celestials. But I believe he can be overcome in single combat. If you have faith in me, give me Bhīma and Arjuna to help me overcome this obstacle."

Yudhiṣṭhira said, "For the fulfilment of our objective let Arjuna follow the best of the Yadus, Kṛṣṇa, and let Bhīma follow Arjuna. Let us hope that tact coupled with prowess will bring about success." Thus blessed by Yudhiṣṭhira, Kṛṣṇa left for Magadha along with Arjuna and Bhīma. In time they entered the kingdom of the great King Jarāsandha, like Himālayan lions entering a cattle pen. When the people of Magadha saw those heroes with broad chests, resembling elephants, they were greatly surprised.

Kṛṣṇa said to Jarāsandha, "O king of Magadha, we challenge you to a duel. Either release all the kings whom you have unjustly imprisoned, or go to the abode of Yama." Jarāsandha replied: "I have never imprisoned any king wrongfully. Who is kept prisoner whom I have

[1] Kuntī was the sister of Kṛṣṇa's father, Vasudeva.

not conquered? I am ready to fight on any terms, an army against an army, or alone against any one, any two, or all three of you."

Kṛṣṇa then said, "O king, name the one amongst us three whom you wish to fight. Who amongst us should be prepared to fight with you?" In reply to Kṛṣṇa, the king of Magadha, Jarāsandha, chose to fight with Bhīma. The combat began on the first day of the month of Kārtika, and continued without any respite, day and night, for thirteen days. On the night of the fourteenth day the Magadha king stopped from exhaustion.

Taking advantage of Jarāsandha's weariness, Bhīma caught hold of him, whirled him by his shoulders a hundred times, dashed him on the ground, and shattered his back. Then he roared in triumph. All the citizens, headed by the Brāhmaṇas, approached Bhīma respectfully and honoured him with every due rite. The liberated kings also offered their respects to Kṛṣṇa and spoke to him in peace. Kṛṣṇa consoled all those who were afraid and at once crowned the son of Jarāsandha as his father's successor to the throne. The Pāṇḍavas and Kṛṣṇa then returned to Indraprastha, and Kṛṣṇa informed Yudhiṣṭhira, "O best among kings, providentially the powerful Jarāsandha was defeated by Bhīma and the imprisoned kings have been released. You may therefore proceed with your plans for the great sacrifice."

Arjuna said to Yudhiṣṭhira: "O best among kings, I think that we should now add to our wealth and exact tribute from other kings." Yudhiṣṭhira approved of this, and Arjuna, accompanied by a large army, set forth on the divine and wonderful chariot given to him by Agni. Similarly the twins Nakula and Sahadeva, and Bhīma, after having been blessed by Yudhiṣṭhira, left with their respective armies. Arjuna reduced the north, Bhīma the east, Sahadeva the south, and Nakula the west. Meanwhile Yudhiṣṭhira stayed at Indraprastha.

After praising his virtues, Kṛṣṇa said to Yudhiṣṭhira, "O emperor, you alone are worthy of performing the great sacrifice. If you complete it satisfactorily and obtain its benefit, then we shall all be happy." Thus advised by Kṛṣṇa, Yudhiṣṭhira, assisted by his brothers, completed the arrangements for the performance of the rājasūya. Vyāsa himself officiated as its high priest, and Susāma, best among the Dhanañjayas, chanted the Sāma Veda. Then Yudhiṣṭhira sent Nakula to Hāstinapura to invite Bhīṣma, Droṇa, Dhṛtarāṣṭra, Vidura, Kṛpa, and all his brothers and relatives, to attend the great sacrifice.

Rivalling Varuṇa in splendour, Yudhiṣṭhira began the sacrifice marked by six sacrificial fires. He propitiated all the visitors with ceremonial offerings and many rich gifts. The mighty Kṛṣṇa, armed with the bow, the cakra, and the club, stood guard over the great sacrifice until its completion. Thereafter Kṛṣṇa and Yudhiṣṭhira took leave of each other and departed to their respective homes. After Kṛṣṇa had left for Dvārakā, only King Duryodhana and his uncle Śakuni stayed on in that celestial hall.

XXI

Lingering in that hall, Duryodhana inspected it at leisure along with Śakuni. He saw many unique things such as he had never beheld in the city of Hāstinapura. Once he reached a transparent surface and, mistaking it for water, drew up his clothes and went around the hall; when he discovered his error he felt ashamed and unhappy. Then he mistook a pond with crystal-clear water, adorned with lotuses, for land and fell into the water fully clothed. The servants laughed at this, but provided him with dry clothes at the royal command of Yudhiṣṭhira. The mighty Bhīma, Arjuna, the twins, and everybody else laughed at Duryodhana's discomfiture.

Duryodhana could not forgive their derision but, to save appearances, he ignored it. He then took leave of the Pāṇḍavas, but having witnessed the wonderful opulence displayed at the great rājasūya sacrifice, he returned to the city of Hāstinapura sad at heart. On his return, Śakuni said, "O Duryodhana, why are you going about sighing like this?" Duryodhana replied, "O uncle, I have observed the whole world brought under the sovereignty of Yudhiṣṭhira by the great Arjuna's skill in the use of arms. I have also seen the great sacrifice of Yudhiṣṭhira, which can be compared only to that performed by the glorious

Iṅdra among the gods. Because of this, I am filled with envy which burns me day and night, and I feel dried up like a small pond in the summer."

"O Duryodhana," said Śakuni, "you should not envy Yudhiṣṭhira. After all, the Pāṇḍavas are enjoying their own good fortune." This was no consolation to Duryodhana, who replied: "If you will let me do so, I shall conquer them with your help and that of the great car-warriors who are our allies. Then the world will be mine, including that opulent assembly hall of great wealth, while all the kings will do me homage." Śakuni said, "The Pāṇḍavas cannot be defeated in battle even by the gods; they are great car-warriors, expert bowmen, learned in the science of arms, and eager for battle. But I know how Yudhiṣṭhira can be overcome."

Duryodhana's spirits picked up on hearing this. He said, "O uncle, tell me how they can be defeated without risk to our friends." Śakuni said, "Yudhiṣṭhira is fond of gambling, though he is no expert at throwing the dice. If he is invited to a game, he will not be able to resist the temptation. I am an expert gambler, without equal in the three worlds. Therefore ask Yudhiṣṭhira to play a game of dice. But, Duryodhana, you must inform the king, your father, about this. With his permission, I shall defeat Yudhiṣṭhira without a doubt."

Duryodhana readily agreed to this plan. Śakuni then went up to Dhṛtarāṣṭra and said, "O great king, you should know that Duryodhana has become pallid, wasted, weak, and absent-minded." Dhṛtarāṣṭra sent for his son and said to him, "O my son, why are you so sad? If you can confide in me, tell me why." "O king," replied Duryodhana, "I am unhappy on seeing the boundless wealth of the enemy. I am obsessed with this thought, so that I cannot obtain any peace of mind."

Śakuni then said, "O king, listen to the stratagem by which you can gain the matchless wealth of Yudhiṣṭhira which you have seen. I am adept in the art of throwing the dice. Yudhiṣṭhira likes to gamble, though he does not know how to throw the dice. If invited to play, he will surely respond. Therefore, ask him to a game." Dhṛtarāṣṭra said, "The wise Vidura is my adviser on whose counsel I act. I shall first consult him and I shall then know how to decide this issue." Duryodhana said, "If Vidura is consulted, this plan will not go through, and, O king of kings, if you stop this, I shall certainly commit suicide."

On hearing these sad words of his beloved son, Dhṛtarāṣṭra ordered his servants, "Let the masons quickly build a commodious and beautiful hall with a thousand pillars and a hundred doors. It must be well built and easily accessible, adorned with gems all over and provided with dice. Let me know when the hall is completed."

When the hall was ready, King Dhṛtarāṣṭra said to Vidura, his chief adviser, "Go to Prince Yudhiṣṭhira and request him on my behalf to come here quickly, along with his brothers, to see this wonderful assembly hall of mine, adorned with costly jewels and furnished with luxurious couches. We shall also have a friendly game of dice."

Vidura said, "O king, I do not like your message. Do not act thus. I apprehend the destruction of the family, for I fear there will soon be a quarrel amongst the brothers." Dhṛtarāṣṭra said, "O Vidura, if fate so ordains, such a quarrel will not trouble me. This world does not act on its own, but only at the will of the Creator and under the influence of fate. Therefore, go to the king as I have directed, and quickly fetch here the invincible Yudhiṣṭhira."

Thus Vidura was forced by Dhṛtarāṣṭra to go to fetch the wise Pāṇḍavas. When he reached Yudhiṣṭhira, the latter said, "I can see that you are unhappy. Vidura, is your mission one of peace? Are the sons of Dhṛtarāṣṭra behaving well? Are the subjects docile?" Vidura replied sorrowfully, "The king is well, as are his sons, but he is obstinate and selfish, and bent on self-aggrandisement. The king of the Kurus asked me to tell you, having first made kind enquiries after your happiness and welfare, 'This hall matches yours in appearance, my son; so come and visit it along with your brothers. In it, O Yudhiṣṭhira, have an enjoyable game of dice with your brothers. We will be delighted if you can come, and so will all the Kurus assembled here.' "

After giving this message, Vidura continued, "You will see gamblers and cheats placed there by King Dhṛtarāṣṭra. I have come to give you this message. Do as you think fit." After considering the situation, Yudhiṣṭhira replied, "Terrible cheats and deceitful gamblers will be there. But we all have to submit to fate and the will of the Creator. I do not wish to play with cheats, and I am reluctant to gamble with Śakuni unless that insolent one challenges me in the hall. If challenged, however, I shall never disregard it. This is my firm vow."

Having said this to Vidura, Yudhiṣṭhira quickly ordered everybody to get ready to depart. The next day he started for Hāstinapura with his family and servants, and also the ladies, led by Draupadī. Having reached Hāstinapura, they spent the night happily. Then, early the next morning, they all completed their daily rites and entered the splendid hall full of gamblers.

XXII

Śakuni said, "O king, here are people gathered to capacity in this hall and ready to play. O Yudhiṣṭhira, now is the time to cast the dice and to agree on the rules of the game." "I have vowed that I shall not refuse to play if I am challenged," replied Yudhiṣṭhira. "O king, destiny is powerful and I am in its grip. Tell me, whom should I take on in this assembly? Who among these players can match my stakes? Answer me, and then let the game begin."

Duryodhana said, "O king, I shall furnish the gems and riches needed for stakes and my uncle Śakuni will play on my behalf." Yudhiṣṭhira replied, "It seems to me that it is wrong for one to play for another. I am sure even you will accept that. However, let it be as you wish." He continued, "O king, this expensive chain, rich with gems and adorned with the finest gold, and obtained from the ocean, this is my stake. What is the stake with which you will match it? I am going to win this stake." So saying, he cast the dice. Then Śakuni, who knew the secret of gambling, grabbed the dice. He cast them and then said to Yudhiṣṭhira, "I have won."

Yudhiṣṭhira said, "You won that stake by cheating. Fie on you, O Śakuni! Let us play staking thousands. I now stake these hundred jars, each filled with a thousand gold coins." They played, and again Śakuni claimed, "I have won." When the game had gone on for a while and Yudhiṣṭhira had lost again and again, Śakuni said, "O Yudhiṣṭhira, you have lost the greater part of the wealth of the Pāṇḍavas. Tell me if you have any assets left." Yudhiṣṭhira said, "O king, my city, my kingdom, my lands, the property that does not belong to the Brāhmaṇas, and the subjects who are not Brāhmaṇas—these are my remaining assets. With this as my stake, O king, I shall now play against you." Once more Śakuni cheated when casting the dice and said to Yudhiṣṭhira, "I have won."

Having lost all his wealth, Yudhiṣṭhira said, "This dark young man with crimson eyes, who looks like a lion and is endowed with mighty shoulders, Nakula, is now my stake." Thereupon, Śakuni cast the dice again and claimed that he had won. Yudhiṣṭhira then said, "Sahadeva dispenses justice and has earned a reputation for wisdom throughout the world; though he does not deserve this and is dear to me, I shall stake him." Again Śakuni cheated when casting the dice, and told Yudhiṣṭhira, "I have won."

"O king," said Śakuni, "I have won both the sons of Mādrī, who are dear to you. Apparently Bhīma and Arjuna are even dearer to you, since you do not wish to stake them." Thus taunted, Yudhiṣṭhira said, "I shall now stake Arjuna who enables us to sail through a battle like a boat, who is the conqueror of enemies, who is a vigorous prince and the hero of the world." Having heard this, Śakuni again cheated when casting the dice, and told Yudhiṣṭhira, "I have won."

"O king," Yudhiṣṭhira said, "I shall now offer as my stake Bhīma, our leader, who leads us singlehanded in battle, who has straight eyes and close-set eyebrows, who has the shoulders of a lion and who never forgives an insult, whose strength is unmatched among humans, who is foremost among club-fighters, and who destroys his enemies." Śakuni, cheating while casting the dice, again said to Yudhiṣṭhira, "I have won."

Yudhiṣṭhira then said, "The only person left is myself, dear to my brothers. If I, too, am won we shall accept our misfortune and the lot of the vanquished." Having heard this, Śakuni cheated again when casting the dice, and told Yudhiṣṭhira, "I have won."

Śakuni then said, "There is one stake left that has not been won as yet—your beloved queen. Stake Draupadī, the daughter of the

Pāñcāla king, and win back freedom along with her." "O wretch," replied Yudhiṣṭhira, "I shall now stake the slender-waisted and beautiful Draupadī, the princess of Pāñcāla, and play with you." When Yudhiṣṭhira said these words, the assembled elders voiced their disapproval. But, flushed with victory and mad with conceit, Śakuni cast the dice once more and said, "I have won."

Duryodhana said, "O Vidura, go and fetch Draupadī, the beloved spouse of the Pāṇḍavas. Let her clean this house and be one of our servant maids." Vidura said, "O fool, you cannot see that by these words you are binding yourself with cords. You do not realize that you are hanging on a precipice. You do not know that you are behaving like a child, like a deer rousing tigers."

Drunk with pride, Duryodhana ignored this warning, saying, "Fie on Vidura." He noticed Prātikāmī in the hall and told him, in the midst of the venerable assembly, "Prātikāmī, fetch Draupadī here, since you are not afraid of the Pāṇḍavas. Vidura speaks in fear, and he never wished us well."

Accordingly, Prātikāmī went to the Pāṇḍavas' residence and told Draupadī of his errand. Draupadī then said, "O son of a charioteer, go and ascertain from the gambler in the hall whether he lost himself, or me, first. When you have this information, return to me and then lead me there." When Prātikāmī returned with this message from Draupadī, Duryodhana said, "O Duḥśāsana, this son of my charioteer is weak-minded and afraid of Bhīma. Go yourself to Draupadī and seize and bring her here. What can these husbands of hers do, having lost their freedom?"

XXIII

His eyes red with anger, Prince Duḥśāsana rose at his brother's words, and entered the residence of those great car-warriors, the Pāṇḍavas. There he said to the Princess Draupadī, "Come, O Pāñcālī, you have been won. Discard your shyness and look at Duryodhana. O lady whose eyes are like lotus petals, respect the Kurus, who have won you fairly, and enter the hall." On hearing these words, the miserable

Draupadī rose up in sorrow and, covering her pale face with her hands, she ran to the ladies' quarters in the palace of the old king. Thereupon Duḥśāsana ran after her in hot pursuit, roaring in anger, and caught hold of her by her long blue wavy tresses. He roughly dragged the defenceless Draupadī by her hair to the hall, while she quivered pitiably like a plantain tree in a storm.

With her hair dishevelled and her dress in disarray, the bashful Draupadī said deliberately, in anger, "O shame! The moral standards of the Bhāratas and of the Kṣatriya code have perished. In this hall everybody assembled looks on while the bounds of virtue are transgressed." So saying, she looked at her helpless husbands. While she was thus invoking virtue, Duḥśāsana shook her with even greater force, repeatedly calling her a slave and laughing aloud. Except for Duryodhana, Duḥṣāsana, Śakuni, and Karṇa, all those present felt very sad on seeing Draupadī thus dragged into the hall.

Bhīma then said to Yudhiṣṭhira, "All the tribute and other wealth you took from the king of Kāśī, all the gems the other kings presented to you, our chariots, our armour and weapons, our kingdom, and even our own selves, have all been lost in gambling. None of this provoked my anger, since you are our lord. But I think you went too far when you played with Draupadī as a stake."

Meanwhile, the evil Duḥśāsana began to pull at Draupadī's clothes, intending to disrobe her by force in the middle of the hall.[1] But as her clothes were thus being pulled off, many similar clothes appeared in their place. There were loud acclamations from all the kings who saw that most miraculous spectacle.

Then Bhīma swore in a loud voice in the presence of those kings, with his lower lip trembling in anger, and squeezing one hand in the other, "O kings, O men, listen to these my words which have never yet been uttered by any man and which will never be said by anyone else. If I do not drink the blood of this sinful, lowborn wretch Duḥśāsana in battle after rending apart his chest, let me forego the path of my ancestors!" Hearing his vow, which astonished everybody,

[1] In other recensions, there is reference to a silent prayer by Draupadī addressed to Lord Kṛṣṇa to come to her rescue. See footnotes to Poona Edition, II, 304.

many in the hall acclaimed Bhīma vigorously and condemned Duḥśāsana. When finally a mass of clothes was heaped in the midst of the assembly, Duḥśāsana, tired and abashed, gave up his evil design and sat down.

Draupadī then said, "I, who was seen only in the svayaṁvara arena by the assembled kings, and was never seen elsewhere in public, have been brought by force to the assembly hall today. I think that these are evil times when the Kurus allow their daughter-in-law to be thus tormented. O Kauravas, say whether this wife of Yudhiṣṭhira, born like him of a royal family, is a slave or not. I shall accept your verdict."

Upon this, Duryodhana said to Yudhiṣṭhira, "Bhīma, Arjuna, and the twins are subject to your command. Reply to Draupadī's question, whether you deem her won or not." Having said this, and with the purpose of encouraging Karṇa and annoying Bhīma, before Draupadī's very eyes Duryodhana bared his left thigh. Bhīma then vowed, "Let me forego the regions of my ancestors if I do not break that thigh of yours in the great battle that is to come."

Meanwhile, thoroughly abashed by Draupadī's appeal, Dhṛtarāṣṭra said, "O Pāñcālī, ask any boon you wish of me. Virtuous and devoted to Dharma as you are, I regard you as the foremost of my daughters-in-law." Draupadī said, "O best of the Bhāratas, if you would give me a boon, I pray that the ever dutiful Yudhiṣṭhira may be set free." Dhṛtarāṣṭra granted her wish and said, "O blessed one, my heart goes out to you. You deserve more than one boon. I wish to give you a second boon; ask of me whatever you want." Draupadī then said, "Let Bhīma and Arjuna, Nakula and Sahadeva be given their chariots and bows: this is my second wish."

Dhṛtarāṣṭra then said, "Ask of me a third boon, for two boons are not enough for you. Truly you are the most virtuous and illustrious of my daughters-in-law." Draupadī said, "O best of kings, avarice kills virtue; I do not wish to be greedy and I do not deserve a third boon. These my husbands, having been rescued from the miserable state of slavery, will win prosperity by their good deeds."

"O king," said Yudhiṣṭhira, "command us and tell us what we should do, for you are our lord. We wish to obey your commands at all times." Dhṛtarāṣṭra said, "O Yudhiṣṭhira, I wish you everlasting prosperity! I give you leave to go in safety and rule your own kingdom with all your wealth intact." Then Yudhiṣṭhira saluted and took leave of everybody, and left with his brothers. Accompanied by Draupadī, they mounted their cars, and with happy minds they left for the most splendid of cities, Indraprastha.

XXIV

After the departure of the Pāṇḍavas, Duḥśāsana said to Duryodhana, Karṇa, and Śakuni, "O great car-warriors, the old man has ruined what was achieved with so much effort and difficulty. The wealth has returned to the enemy." Then Duryodhana said to Dhṛtarāṣṭra, "O father, having got back their weapons and cars, the Pāṇḍavas will kill us like angry serpents. O best of the Bhāratas, there is only one solution: we should again gamble with the Pāṇḍavas, the penalty for the losers being exile to the forest, and we shall thus be able to control them. Either one of us, having lost at dice, shall enter the thick forest, dressed in skins, and live there for twelve years. In the thirteenth year the losers shall live in hiding amid the people. If recognized during this period, they shall return to the forest for another twelve years."

"One or the other of us shall live in this way," Duryodhana continued. "Therefore let the game commence once more. Let the dice be cast, and let the Pāṇḍavas be invited again to play. O king, this is our most important task. You know that Śakuni is skilled in the art of gambling. O king, if at the end of the thirteenth year the Pāṇḍavas return after having kept the vow, we can easily conquer them. By then we will be firmly established in our kingdom, and meanwhile we shall have gained allies and built up a strong, big, and invincible army. O destroyer of foes, consider this." Dhṛtarāṣṭra said, "Ask the Pāṇḍavas quickly to come back, even if they have gone some distance. Let them return and play again."

Prātikāmī was then dispatched to invite Yudhiṣṭhira to come and play again. Prātikāmī said, "O King Yudhiṣṭhira, the assembly is gathered and your father has asked me to invite you again to come and play at dice." "All creatures receive good or evil at the command of the Creator," said Yudhiṣṭhira. "If I have to play once more, it is inevitable. I know that this command of the king, this fresh invitation to a game of dice, will cause desolation all round. But even so, I am not able to disregard it." So saying, he returned to the gambling hall.

Śakuni then said, "The old king returned your wealth, and that is truly commendable. But listen to me carefully, for I am going to propose another very high stake. If you defeat us at dice we shall be exiled in the forest for twelve years, clad in deerskins, and shall live in hiding during the thirteenth year. If recognized during this period, we shall go into exile in the forest for another twelve years. On the other hand, if we defeat you, you shall likewise live in exile in the forest for twelve years, dressed in deerskins, and accompanied by Draupadī. At the end of the thirteenth year, one or the other shall regain his own kingdom. O Yudhiṣṭhira, with this compact between us, cast the dice for the game, and let us play."

"O Śakuni," said Yudhiṣṭhira, "how can a dutiful king like me refuse to accept such a challenge? I shall play with you." Thereupon Śakuni, casting the dice again, said to Yudhiṣṭhira, "I have won."

Then the defeated Pāṇḍavas prepared to go to the forest. They wore upper garments of deerskin, according to the compact. When the Pāṇḍavas were leaving the hall the foolish Duryodhana imitated the gait of Bhīma who walked like a lion. Bhīma said, "I shall kill Duryodhana, and Arjuna shall slay Karṇa, while Sahadeva will kill the deceitful Śakuni. I shall kill the evil Duryodhana in a club-fight. I shall stand with my foot on his head while he lies on the ground. Like a lion I shall drink the blood of the sinful Duḥśāsana, who is brave only in words."

When the Pāṇḍavas were getting ready to leave, Vidura said: "It is not right that the revered Princess Kuṅtī should go to the forest. She is delicate and aged, and should ever be comfortable. The blessed Kuṅtī will live in my house as an honoured and welcome guest. Know this, O Pāṇḍavas, and I bless you that you may always be safe!"

As she was about to depart, Draupadī was oppressed by sadness. She took leave of the illustrious Kuṅtī and the other ladies there. Kuṅtī, also greatly disturbed on seeing Draupadī ready to leave, spoke a few sad words with difficulty. "Good women are never worried about the future," she said. "Your great virtue will protect you and you will soon gain prosperity." Having consoled the weeping Kuṅtī and saluted her, the unhappy Pāṇḍavas left for the forest. When they had gone, King Dhṛtarāṣṭra's mind was overcome with worry. He asked Vidura to join him immediately.

Āraṇyaka Parva

XXV

Yudhiṣṭhira said to the sage Dhaumya who was accompanying him to the forest, "The Brāhamaṇas, learned in the Vedas, are following me to the forest. Afflicted as I am by so many misfortunes, I will be unable to look after them. I cannot abandon them, but I do not have the means to give them food and sustenance. O holy one, tell me what I should do." After a moment's reflection on the proper course, Dhaumya, foremost of virtuous men, said to Yudhiṣṭhira, "The food which supports the lives of all creatures derives from the Sun, who is the father of all creatures. Therefore seek his protection." Thereupon, the virtuous Yudisṭhira purified himself by touching the waters of the Gāngā and undertook a fast. He worshipped the Sun with flowers and other offerings. Next he brought his senses under control, and, having reached the stage of Yoga, he practised Prāṇāyāma.[1] He then recited the one hundred and eight names of the Sun, as taught to him by Dhaumya.

Thereupon the Sun was pleased. Radiant and blazing like fire, he appeared before Yudhiṣṭhira. "You shall obtain all that you wish," said the Sun. "I shall furnish you with sustenance for the entire twelve years of your exile. Cooked in your kitchen, the four kinds of food—fruit, roots, meat, and vegetables—shall from this day be abundant and never be depleted. You shall also have all kinds of wealth." Having said this, the Sun disappeared.[2] Thereupon the Pāṇḍavas performed

[1] One of the processes of Yoga.

[2] In other recensions, there is a reference to an inexhaustible copper vessel that the Sun-god bestowed on Yudhiṣṭhira. See footnote to verse 3 of Poona Edition, III, 17.

certain auspicious rites and proceeded to the forest of Kāmyaka, accompanied by Dhaumya and surrounded by the Brāhamaṇas.

Having heard of the exile of the Pāṇḍavas, the Bhojas, along with the Vṛṣṇis and the Aṅdhakas, went to see the grieving Pāṇḍavas in the forest. The relatives of the king of Pāñcāla, Dhṛṣṭaketu, the king of Cedi, and the mighty and famous brothers, the Kekayas, also went to visit the Pāṇḍavas in the forest. They censured the sons of Dhṛtarāṣṭra angrily and indignantly, and asked, "What should we do?" All those illustrious Kṣatriyas led by Kṛṣṇa sat around Yudhiṣṭhira. Kṛṣṇa then said, "The earth will drink the blood of Duryodhana, Karṇa, Śakuni, and Duḥśāsana. We shall kill their followers, and Yudhiṣṭhira shall again wear the crown. This is everlasting morality."

Having thus spoken to Yudhiṣṭhira, that foremost of men, the mighty and wise Kṛṣṇa saluted the Pāṇḍavas and prepared to leave. And after Kṛṣṇa's departure Dhṛṣṭadyamna also left for his own city, taking Draupadī's sons with him. Though the Brahmaṇas, the Vaiśyas, and the other subjects of his kingdom, were repeatedly urged to depart, they would not leave the Pāṇḍavas. The retinue of the illustrious Pāṇḍavas in the forest of Kāmyaka was truly extraordinary.

The Pāṇḍavas used to have long discussions as to their future course of action. While one such discussion was going on, there came to that place the great sage Vyāsa. He said, "O best of the Bhāratas, the time is propitious. Arjuna will eventually kill your enemies in battle. Let him receive from me this knowledge, called Pratismṛti, which is the embodiment of success. I shall teach it to him. Learning it, the mighty Arjuna will be able to achieve his desire. In order to acquire weapons, he should seek Iṅdra, Rudra, Varuṇa, Kubera, and Yama. He will be enabled to meet these celestials by virtue of his austerity and valour. He is a sage of great eminence; he is an intimate friend of Nārāyana [Kṛṣṇa]; he is timeless, deathless, divine, unconquerable, and an aspect of Viṣṇu, the Preserver. O mighty hero, he will perform great feats by obtaining weapons from Iṅdra, Rudra, and the Regents of the World."[3]

[3] I have translated as "Regents of the World" the Sanskrit expression *Lōkapālāh*, which is further explained in the Glossary.

After Vyāsa's departure Yudhiṣṭhira said to Arjuna, "O Arjuna, Iṅdra is in charge of all celestial weapons. The gods left their weapons in his safekeeping on account of their fear of the demon Vṛtra. They are all assembled in one place, and you can thus obtain them all at the same time. If you meet Iṅdra, he will give you all his weapons. Get ready to go this very day to see Iṅdra." At the command of Yudhiṣṭhira, the mighty Arjuna went to see Iṅdra. Before leaving, he put on his armour, gauntlets, and finger-protectors, and also took the Gāṇḍīva bow and his inexhaustible quivers. Then, having poured offerings into the fire and made gifts to the Brāhmaṇas and obtained their benedictions, Arjuna set out for his meeting with Iṅdra.

XXVI

Walking day and night, Arjuna crossed the Himālayas, the Gaṅdhamādana, and many other uneven and dangerous passes, and finally reached Iṅdrakīla, where he paused. He heard a voice out of the sky, which asked him to halt. The ambidextrous Arjuna then saw an ascetic seated at the foot of a tree, shining with Brāhmaṇa radiance. His body was tawny, thin, and spare, and his locks were matted. Arjuna saluted the ascetic, who was pleased with him and said, smilingly, "O slayer of foes, I bless you. I am Iṅdra. You may request a boon." With joined hands and bowed head, the preserver of the Kuru race, the heroic Arjuna, replied to Iṅdra, the deity of a thousand eyes, "O holy one! My greatest wish is to learn from you the secret of all the weapons. Give me this boon." Iṅdra replied, "O child, you shall first meet the three-eyed deity, Śiva, the holder of the trident and the lord of all creation; only after that shall I give you all my weapons. O Arjuna, try to see the greatest of all the deities, for only when you have met him will your wishes be accomplished."

While Arjuna was seeking Śiva, as directed by Iṅdra, that benign god took on the form of a Kirāta and, radiant as a golden tree, he loomed as large as a second Meru mountain. He was accompanied by Umā who was in the same hunting costume as that of her consort,

Śiva, and was followed by many merry goblins in a variety of forms and dresses. Coming near Arjuna of immaculate deeds, Śiva observed that a demon, named Mūka, had assumed the form of a boar, intending to kill Arjuna. Taking up his Gāṇḍīva bow, and venomous snakelike arrows, Arjuna said to Mūka, "As you intend to kill me who have done you no harm, I shall today send you to the abode of Yama."

Seeing the mighty archer Arjuna about to kill the boar, Śiva, in the guise of the hunter, suddenly asked him to stop. He said, "I was the first to see this boar; he is therefore my rightful trophy." But ignoring his words, Arjuna shot at it. At that very moment the hunter also discharged an arrow at the boar, like a blazing fire or a flaming thunderbolt. The two bolts thus discharged by the two men hit the mountainous body of Mūka simultaneously. Thus struck by more than one arrow, Mūka resumed his terrible rākṣasa form, and gave up his life.

Arjuna then looked at the being, resplendent as gold, dressed as a hunter, and accompanied by a woman, who had shot at the boar. With joy in his heart Arjuna smilingly said to him: "O you golden creature! Who are you, and why are you roaming in the deserted forest along with so many women? Are you not afraid of this dreadful forest? I was the first to take aim at the rākṣasa who came here in the form of a boar. Why did you shoot at him when I had marked him first?"

Thus questioned by Arjuna, the hunter smilingly replied, in soft words, "I first saw him, I first claimed him, and it was my shot that killed him." Then an argument developed between Arjuna and the hunter, who said, "Be firm. I shall shoot arrows like thunderbolts at you. Use your strength and aim your arrows at me." Arjuna rained arrows on the hunter, who bore them all cheerfully.

Seeing the ineffectiveness of his downpour of arrows, Arjuna was greatly astonished and said, "Well done, well done." He asked himself, "Who could this be? A god, a yakṣa, Iṅdra, or even Rudra himself? The gods do visit this noblest of mountains sometimes." Wondering who his opponent could be, Arjuna continued to engage him in hand-to-hand fighting. Finally, the great god angrily smote the already weakened Arjuna with all his might. Thus struck by the powerful god, Arjuna became breathless and fell down unconscious. Thereupon Śiva was pleased, and said, "O Arjuna, I am pleased with you and your unparalleled feat. There is no warrior equal to you in heroism and courage."

The holy one continued, "O Pāṇḍava, I shall bestow on you my favourite weapon, the great Pāśupata. You alone are capable of wielding, hurling, and withdrawing it." Then Śiva, the lord of all the denizens of heaven, the mountain-dweller, the consort of Umā, conferred on Arjuna, most illustrious of men, the great bow called Gāṇḍīva,[1] capable of destroying the Daityas and the Piśācas.

After receiving Śiva's blessings, Arjuna set out to meet Iṅdra. Having passed through many worlds, the lotus-eyed Arjuna at last saw Iṅdra's capital Amarāvatī. He approached Iṅdra, greeting him respectfully with bowed head. Iṅdra enfolded him in his big arms and, taking him by the hand, made him share his own sacred throne, while the celestials and royal sages worshipped him. And Arjuna received at the hands of Iṅdra his favourite and invincible weapon—the Vajra—and other terrible weapons such as the thunderbolts.

Meanwhile, in the Kāmyaka forest, the sage Bṛhadaśva consoled the Pāṇḍavas by telling them the story of Nala who also lost his kingdom by gambling at dice, and subsequently recovered it. At the end of the account, Bṛhadaśva said to Yudhiṣṭhira: "O king, I shall now dispel, once and for all, your apprehension lest some one may again challenge you to a gambling game! O great hero, I am an authority on gambling. Being pleased with you, I shall teach you the whole science of gambling, if you would learn it from me." Thereupon King Yudhiṣṭhira was overjoyed and said to Bṛhadaśva, "O holy one! Indeed I wish to learn it from you." The sage then taught the science of gambling to the illustrious Pāṇḍava.

The sage Dhaumya used to give many learned discourses to the Pāṇḍavas in the forest. Once, when he was thus discoursing, the holy Lomaśa came there. After kind greetings and enquiries by

[1] According to statements made on pp. 60 and 61, Arjuna already had this bow when he set out to find Iṅdra.

Yudhiṣṭhira, the high-minded sage, well pleased, spoke in sweet words that delighted the Pāṇḍavas. He said, "O sun of Kuntī, travelling over all the three worlds at will, I had occasion to go to the kingdom of Indra, where I saw the king of the celestials himself. I also saw your brother, the heroic and ambidextrous Arjuna, sharing Indra's seat, and I was greatly surprised to see him there."

"O lord," Lomaśa continued, "he has asked me to inform you that he has obtained from Rudra that matchless weapon called Brahmaśiras which Rudra himself obtained only after much penance. He has received this terrible weapon which emerged from the divine nectar, and he has also learnt the spells for discharging and withdrawing it, as well as the rites of expiation and revival. O Yudhiṣṭhira, Arjuna has been given the Vajra, Daṇḍa, and other weapons by Yama, Kubera, Varuṇa, and Indra. Viśvāvasu's son Citrasena has taught him both vocal and instrumental music, as well as dancing, and also the reciting of the Sāma Veda. All these he has learnt thoroughly, as they should be learnt. Having thus obtained all weapons and learnt music and dancing, your second brother Arjuna is living happily in heaven."

Lomaśa then said, "Indra told me: 'You will certainly go to the world of human beings. O foremost of men, give Yudhiṣṭhira this message: Your brother will soon return to you after having received all weapons and after having achieved a great feat on behalf of the celestials which they themselves are incapable of doing.' "[2]

"O Yudhiṣṭhira," Lomaśa went on, "hear now what Arjuna told me. He said, 'Let my brother Yudhiṣṭhira follow all the rules of ethics. You know how men may purify themselves. Therefore, persuade the Pāṇḍavas to acquire religious merit by visiting the holy waters.' " He added, "O Yudhiṣṭhira, I have already twice visited the holy places. I shall, however, visit them with you for the third time, if you so desire."

Yudhiṣṭhira said: "I am speechless and overjoyed. Who can be more fortunate than one whom Indra remembers? O Brāhman, I shall join you on the pilgrimage to the holy waters whenever you wish."

[2] The defeat of the Nivātakavacas. This episode has been omitted from the present translation.

XXVII

The Pāṇḍavas then started on their pilgrimage. Accompanied by the sage Lomaśa, and by their followers, the heroic Pāṇḍavas went from place to place, until at last they reached the Naimiśa forest. There they bathed in the holy waters of the Gomatī and then made gifts of cattle and money to the deserving. The truthful Pāṇḍavas also bathed at the confluence of the Gaṅgā and the Yamunā and, thus purified, presented rich gifts to the Brāhmaṇas.

After visiting many places of pilgrimage, they came to the kingdom of Subāhu, close to the Himālayas. Subāhu, king of the Kuṇiṅdas, received them with due honours and great affection, and they rested comfortably in his palace. They left in his care all their servants such as Iṅdrasena, as well as the cooks and stewards, and also the dresses of Draupadī, and everything else. Thereafter, when the sun was shining brightly, those mighty car-warriors set out towards the Himālaya mountains. They proceeded cautiously, with Draupadī following; they were all cheerful and looking forward to meeting Arjuna again.

Though they saw many beautiful forests on the mountain, they could not help thinking of Arjuna constantly, and so every day and every night appeared to them as long as a year. In this way the Pāṇḍavas passed a month there with great impatience, their thoughts constantly on Arjuna who had gone to Iṅdra with the desire to learn the science of arms. While those mighty car-warriors were thus thinking of Arjuna they were delighted on seeing the car of Iṅdra, yoked with splendid horses and bright as lightning, approaching them all of a sudden. Arjuna was sitting in the car, wearing garlands and rare ornaments. Then, powerful as Iṅdra himself and radiantly beautiful, he alighted on the mountain.

Still wearing a coronet and garlands, Arjuna then descended from Iṅdra's car. First he saluted the feet of the holy Dhaumya and then those of Yudhiṣṭhira. He also bowed to Bhīma and was himself saluted by the twins Nakula and Sahadeva. He then went over to Draupadī and, after greeting and consoling her, he respectfully stood before his brother Yudhiṣṭhira. They were all highly delighted at being reunited with the peerless Arjuna.

After Mātalī, Indra's charioteer, had departed in the celestial chariot, Arjuna presented to his beloved Draupadī many beautiful and precious gems and ornaments, bright as the sun, which had been given to him by Indra. Then Arjuna sat amidst his brothers and those illustrious Brāhmaṇas and told them of all that had happened to him in heaven. He concluded, "In this way, I learnt the science of arms from Indra, Vāyu, and Śiva himself; and all the gods were pleased by my conduct and attention."

After hearing Arjuna's account, Yudhiṣṭhira said, "O Arjuna, it is fortunate that you have obtained these powerful weapons from the king of the celestials. Now I am curious to see them." "You will see tomorrow morning," promised Arjuna, "all those celestial weapons whereby I slew the terrible Nivātakavacas." At that very moment Nārada, deputed by the celestials, arrived there. The sage spoke to Arjuna these words of caution: "O Arjuna, do not discharge these celestial weapons for the purpose of showing them off. These weapons should not, under any circumstances, be discharged aimlessly. And unless sorely afflicted, one should not aim them even at an object. O Arjuna, it will be a great sin if these weapons are let loose without cause." Then turning to Yudhiṣṭhira, Nārada said, "O Yudhiṣṭhira, you will see these weapons in due course, when Arjuna uses them for the destruction of your enemies in battle."

XXVIII

Karṇa said to Duryodhana, "Having sent the heroic Pāṇḍavas into exile, you now rule this earth without a rival, as the slayer of Śaṁbara, Indra, rules in the heaven. Let us go and visit the Pāṇḍavas who are now bereft of their prosperity and are living in the forest. O Duryodhana, it is said that the sight of the adversity of one's enemies brings greater joy than the attainment of wealth, the birth of a son, or even reigning over a kingdom."

Duryodhana replied, "O Karṇa, what you say has always been on my mind. But I will not be allowed to go where the Pāṇḍavas are. King Dhṛtarāṣṭra is always sorry for those heroes. He considers them to be more powerful now than ever before by their practice of asceticism." Thereupon Karṇa smilingly spoke thus to Duryodhana, "O king, please listen to the plan I have thought of. You know our herds of cattle are now in Dvaitavana awaiting your inspection. No one can object to our going there on the pretext of seeing our cattle. O king, it is always considered proper to go and inspect the herds; if you mention this reason to your father, you will be able to obtain his permission."

They agreed upon this course. While they were all with the king one day, a cowherd named Samaṅga, who had been instructed beforehand, came to King Dhṛtarāṣṭra and spoke about the cattle. Then Karṇa and Śakuni said to that foremost of kings, "O king, our cattle are now stationed in charming places, and it is also the time for marking the calves. This is a suitable time for your son Duryodhana to go hunting. Therefore please allow him to go." The king replied: "O child, hunting and inspecting the cattle are both very proper pursuits. I agree that the herdsmen should not be completely trusted. I have, however, heard that those foremost of men the Pāṇḍavas are living somewhere near that place; because of this I will not let you go there." Śakuni then promised, "We shall not go anywhere near the Pāṇḍavas. Therefore there can be no possible misconduct on our part." When Śakuni made this promise, Dhṛtarāṣṭra reluctantly gave permission to Duryodhana and his counsellors to go. Duryodhana then went to the lake of Dvaitavana with his followers and conveyances, and encamped some two leagues away from the lake.

Duryodhana ordered his servants to build pleasure houses on the spot with the least delay. Meanwhile, the Gandharva king along with his followers had already travelled there from the abode of Kubera, the paramount sovereign of the Gandharvas. As the vanguard of Duryodhana's army was about to enter the forest, many Gandharvas came forward and stopped them. The soldiers ran back to King Duryodhana and informed him of this.

On hearing that his soldiers had been stopped by the Gandharvas, the mighty Duryodhana was filled with anger and thus directed his followers, "Chastise the wicked people who do what is disagreeable to me, even if they be the celestials, with Indra at their head." Thereupon Duryodhana's soldiers entered that great forest, disregarding all those Gandharvas. The ten directions resounded with their war cries.

Since Duryodhana's soldiers did not heed their words and would not desist, the Gandharvas went and spoke to their lord Citrasena. When he heard their story, the Gandharva king was angry at the Kauravas and ordered his followers to punish and chastise the wicked intruders. Thus commanded by him, the Gandharvas hurled themselves against Duryodhana's men, with weapons raised for attack. Seeing the Gandharvas rushing towards them at great speed and with raised weapons, Duryodhana's warriors fled in all directions.

While Duryodhana's soldiers were thus fleeing before the enemy, the heroic Karṇa alone stood his ground. The great army of the Gandharvas converged on him, and Karṇa attacked them with a tremendous shower of arrows. Encouraged by Karṇa's stand, Duryodhana, Karṇa, and Śakuni all fought with the Gandharvas, though they were all severely wounded. All the Gandharvas concentrated their attack on Karṇa and rushed upon him in hundreds and thousands.

The unequal struggle could not last long, and the great car-warrior Karṇa was routed by the Gandharvas. Thereupon the rest of Duryodhana's army took to their heels before his very eyes. Even though his soldiers were thus fleeing from the enemy, the great king Duryodhana refused to run away. The mighty Citrasena forced Duryodhana to descend to the ground and then captured him alive. After he had been taken prisoner, the Gandharvas surrounded the car on which Duḥśāsana was seated, and took him prisoner also.

The soldiers of Duryodhana who were routed by the Gandharvas then came to the Pāṇḍavas. They lamented, "The Gandharvas are taking away the handsome and mighty Duryodhana as prisoner. O Pāṇḍavas, pursue them." On hearing their appeal, Yudhiṣṭhira asked his four brothers, led by Bhīma, to undertake the rescue of the Kauravas. He said, "Try by all means, O Bhīma, to rescue

Duryodhana. First, you may try conciliation. If, however, the Gandharva king cannot be brought round by this, then you must try to rescue the Kauravas by light fighting. If even this does not succeed, then you should save them by using all the means in your power."

Those great car-warriors, the four Pāṇḍavas, then put on impenetrable armour decked with gold. In accordance with the words of the wise Yudhiṣṭhira, they gradually began to engage in a gentle skirmish with the Gandharvas. In the course of the skirmish, the unconquerable and ambidextrous Arjuna said to the Gandharvas, "As commanded by Yudhiṣṭhira, release the mighty heroes, the sons of Dhṛtarāṣṭra, and their ladies." The Gandharvas replied, "There is but one in this world whose orders we obey; living under his rule, we pass our days free from all ills. We do not recognize any other command except that which is given to us by the king of the Gandharvas."

Then the Pāṇḍavas began to fight the Gandharvas in good earnest. Thereupon the Gandharvas, armed with celestial weapons and adorned with golden garlands, showered innumerable blazing arrows on the Pāṇḍavas from all sides. There were but four Pāṇḍava heroes; there were thousands of Gandharvas. The battle between them was extraordinary. In the course of that battle the powerful Arjuna with his Āgneya weapon sent thousands upon thousands of Gandharvas to their death. That great bowman, Bhīma, foremost of all strong men, killed hundreds of Gandharvas with his sharp arrows. The twins, too, fighting with great prowess, formed the vanguard and killed hundreds of the foes.

Seeing the Gandharvas thus routed by the wise Arjuna, Citrasena took up a mace and rushed toward him. As he was rushing forward, Arjuna shot some arrows and broke that iron mace into seven pieces. Then his dear friend Citrasena reappeared before Arjuna. On seeing him, fatigued and weary of fighting, Arjuna withdrew his weapons while his brothers checked their flying horses and put away their bows and arrows. Citrasena, Bhīma, Arjuna, and the twins enquired after one another's welfare, and sat down on their respective chariots.

The supreme bowman Arjuna then said to Citrasena, in the midst of the Gandharva army, "O hero, what purpose is served by punishing the Kurus? Why do you persecute Duryodhana and his wives?" Citrasena replied, "O Arjuna, I knew the real purpose of the visit of the wicked Duryodhana and the wretched Karṇa. Knowing that you and the illustrious Draupadī were undergoing undeserved suffering in the forest, they wished to mock you." Thereupon they all went to King Yudhiṣṭhira and told him of Duryodhana's evil intention. Yudhiṣṭhira, however, asked Citrasena to set them all free, and he also praised the Gandharvas. He said, "It is fortunate for us that, though you possess such great strength, you did not injure the wicked sons of Dhṛtarāṣṭra or their counsellors and relatives."

Indra now came there and revived by a shower of the celestial ambrosia all those Gandharvas who had been killed in the encounter with the Pāṇḍavas. Having rescued their relatives, along with the ladies of the royal household, the Pāṇḍavas too were happy over the great feat they had achieved. Yudhiṣṭhira spoke affectionately to the liberated Duryodhana in the midst of his brothers: "O child, do not commit such a rash act again. A rash man never attains happiness. O Kuru prince, I bless you and all your brothers. Go back home when it pleases you, without feeling despondent."

XXIX

And so the twelve years dragged on. On the expiration of the twelfth year of their forest life and as the thirteenth was due to begin, Indra, the well-wisher of the Pāṇḍavas, resolved to get Karṇa's earrings. But the Sun-god,[1] aware of Indra's intentions, appeared before Karṇa and advised him as follows: "O son, you bestow on the Brāhmaṇas anything they ask of you and never refuse a gift to any one. Aware of this habit of yours, Indra will come to you in person, in order to beg of you your earrings and armour. When he asks for the earrings, you must not part with them, but entreat him to desist. These two jewelled earrings originate from ambrosia, and if you value your life you should carefully preserve them."

[1] The begetter of Karṇa.

Karṇa said, "O Sun, all the world is aware of this vow of mine, that I am ready to give my very life to the best of Brāhmaṇas. If Indra disguises himself as a Brāhmaṇa and comes to me in quest of the earrings for the good of the Pāṇḍavas, then I will give him the earrings and the excellent armour. In that case my fame, which has spread over the three worlds, will not suffer. O Sun, I long for fame in this world even at the sacrifice of my life. Men of renown attain heaven while those having none are lost. So I will win everlasting fame by giving my earrings, with which I was born, to the Brāhmaṇas."

Seeing that Karṇa was adamant, the Sun-god said, "O mighty son, if you give away your beautiful earrings to Indra the wielder of the thunderbolt, you should, in order to secure victory, say to him, 'O thousand-eyed lord, I will give you my two earrings and my excellent armour, if you will bestow on me an infallible dart destructive of enemies.' " Having thus advised Karṇa, the Sun-god departed.

In due course, Indra visited Karṇa, as foretold by the Sun. Karṇa saw that the king of the celestials had come to him disguised as a Brāhmaṇa and said, "You are welcome." The Brāhmaṇa said, "O sinless one, if you will truly observe your vow, then cut off from your body the armour and earrings with which you were born and give them to me." Karṇa replied, "O god of gods, I knew that you would come. It is not proper for me to bestow on you a boon without return, because you are the very lord of the celestials. It is for you to confer boons on me, as you are the lord of all creation. In exchange for my armour and earrings, O Indra, bestow on me the Śakti weapon which is capable of destroying all hostile forces in battle."

Thereupon, Indra pondered for a moment regarding the Śakti weapon, and spoke these words to Karṇa: "Give me your earrings and the armour which you wore even at birth, and take the Śakti weapon, under one condition. O Karṇa, hurled by your hand, roaring and flaming like fire, it shall kill one powerful enemy and shall then return to me." Karṇa then said, "I accept the Śakti weapon on that condition. I shall now cut the earrings and the mail from my body, and give them to you. But let not my limbs, thus wounded, look scarred." Indra said, "O Karṇa, since you are desirous of observing your vow, you shall not look ugly nor shall there be any scars on your body. Remember: if you hurl this infallible Śakti weapon, maddened with rage, when your life is not in danger, and when you have other weapons with you, then it will turn against you."

Karṇa replied: "I tell you truly, O Iṅdra, that I shall discharge this celestial weapon strictly according to your directions, only when my life is in grave danger." Then, accepting that blazing Śakti weapon, Karṇa began to cut off the armour from his body with sharp weapons. The gods, the mortals, and the Dānavas, seeing Karṇa cut off part of his own body, roared with approbation, because no signs of pain were visible on his face, nor were any scars left on his body.

Meanwhile, having completed their twelve years of exile in the forest in accordance with their pledge, the Pāṇḍavas prepared to spend the thirteenth year of their exile incognito. Those foremost of men proceeded the next day to the distance of a league and sat down there in order to hold a consultation with one another, so to how they should spend their year in disguise.

Virāṭa Parva

XXX

The high-souled King Yudhiṣṭhira, born of Dharma, summoned all his brothers together and said to them, "For these twelve years we have been banished from our kingdom. We have come to the thirteenth year, which will be very hard to pass. The elderly Virāṭa, king of Matsya, is powerful, charitable, and righteous, and formerly a friend of the Pāṇḍavas. In his city, O dear ones, we may spend the whole of this year in his service without being recognized. I shall now tell you what work I shall offer to do when I appear before King Virāṭa, best among men. I shall pretend to be a Brāhmaṇa, Kaṅka by name, expert in dice and fond of gaming; I shall offer my services as a companion to that high-souled king. If he questions me closely, I shall say, 'Previously I was a friend of Yudhiṣṭhira, dear as life itself to him.' "

In his turn, Bhīma said, "O Bhārata, I shall appear before King Virāṭa and present myself as a cook, named Ballava. If questioned, I shall say, 'Formerly I was the cook, and also tamer of animals and court wrestler, of Yudhiṣṭhira.' " Arjuna said, "O king, I shall pretend to be one of the neuter sex, though it is very difficult to conceal the big scars of the bowstring on my arms. I shall offer to instruct the ladies of Virāṭa's palace in singing, dancing, and similar musical exercises. If the king questions me, I shall say, 'I used to be a servant of Draupadī in the palace of Yudhiṣṭhira.' "

Nakula then said, "I shall offer to be the keeper of the king's horses, a work I like. I shall call myself Granthika. I am expert both in training horses and treating them; and I have always loved horses, even as you, O king." Sahadeva said, "I shall offer my services as accountant of the cows of the king; I am skilled in taming, milking, and keeping count of them. I shall give my name as Tantripāla, and under that name I shall do my duty well. Do not have any anxiety on my score."

Yudhiṣṭhira then asked, "In what capacity will Draupadī appear? She does not know how to do ordinary housework like other women." Draupadī replied, "O Bhārata, there is a class of maidservants called sairandhrī employed in the service of others. It is common knowledge that no respectable ladies will enter such service. Since you ask me, I shall call myself a sairandhrī, skilled in hairdressing; I shall pass my days in concealment, serving Sudeṣṇā, the famous queen of Virāṭa. Once I obtain service under her she will protect me. Let your anxiety on my account be set at rest."

Having thus settled the disguises they would adopt, the Pāṇḍavas and Draupadī proceeded to Virāṭa's kingdom. When they were approaching the capital, Yudhiṣṭhira asked Arjuna, "Where shall we leave our weapons before we enter the city?" Arjuna said, "O king, close by the cremation ground, on a hill, there stands a huge śamī tree, hard to climb and with tremendous boughs. We shall deposit our weapons in that tree and then go to the city where we shall pass our days in the guise befitting us."

Then, one by one, the Pāṇḍavas appeared in the royal court. Yudhiṣṭhira, the best of men, approaching King Virāṭa first, addressed him thus: "O great king, know me to be a Brāhmaṇa who has lost his all and has come to you in search of livelihood. If you permit me, I wish to stay with you and to follow all your desires, O Lord!" After having accorded him a due welcome the king, well pleased, said, "You may have any post you seek." Yudhiṣṭhira said, "I was once a friend of Yudhiṣṭhira. I am a Brāhmaṇa belonging to the family known as Vaiyāghrapadya. I am expert in throwing dice, and my name is Kanka." Virāṭa said, "Kanka, you shall be my constant companion; your car shall be the same as mine; you shall have plenty of clothes, food, and drink. You shall know all my affairs, and my doors shall ever be open to you."

Then Bhīma approached King Virāṭa, looking like a poor man, and said, "O king, I am a cook named Ballava; pray appoint me as your chef. I am also a wrestler, and I have no equal in strength. I shall ever be ready to entertain you by fighting with elephants and lions." Virāṭa said, "What you desire is done, and I appoint you as my chef. You shall be at the head of all those whom I have already appointed to serve in the kitchen."

Next came Draupadī. Wearing a dirty piece of cloth, and dressed as a sairaṅdhrī, Draupadī wandered round the palace like one in a miserable plight. While looking out of the palace, Virāṭa's beloved wife Sudeṣṇā, daughter of Kekaya, saw Draupadī. Seeing her in that state, unprotected and clad in a single piece of cloth, the queen called her and said, "Who are you and what do you wish to do?" Draupadī replied, "I am a sairaṅdhrī; whoever will protect me, I shall do her work. I know how to dress the hair, as well as how to pound fragrant stuff to make unguents and to prepare a variety of beautiful garlands. Formerly I served Satyabhāmā, the beloved queen of Kṛṣṇa, and also Draupadī, the wife of the Pāṇḍavas and the supreme beauty of the Kuru family. I serve only in those houses where I get good reward and clothes. Draupadī called me by the name of Mālinī, O lady Sudeṣṇā; I, her serving maid, have come to your house today."

"I shall be happy to give you employment and treat you with the greatest respect," said Sudeṣṇā. "My only anxiety is that the king's heart may be captivated by you." Draupadī replied, "Neither Virāṭa nor any other man can win me, O fair lady, for I have five youthful husbands who are all Gaṅdharvas. Anyone who desires and pursues me as though I were a common woman will meet with destruction that very night." "O charming one," Sudeṣṇā said, "in that case, I will allow you to reside in my palace, as you desire. You will have plenty of fresh food and you will never be asked to perform any menial tasks."

Wearing the dress of a cowherd and speaking their dialect, Sahadeva also arrived at the city of King Virāṭa. Coming to the king, he said in a voice deep as thunder, "I am a Vaiśya known by the name of Ariṣṭanemi; I served as an accountant of the cows of those best of the Kuru race, the Pāṇḍavas." Virāṭa said, "I have a hundred thousand kine of various categories which have not yet been classified. I place those animals along with their keepers in your charge. Let my cattle henceforth be in your care."

Then there appeared at the gate of the ramparts another person, of colossal form, rich in beauty, bedecked like a woman, and wearing large earrings and fine conch bracelets set with gold. That long-armed one, powerful as an elephant, with abundant flowing hair, came to Virāṭa's court, making the very earth tremble under his tread, and stood before the king. Arjuna (for it was he) then said, "I can sing, dance, and play on instruments. I am skilled in dancing and expert in singing. O king, assign me to your daughter Uttarā.[1] I shall be the dancing master of the princess. Please do not ask how I have come by this form. It will merely increase my pain, O lord of men; know me to be Bṛhannaḍā, a son or daughter without father or mother." Virāṭa said, "O Bṛhannaḍā, I grant your prayer; I appoint you to instruct my daughter and her friends in dancing. However, it seems to me that this job is hardly worthy of you."

Then another mighty son of Pāṇḍu could be seen approaching King Virāṭa. To the common people he appeared like the sun emerging from the clouds. Nakula came to the king and said, "O king, may victory be yours and good betide you! I am well known for my handling of horses. I know their nature and the complete art of breaking them in. I know how to correct wicked animals and to treat ailments of all kinds. Pray appoint me as the keeper of your horses." Virāṭa said, "All my horses shall be entrusted to your care from today, and all my charioteers and those who yoke my horses shall henceforth be subordinate to you."

XXXI

Those mighty warriors, the Pāṇḍavas, spent ten months living thus in disguise in Virāṭa's capital. One day the commander of Virāṭa's forces, Kīcaka, happened to see the lotus-like face of Draupadī as she

[1] Uttarā's brother Bhumiñjaya was known as Uttara. See p. 81, n. 2.

went about her work in Sudeṣṇā's palace. Burning with the flame of lust, Kīcaka went to his sister Sudeṣṇā and smilingly said to her, "O blessed one, who is this celestial beauty who has entered my heart? Tell me who she is and where she comes from. She agitates my mind, which is no longer in my control. There is no remedy for it. This fine maid of yours seems to me to have the blooming beauty of a goddess. The service which she gives you is quite unsuitable to her. Let her rule over me and all that is mine."

Having consulted Sudeṣṇā, Kīcaka approached the princess Draupadī and spoke to her in gentle words, like a jackal addressing a lioness in the forest, "O lady of sweet smiles! I shall give up all my old wives. Let them be your serving maids. O beautiful one, I will be your slave and ever obedient to you." Draupadī replied to Kīcaka; "In desiring me, you desire someone who is not worthy of such honour, a low-caste sairaṅdhrī engaged in the menial task of a hairdresser. Such conduct does not become one in your position. Besides, I am married to others. The wives of others are dear to them. Think of this moral rule." Her final warning to Kīcaka was, "Do not play the fool and throw away your life today; know that I am unattainable, and protected by heroes."

Rejected thus by the princess, Kīcaka, overcome by lust and forgetful of all sense of propriety, said to Sudeṣṇā, "O Kaikeyī, do that by which the sairaṅdhrī may be united with me. O Sudeṣṇā, please persuade her. Do not make me throw away my life." Accordingly, Sudeṣṇā said one day, "O sairaṅdhrī, I am thirsty. Please go to my brother Kīcaka's residence and bring me some wine." Draupadī tried to avoid this errand, saying, "O princess, I shall not go to his house; you yourself know how shameless he is." In the end, however, she was forced to go.

When she reached Kīcaka's house, Draupadī said to Kīcaka, "The queen has sent me to you for wine; give it to me quickly, for she told me she is very thirsty." Kīcaka replied, "O gentle one, I shall send someone else to take the wine that has been promised to the queen." Saying this, he seized her by the right arm. She threw him to the ground and ran trembling to the court, where Yudhiṣṭhira was, to seek his protection. Kīcaka ran in pursuit, seized her by her locks while she was running, and brought her down with a kick in the very presence of the king. Both Bhīma and Yudhiṣṭhira, who were seated there, witnessed helplessly, but with burning resentment, the outrage Kīcaka committed on Draupadī.

The weeping Draupadī approached the court, where she beheld her lords Bhīma and Yudhiṣṭhira in a melancholy mood, but determined to keep up their disguise. Then, with flashing eyes, Draupadī said to the king of the Matsyas, "O Matsya, it is highly improper that I should thus be outraged by this villain in your very presence. Let all the assembled courtiers mark this wicked behaviour of Kīcaka's." Virāṭa replied, "I do not know anything of the rights and wrongs of your quarrel. How can I render justice without knowing the true facts?" In the face of the king's indifference, Draupadī could not get any justice in the royal court.

The illustrious and exceedingly beautiful princess Draupadī returned to her quarters brooding over the outrage she had suffered and planning the destruction of the leader of Virāṭa's forces. Weeping and resolved to bring about Kīcaka's downfall, she thought, "What shall I do? Where shall I go? How can my desire be fulfilled?" While she was brooding thus, she thought of Bhīma. "No one but Bhīma," she reflected, "can accomplish my desire in time."

That very night, after everyone had retired, Draupadī went to see Bhīma. Being awakened by the princess, he got up from his bed and sat on the couch. "Why have you come here in such haste?" he asked his beloved consort. Draupadī replied, "O Bhārata, the wicked Kīcaka, who is the leader of Virāṭa's army, pursues me every day, while I live in the royal palace in the guise of a sairandhrī, and pesters me to become his wife." Draupadī then related her woes to Bhīma, weeping all the while, with her glance fixed on him. She ended with this appeal, "Kill this wretch who has outraged me, and who torments me in the confidence that he is a favourite of the king. Smash this creature maddened with lust, as you would dash an earthen pot against a stone."

Bhīma replied, "O gentle one, I shall do as you say. I shall soon kill

Kīcaka with all his kinsmen. Give up your sorrow, and bring him round so that he is on good terms with you by tomorrow evening. There is the dancing school which Virāṭa has built; the girls dance there during the day but retire to their respective homes at night. In that hall there is a bedstead firmly fixed and conveniently placed; there I will make Kīcaka see the spirits of his deceased ancestors. When talking to him, make sure that no one sees you, and manage things in such a way that he may come near you, when he thinks you are alone."

Having thus exchanged their thoughts and shed tears of grief, they both awaited the dawn with anxious hearts. Early the next day, Kīcaka rose up and went to Sudeṣṇā's palace, where he said to Draupadī, "I threw you down in the court and kicked you in the very presence of the king. And yet you could not obtain any protection or redress. Virāṭa is said to be the king of the Matsyas, but that is only in name; I am the commander of the forces, and I am verily the king of the Matsyas. O bashful one, accept me happily; I shall become your slave. I shall give you this very day a hundred niṣkas[1] and a hundred men and a hundred maidservants; I shall also present you with a chariot yoked with female mules. O beautiful one, let us be united."

"O Kīcaka," replied Draupadī, "there is one condition that you should accept; neither your friends nor your brothers must know that we are united. I am really afraid of being discovered by those renowned Gandharvas, my husbands. If you promise me this, I shall be yours." "O beautiful creature," Kīcaka replied, "I will do as you say; overcome by the god of love, I shall go alone to any lonely place for the purpose of being united with you, so that your husbands, the Gandharvas, brilliant as the sun, may not be able to see you." Draupadī said, "There is the dancing hall erected by King Virāṭa. Here the girls dance during the day and return home at night. If you go there, the Gandharvas will not know it. There will be no suspicion and no blame."

Kīcaka readily fell in with this plan. That night Bhīma went early to the dancing hall under cover of darkness, and sat there awaiting

[1] "Niṣka" may mean either a golden ornament or a particular coin.

Kīcaka like an unseen lion waiting for a deer. Having preened himself to his liking, Kīcaka arrived at the dancing hall at the appointed hour, desirous of union with Draupadī. The powerful Bhīma of mighty arms, laughing at the meanest of men, seized him by the hair which was adorned with fragrant garlands. Though caught with force by the hair, the powerful Kīcaka speedily freed himself and grasped the arms of Bhīma. The two lions among men, worked up with anger, fought hand-to-hand like two powerful male elephants fighting for a female elephant in the spring season. After a long and desperate struggle, Bhīma finally killed Kīcaka.

Then, having broken all Kīcaka's limbs and reduced him to a lump of flesh, the mighty Bhīma showed him to Draupadī, the ornament of her sex, who was highly delighted at the destruction of Kīcaka. Her sorrow dispelled, she said to the guards of the assembly hall: "This Kīcaka who lusted after another's wife has been slain by my Gaṅdharva husbands; come and see for yourselves." Hearing her words, the guards of the dancing hall came there by the thousand, carrying torches in their hands. Going into the room, they saw Kīcaka fallen on the ground lifeless, bathed in a pool of blood. They asked: "Where is his neck, where are his feet and arms, and where is his head?" They then concluded that he must indeed have been slain by the Gaṅdharvas.

XXXII

All over the Matsya kingdom, people were astonished at the destruction of Kīcaka. They said among themselves, "The wicked Kīcaka was the oppressor of men and the ravisher of others' wives; that sinful, evil man has been killed by the Gaṅdharvas." Meanwhile Duryodhana's spies looked for the Pāṇḍavas in many villages, cities, and provinces, and finally returned to the city of Hāstinapura with anxious minds, because they could not find them. Thereupon Karṇa said, "O king, let us send other spies, more cunning and capable and better fitted for this work, in disguise, to look for the Pāṇḍavas."

Meanwhile Suśarmā, the powerful king of the Trigartas, said, "My kingdom has been invaded many times by the king of the Matsyas. Formerly the powerful Kīcaka was his commander in chief. Now that he has been killed, I believe that King Virāṭa will be without adequate protection. I consider this circumstance to be favourable to us. Let us all proceed to the Matsya kingdom, which has plenty of corn. We shall invade his city and carry away by force the many varieties of excellent cattle that he owns by the thousand."

While Suśarmā was thus planning an invasion, the high-souled Pāṇḍavas passed the stipulated period in disguise, without being detected. It was therefore after the expiration of the thirteenth year that Suśarmā seized many of Virāṭa's kine by force. Virāṭa said to his younger brother Śatānīka; "I feel sure that Kaṅka, Ballava, Gopāla,[1] and the greatly energetic Dāmagraṅthī will fight. Give them chariots adorned with flags and pennons, and various sets of armour which are invulnerable and easy to wear, and also the weapons they may need."

Suśarmā had meanwhile invaded Matsya. Having attacked and defeated quickly the entire army of Virāṭa, Suśarmā rushed furiously at Virāṭa himself. He killed Virāṭa's two horses, his charioteer, and also the soldiers who protected him in the rear, and then captured King Virāṭa alive. Bhīma, however, rallied Virāṭa's forces. Alighting from his car, the powerful Bhīma seized the king of Trigarta like a lion grasping a small deer. Thereupon the entire army of Trigarta was afflicted with fear and soon dispersed.

Thus the mighty Pāṇḍavas prevented the cattle from being taken away, overpowered Suśarmā, and seized all his wealth. Having killed their enemies by the strength of their own arms, the modest Pāṇḍavas passed that night happily in the battlefield. Virāṭa honoured those mightly car-warriors with wealth and every mark of respect.

While King Virāṭa had gone after the Trigartas to recover his cattle, Duryodhana with his counsellors had attacked Virāṭa's kingdom. Encircling the realm on all sides with a huge array of chariots, the Kauravas seized sixty thousand kine. Grief-stricken, the chief of the cowherds quickly mounted a chariot and started for the city. On reaching the

[1] Literally the protector of cows—the role assumed by Sahadeva.

capital, he went, in the absence of the king, to Prince Bhūmiñjaya[2] and told him in detail of the capture of the royal cattle.

Uttara said, "Expert in the use of bow as I am, I shall today go out in pursuit of the kine, if only somebody skilled in the management of horses will be my charioteer. The assembled Kurus shall see my prowess today. They shall ask each other, 'Is it Arjuna himself?'" These words of the young prince were being repeated among the ladies of the royal household. Draupadī could not bear these references to Arjuna. She sought the prince in the middle of the ladies, and gently and shyly told him, "The young and handsome man, splendid as an elephant, who goes by the name of Bṛhannaḍā, used to be the charioteer of Arjuna himself." Uttara then arranged that Bṛhannaḍā should be his charioteer.

Uttara said, "O Bṛhannaḍā, singer or dancer or whatever you may be, make haste to ascend my chariot and guide my fine horses." With Bṛhannaḍā as his charioteer, and taking many costly bows and beautiful arrows, the hero sallied forth. Having come out of the city, the prince said to his charioteer, "Go where the Kurus are." But when he got there and saw the huge army, equipped with elephants, horses, and chariots, and led by Karṇa, Duryodhana, Kṛpa, Bhīṣma, Droṇa, and his son the wise and great bowman Aśvatthāmā, the prince became frightened. His hair standing on end, he said to Bṛhannaḍā, "I do not have the heart to fight with the Kurus: see how the hairs of my body stand on end! I am unable to fight with the vast Kuru army, led by so many splendid heroes, whom even the celestials could hardly vanquish. I dare not enter the army of the Bhāratas consisting of bowmen, chariots, horses, elephants, infantry, and flags. My soul is discouraged even by the sight of the enemy. I am all alone and a mere stripling, without much practice in the use of arms. I cannot fight all these warriors skilled in arms; desist, O Bṛhannaḍā." So saying, the foolish prince, adorned with earrings, dismounted from the chariot and, leaving behind his bow and arrows, fled away in fear without any regard to his honour and pride.

Bṛhannaḍā [Arjuna] said, "It is not the habit of a Kṣatriya to flee

[2] Also named Uttara. His sister was known as Uttarā. See p. 75, n. 1.

like this; death in battle is preferable to flight in fear." So saying, he came down from the car, and pursued the prince who was running away, his own long braid and blood-red garments fluttering behind him in the air. When he caught up with the prince, who had lost heart and was much afraid, Arjuna said, "If you have no desire to fight the foe, come and be my charioteer while I give battle to the enemy. Be not afraid, O prince! Remember, you are a Kṣatriya. Let me give battle to the Kurus and rescue the cows." Then Arjuna, foremost of warriors, made the prince—who had lost heart, who was sorely afraid, and who had no desire to fight—mount the chariot again.

XXXIII

Arjuna's first task was to secure the weapons he had hidden earlier. Together the prince and Arjuna approached the śamī tree, and Arjuna then said to the young prince, who was delicate and inexperienced in battle, "O prince, go up this tree, for the banners, shafts, and celestial armour of the heroic sons of Pāṇḍu—Yudhiṣṭhira, Bhīma, Arjuna, and the twins—have been left in it." Thus requested by Arjuna, the prince dismounted from the chariot and somewhat reluctantly climbed the śamī tree. He took out the weapons and, as he removed their wrappings, saw the Gāṇḍīva and also the bows of the four others.

Uttara then asked, "Who is the illustrious hero who owns this excellent bow, having a hundred golden bosses and shining ends?" Bṛhannaḍā replied, "The bow about which you first asked is the world-famous Gāṇḍīva bow of Arjuna, which is capable of destroying the enemy's army." Uttara exclaimed, "Truly these golden arms, belonging to the noble Pāṇḍavas, are beautiful! But where are Arjuna, Yudhiṣṭhira, Nakula, Sahadeva, and Bhīma?" Arjuna replied, "I am Arjuna, the son of Pṛthā; your father's courtier is Yudhiṣṭhira, and Ballava, the clever cook of your father, is Bhīma. Nakula is in charge of the horses and Sahadeva is in the cowshed; you should also know that the sairandhrī, on whose account Kīcaka and his followers were slain, is Draupadī. Listen now to my ten names: Arjuna, Phalguna,

Jiṣṇu, Kirīṭī, Śvetavāhana, Bībhatsu, Vijaya, Kṛṣṇa, Savyasācī, and Dhanañjaya."

At this revelation, the prince, son of Virāṭa, was greatly impressed. Then, saluting Arjuna, he said, "My name is Bhūmiñjaya; I am also called Uttara. By good luck I see you, O Arjuna. Welcome to you! Whatever I may have said to you in my ignorance, please forgive me for it.

"O hero," he continued, "mount this beautiful car with me as the charioteer, and tell me which division you would like to attack. I shall drive you there." Making Uttara his charioteer, Arjuna set out, armed with his own weapons. He raised over his chariot the golden flag with the emblem of a monkey which was a celestial design created by Viśvakarmā. Then he blew a mighty blast on his conch, producing a thunderous sound, capable of making the hairs of his enemies stand on end. Uttara said, "I have heard the sound of many a conch and trumpet, and the roar of many an elephant on the battlefield, but never have I heard a sound like this. Nor have I ever beheld a flag like this."

On hearing the sound of Arjuna's conch, Droṇa said, "From the rattle of the car, from the way in which the conch was blown, and from the fact that the earth quakes, I conclude that he is none other than Arjuna." Thereupon King Duryodhana said in the battlefield to Bhīṣma and Droṇa, foremost of car-warriors, and also to the mighty Kṛpa: "It was agreed that if they were defeated at dice, the Pāṇḍavas should live in the forest for twelve years, and incognito for one more year. The thirteenth year is not yet over. And yet Arjuna, who was living in disguise, has come to fight us. Now if Arjuna shows himself before the term of exile is over, the Pāṇḍavas will have to pass another twelve years in the forest."

"I see all of you looking as if you are terrified and afraid for your lives, irresolute and unwilling to fight," said Karṇa. "Today I shall kill Arjuna in battle and thus discharge the debt which is so hard to repay, the promise I made formerly to Duryodhana."

Bhīṣma said, "In consequence of fractional excesses, as well as the deviations of the heavenly bodies, there is an excess period of two months once every five years. Thus calculated, there will be an excess of five months and twelve days in thirteen years. The Pāṇḍavas have therefore fully met the conditions agreed upon. Being sure of this, Arjuna has now come out into the open."

Bhīṣma then outlined the following strategy: "Quickly proceed towards the capital city with one fourth of the army. Let another quarter take away the cattle. With the remaining half of the army we shall give battle to Arjuna, or to Virāṭa if he comes back. Let the preceptor Droṇa stand in the middle; let Aśvatthāmā guard the left wing and Kṛpa the right wing. Let Karṇa, clad in armour, stand in the van. And I shall command the entire army in the rear."

Arjuna could divine Bhīṣma's strategy. He said: "I do not see King Duryodhana. I am afraid that, anxious to save his life, he is escaping by the southern road with the cattle. Leaving the car-warriors here, let us pursue Duryodhana. I shall fight him there, vanquish him, and return with the kine, O son of Virāṭa!"

Having quickly defeated the enemy's host and recovered the cattle, that foremost of archers Arjuna proceeded towards Duryodhana with a view to giving him battle. Seeing the kine run towards the city and concluding that Arjuna was successful, the heroic Kurus all of a sudden opposed him while he was pursuing Duryodhana. Beholding their army with its various well-arranged divisions flying numberless flags, Arjuna said to Prince Uttara, "Take these white horses, driven by golden reins, by this route, to where the leading Kuru heroes are stationed. The wicked Karṇa wishes to fight with me, as an elephant does with another. O prince, take me to him who has grown arrogant on account of Duryodhana's patronage."

Then took place the duel between Arjuna and Karṇa. With twelve shafts Karṇa quickly pierced Arjuna, as well as the horses and Prince Uttara. In his turn Arjuna, in the course of the combat, pierced Karṇa's arms, thighs, head, forehead, and other parts of his body with sharp arrows, bright as the thunderbolt, shot from his Gāṇḍīva bow. Thus wounded by the arrows shot by Arjuna, Karṇa left the battlefield and took to his heels, like an elephant defeated by another.

After Karṇa's flight from the battlefield, all the other heroes, headed by Duryodhana, attacked Arjuna with their arrows. But that hero covered all those mighty car-warriors with clouds of arrows, even as the mist covers the mountains. Hearing the twang of the Gāṇḍīva bow, echoing like thunder, many fled in fear from that terrible battle. Seeing his power scorching the hostile army, they all became reluctant to fight, in the very sight of Duryodhana.

The heroic Arjuna suddenly blew on his conch Devadatta a mighty blast of victory. The enemy were humbled before him. Beholding the flight of the Kurus, Arjuna, resplendent with his golden flag, said joyfully to Uttara, "Turn back the horses. Your cows have been recovered. Return to the city in triumph."

Arjuna, now that the Kurus were defeated, also retrieved the immense wealth of Virāṭa. Having dispersed the Kuru army, like a violent storm scattering the clouds, Arjuna respectfully said to Uttara, "Send the cowherds quickly to the city to announce the joyful news and your victory." As advised by Arjuna, Uttara quickly despatched messengers to announce his triumph.

XXXIV

Virāṭa, who had so speedily recovered his wealth from Suśarmā, was delighted as he reentered his capital, along with the four Pāṇḍavas. But when he heard on arrival that his brave son had gone out with only one car and Bṛhannaḍā as his charioteer, Virāṭa was filled with sorrow and said to his leading ministers, "Let those of my soldiers who have not been wounded by the Trigartas proceed with a strong force to rescue Uttara." Yudhiṣṭhira smilingly said to the king, who was greatly afraid of the Kauravas, "O king, if Bṛhannaḍā is the prince's charioteer, the enemies will not be able to take away the cattle."

Meanwhile, the messenger despatched by Uttara quickly reached the city and proclaimed the victory. Greatly relieved, Virāṭa began to play a game of dice with Kañka. In the course of the play, Virāṭa said to Yudhiṣṭhira, "Even the terrible Kauravas have been defeated in battle by my son." To this Yudhiṣṭhira replied, "Why should he not conquer the Kurus, when he has got Bṛhannaḍā as his charioteer?"

At this, Virāṭa was enraged and said to Yudhiṣṭhira, "O Brāhman, you speak as though my son and this eunuch are equals. Out of regard for our friendship, I forgive you this offence. Do not speak in this vein again, if you wish to live."

Yudhiṣṭhira repeated: "Droṇa, Bhīṣma, Aśvatthāmā, Karṇa, Kṛpa, and other kings and car-warriors were protecting Duryodhana, like hordes of Maruts protecting Iṅdra. Who else, save Bṛhannaḍā, can fight them all together?" Virāṭa exclaimed wrathfully, "I have cautioned you repeatedly, and yet you do not control your speech." Saying this, the king, excited with anger, struck Yudhiṣṭhira on the face with one of the dice. The pious Yudhiṣṭhira then looked at Draupadī who was standing beside him. That faultless one, ever obedient to her husband, divined his intention; she brought a golden vessel filled with water, and caught the blood that flowed from his nose.[1]

In the meantime Uttara, redolent with various perfumes and covered with garlands, slowly and joyfully entered the city, and proceeded to the royal court. Having saluted the feet of his father, he saw Yudhiṣṭhira, covered with blood, sitting by himself on the floor at one end of the court, attended by the sairaṅdhrī [Draupadī]. Uttara then asked his father hurriedly, "Who has struck him, O king? Who has committed this great wrong?" "It was I who struck this wily Brāhmaṇa," said Virāṭa. "He deserves even worse. When I was applauding you, heroic as you are, he praised a eunuch." Uttara said, "You have committed a great sin. Propitiate him soon so that the deadly poison of a Brāhmaṇa's curse may not destroy you to the very roots.

"The cattle were not rescued by me nor was the enemy defeated by me," continued Uttara. "All that was the achievement of the son of a celestial. Seeing me running away in fear, the youth, splendid as Iṅdra, stopped me, and got on my chariot. By him were the cattle rescued and the Kauravas routed. This is the work of that hero and not mine." Uttara, however, in deference to Arjuna's wishes, did not identify Arjuna, Yudhiṣṭhira, or the other Pāṇḍavas.

[1] Arjuna had taken a vow that he would kill anyone who wounded Yudhiṣṭhira and caused his blood to fall on the earth, except in battle.

Two days later the five brothers, great car-warriors all, bathed and put on white clothes adorned with all kinds of ornaments. They observed their rites in due time and, with Yudhiṣṭhira leading them, they appeared, resplendent, like elephants having red spots.[2] Entering the assembly hall of King Virāṭa, they sat on thrones reserved for kings and glowed there like fire on the sacrificial altar.

After they had taken their seats King Virāṭa entered to perform his varied royal duties. When he saw the beautiful Pāṇḍavas, who shone like burning fire, the king said to Kaṅka [Yudhiṣṭhira], who looked divine as Iṅdra surrounded by maruts, "You were a player at dice whom I appointed as a courtier. Why do you presume to sit on a royal throne, adorned with ornaments?" Hearing the words of Virāṭa, Arjuna smiled and said, "This man, O king, is fit to sit even on Iṅdra's throne. Respectful toward Brāhmaṇas, well read in the Scriptures, engaged in the performance of sacrifices, self-sacrificing, of firm vows, he is the first of the Kurus—the son of Kuṅtī, Yudhiṣṭhira. His fame has spread over the earth as the sun's effulgence spreads over the skies. O king, how can there be any question that such a person, the son of Pāṇḍu, foremost of all kings, deserves a royal throne?"

Virāṭa exclaimed, "If this be indeed the king of the Kurus, Yudhiṣṭhira, the son of Kuṅtī, who amongst you is his brother Arjuna and who the mighty Bhīma? Which of you is Nakula, who is Sahadeva, and where is the illustrious Draupadī? From the time of their defeat in gambling, no one has seen the Pāṇḍavas."

"O king," replied Arjuna, "this your cook, known as Ballava, is Bhīma, feared for his prowess and energy. The keeper of your horses is Nakula, the slayer of enemies. The one in charge of your cattle is Sahadeva. Both the sons of Mādrī are great car-warriors. This lotus-eyed, slender-waisted sairaṅdhrī of sweet smiles is Draupadī, O king, on whose account Kīcaka met his death. I am Arjuna, O king, of whom you have heard. We have spent the last year of our exile happily, undiscovered in your house, like creatures living in the womb."

After Arjuna had thus disclosed the identity of the five heroic sons of Pāṇḍu, Uttara described Arjuna's prowess. Hearing the words of

[2] Supposed to be the mark of superior elephants.

Uttara, Virāṭa, who had so recently insulted Yudhiṣṭhira, said to him, "The time has come to please the Pāṇḍavas. If you agree I shall confer my daughter Uttarā upon Arjuna." Virāṭa, highly pleased, also offered Yudhiṣṭhira his entire kingdom including his sceptre, treasury, and city.

Thereupon the pious King Yudhiṣṭhira glanced towards Arjuna. Responding to his brother's look, the latter said to Virāṭa, "O king, I shall accept your daughter as my daughter-in-law. Such an alliance between the Matysas and Bhāratas is indeed suitable." Virāṭa asked, "O foremost of Pāṇḍavas, why do you not want to accept as your wife my daughter whom I desire to confer upon you?" "Living in your inner apartment," Arjuna replied, "I saw your daughter all the time. Alone or in the presence of the others she always used to confide in me as in a father. Well versed as I am in dancing and singing, your daughter always regarded me as her preceptor and liked me much. O king, I would therefore prefer to have your daughter as my daughter-in-law. My son, the mighty Abhimanyu, is a proper son-in-law for you and a suitable match for your daughter."

Virāṭa was satisfied and said, "It is indeed fitting that the foremost of Kurus, the virtuous and wise Arjuna, should say so." After King Virāṭa had spoken, Yudhiṣṭhira gave his blessing to the alliance. Arjuna then brought over Abhimanyu, Kṛṣṇa, and many members of the Dāśārha family from the Ānarta country. The Matsya king duly honoured them all. He gave away his daughter to Abhimanyu, well pleased with the match.

Udyoga Parva

XXXV

In due course the heroes joyfully celebrated the wedding of Abhimanyu. After resting that night, they proceeded early the next day, in a cheerful frame of mind, to Virāṭa's court, which was richly decorated and adorned with precious stones and selected gems, having seats festooned with fragrant garlands. Then the kings came and sat there. In front sat the two kings Virāṭa and Drupada, as well as the aged and revered grandfather of Balarāma and Kṛṣṇa. Near Drupada sat Sātyakī, the brave ruler of Śini, along with Balarāma; and next to Virāṭa sat Kṛṣṇa and Yudhiṣṭhira. The sons of King Drupada, as well as Bhīma and Arjuna; the two sons of Mādrī; Pradyumna and Sāṁba, who were brave in battle; and Abhimanyu, in company with Prince Uttara, were all present. The heroic sons of Draupadī, who were equal to their fathers in valour and beauty, sat on golden seats by themselves.

Kṛṣṇa said, "You all know how Yudhiṣṭhira was tricked at a game of dice by Śakuni, how he was robbed of his kingdom, and how he accepted a condition regarding his exile. True to their words, the sons of Pāṇḍu, who are capable of conquering the world by sheer force of arms, have fulfilled that terrible vow for thirteen years. We are not aware of Duryodhana's intentions, nor do we know what he will do. In the circumstances, it is difficult to decide what we should do ourselves. I therefore suggest that we send a man, virtuous, holy, and of good parentage and sobriety from here—a capable emissary who can persuade Duryodhana to surrender half of Yudhiṣṭhira's kingdom."

"If these heroes among men obtain half of the kingdom," said Balarāma, "they will lead a quiet life, if the other party does the same; peace between them spells the good of their subjects. I should be glad if somebody were to be sent to bring about good relations between the Kauravas and the Pāṇḍavas, and also to ascertain Duryodhana's intentions, and to tell him of Yudhiṣṭhira's views."

"It is not wrong to kill one's enemies," Sātyakī said, "while it is both impious and shameful to beg from one's enemies. Let us therefore do quickly what is Yudhiṣṭhira's heartfelt wish. Let Dhṛtarāṣṭra surrender the kingdom and let the Pāṇḍavas take it. This day, either Yudhiṣṭhira should get the kingdom or all our enemies should fall on the ground slain in battle."

Drupada said, "O Sātyakī, it will no doubt turn out as you have said. Duryodhana will not restore the kingdom by peaceful means. I therefore agree that he should by no means be addressed in a conciliatory tone. I believe that it is impossible to bring the ill-natured Duryodhana to reason by gentle means. We should therefore make preparations for war and send word to our friends to collect armies for us."

"These words befit Sātyakī," said Kṛṣṇa, "and will no doubt promote the best interests of Yudhiṣṭhira. The course suggested by him is our first duty, since we desire to act on the principles of politics; and the man who acts otherwise is a fool. Let us, however, follow both courses at the same time. If the Kaurava leader agrees to a just peace, there will be no harm done to the fraternal feelings between the Kauravas and the Pāṇḍavas. If, however, impelled by pride and folly, Duryodhana should refuse, then summon your other allies, and us too."

Then Virāṭa and his relatives and King Drupada too sent word to all the rulers. At the request of the Pāṇḍava heroes and of the rulers of Matsya and Pāñcāla, many kings came cheerfully with large armies. The news reached Dhṛtarāṣṭra that a large army was being collected for the Pāṇḍavas, and he too brought together many rulers. At that time the earth became crowded with the assemblage of kings who had come on behalf either of the Kauravas or of the Pāṇḍavas.

Meanwhile Drupada, who shared Yudhiṣṭhira's views, sent his own priest, who was old both in wisdom and in age, on a mission to the Kauravas. Receiving his instructions from the great Drupada, the learned priest, accompanied by his followers, went to the city of Hāstinapura.

XXXVI

By sending out scouts privately, Duryodhana learnt all that had been done by the Pāṇḍavas. Hearing that Kṛṣṇa was on his way to Dvārakā, he set out for that city, with a modest retinue borne by horses speedy as the wind. Arjuna arrived at Dvārakā, the beautiful city of the Ānartas, on the same day. The two descendants of Kuru, foremost among men, reached Dvārakā at about the same time, and saw Kṛṣṇa asleep. As Kṛṣṇa slept, Duryodhana entered the bedroom and sat on a fine seat near Kṛṣṇa's head. Then entered the great-souled Arjuna; with folded hands he stood near Kṛṣṇa's feet. When Kṛṣṇa awoke, he naturally saw Arjuna first, and Duryodhana only second. He welcomed them both, did them due honours, and then made inquiries as to the occasion for their visit. Duryodhana said smilingly; "It is proper that you should help me in this war, for your friendship with myself and with Arjuna is equal. Our relationship with you is also equally close. Furthermore, today I have come to you first. Our good ancestors always honoured those who came first."

Kṛṣṇa said, "I have not the slightest doubt that you came here first, but I first set eyes on Arjuna. O Duryodhana, since you arrived here first and I saw him first, I shall help both of you. But the holy books say that younger persons should be aided first; therefore I should first assist Arjuna. I have a large army of ten million gopas, each of whom is capable of slaying me, who are known as the Nārāyaṇas. I shall place this invincible army at the disposal of one party among you; I myself, noncombatant and unarmed, shall take the side of the other. Of these two, O Arjuna, make your choice as you please, since customary law gives you the right of choosing first."

Thus addressed by Kṛṣṇa, Arjuna unhesitatingly chose Kṛṣṇa, who was not to fight in the battle. And Duryodhana for his part chose the whole of that army. Since he had got thousands upon thousands of warriors, even though Kṛṣṇa was lost to him, he was well pleased.

Having obtained the whole army of Kṛṣṇa, Duryodhana went to see Balarāma. He told him why he had come, upon which Balarāma said in reply, "I will not help either you or Arjuna; such is the unalterable conclusion I have reached, after taking into account Kṛṣṇa's views. You are born in the race of Bharata, honoured by all rulers of the earth; go and fight in strict accordance with the code of honour and chivalry."

After Duryodhana's departure, Kṛṣṇa said to Arjuna: "Why have you chosen me, knowing that I shall not take any part in the battle?" "There is no doubt that you can slay them all," said Arjuna. "O foremost among men, I too can slay them all singlehanded. It has been my yearning to have you as my charioteer and it behoves you to fulfil this longfelt desire of mine." Kṛṣṇa replied, "It is but fair that you should compare yourself with me. I shall be your charioteer in fulfilment of your wish."

XXXVII

Śalya too heard the news and went to help the Pāṇḍavas, surrounded by a large army and accompanied by his sons who were mighty car-warriors. He proceeded by slow marches toward the camp of the Pāṇḍavas, resting his army en route. Duryodhana learned that the great Śalya was coming with a large army and hastened to welcome him in person. He also had pavilions erected in charming spots, ornamented with gems and well decorated, for Śalya's accommodation and in his honour. Well pleased with these attentions, Śalya asked the servants, "Who are the men of Yudhiṣṭhira who built these palaces? Bring them to me. I think it is meet that I reward them."

Duryodhana, who had concealed himself, then appeared before Śalya. On seeing him, Śalya knew that all these attentions came from him. Embracing Duryodhana, he said, "Accept whatever you desire." "May your words come true!" said Duryodhana. "Grant me this auspicious boon. It is proper that you should lead all my armies."

"It is done," said Śalya. "Is there anything else?" Duryodhana had no other wish. He took leave of Śalya, and returned to his own city.

Śalya went on to see Yudhiṣṭhira and to inquire what he wished to have done. In the course of time, he reached Upaplavya, and entered the Pāṇḍava encampment, where he spoke about his meeting with Duryodhana, and the great boon he had given because of the attentions he had received.

Yudhiṣṭhira said, "O king, what you have done is good; you have fulfilled a promise made when you were well pleased in the innermost recesses of your heart. I want you to do only one thing for me. You are the best among kings, you are Kṛṣṇa's equal in battle; when the two, Karṇa and Arjuna, riding their chariots, meet in battle, I have no doubt that you will fill the office of Karṇa's charioteer. O king, if you wish me well, you must protect Arjuna, and do whatever is necessary to kill the energy of Karṇa, and whatever is calculated to bring us victory. Though this is improper, yet must you do it, uncle mine!" "O son," replied Śalya, "I shall do what you have asked me to do, and anything else which I can see is for your good." The ruler of Madra, the noble Śalya, then took leave of the sons of Kuṅtī and went with his army to Duryodhana, as he had promised.

XXXVIII

In due course Drupada's priest reached Hāstinapura and was greeted by Dhṛtarāṣṭra, Bhīṣma, and Vidura, to whom he said, "It is well known that Dhṛtarāṣṭra and Pāṇḍu are brothers, and there is no doubt that the kingdom of their fathers should be shared by them equally. The heroic sons of Pāṇḍu have no desire to wage war with the Kauravas. They do not wish to regain their own kingdom by ruining the world. Therefore, as virtue dictates and as is timely, restore that which should be given back. Do not let this opportunity slip."

Bhīṣma said, "It is fortunate that our brothers, the Pāṇḍavas, desire peace; it is lucky that they and Kṛṣṇa do not desire war." But while Bhīṣma was speaking, Karṇa interrupted him angrily. Addressing Duryodhana, he said, "If they want the restoration of the kingdom of their forefathers let them, as stipulated, live in the forest to the end of the period that was agreed upon."

Dhṛtarāṣṭra appeased Bhīṣma by approving of his sentiments. In rebuke of Karṇa, he said, "What Bhīṣma, the son of Śaṅtanu, has said is designed to advance our interests and the interests of the Pāṇḍavas as well as those of the entire world. After mature consideration, I have decided to send Sañjaya to the Pāṇḍavas." Addressing Drupada's priest, the king said, "Return today to the Pāṇḍavas, and tell them of Sañjaya's mission."

Dhṛtarāṣṭra gave necessary instructions to Sañjaya before the latter's departure. He said, "Proceed quickly in a chariot to the place where the army of the Pāñcālas is encamped. Ask about the welfare of Yudhiṣṭhira, and address him repeatedly in affectionate terms. Meet also the great Kṛṣṇa, foremost of all heroic men. Inquire about his welfare too, and assure him that Dhṛtarāṣṭra desires peace with the Pāṇḍavas. There is no word of Kṛṣṇa's that Yudhiṣṭhira will not heed. Kṛṣṇa is as dear to them as their own selves. He is learned, and devoted to their welfare. Say whatever you think may properly be said to the enemy, as occasion arises, and also whatever you judge to be conducive to the interests of the race of Bharata. Do not say anything which may give cause for war."

Having taken note of the words of King Dhṛtarāṣṭra, Sañjaya went to Upaplavya to see the Pāṇḍavas. On seeing him, Yudhiṣṭhira said, "O son of Gavalgaṇa, O Sañjaya, you are welcome. We are happy to see you. In return I wish to know about your health. For our part my younger brothers and I are well, O learned man."

"It is as you have said, O son of Pāṇḍu," replied Sañjaya. "You ask about the Kurus, of whom you are the foremost. Those about whom you inquire are in good health and excellent spirits. King Dhṛtarāṣṭra, welcoming the chance of peace, had my chariot speedily got ready. Therefore, Yudhiṣṭhira, may you, with your brothers, sons, and friends, find these words acceptable: Let there be peace!"

Yudhiṣṭhira said, "What words have you heard me say, O Sañjaya, indicating that I desire or expect war? Peace is preferable to war. Who, having the choice, would prefer to fight? You know what sufferings we have undergone. Out of my respect for you, I would forgive them. You know well what has taken place between us and the sons of Kuru, and also how we have conducted ourselves towards Duryodhana. May that continue today! I shall make peace, as you ask me to do. Let Indraprastha be my kingdom. Let Duryodhana restore it to me."

Sañjaya replied, "After having allowed the strength of your enemy to increase and after weakening your own friends, and after having lived in banishment in the forest for several years, why do you now desire to fight at such an inopportune time, O son of Pāṇḍu? Who would be inclined to anger which leads to sin? Forbearance is better for you than enjoyment, if Bhīṣma the son of Śantanu will be killed, and Droṇa and his son slain."

At this, Yudhiṣṭhira declared, "Let the illustrious Kṛṣṇa, the son of Vasudeva, who desires the welfare of both parties, say if I am to blame by not making peace, and if I swerve from the duties of my princely order because I wish to fight for my rights."

In response to this appeal to him, Kṛṣṇa said, "I wish, O Sañjaya, that the sons of Pāṇḍu may not be destroyed. I desire their prosperity and their good; and in the same way do I desire the prosperity of King Dhṛtarāṣṭra, who has many sons. It has ever been my purpose to adjure them to be peaceful. I hear that this is also the wish of the king and I believe that it is equally advantageous to the Pāṇḍavas. Yudhiṣṭhira is ever devoted to the study of the Vedas and you know he is also attached to Aśvamedha and Rājasūya sacrifices. At the same time he also shoots with the bow and dons armour; he rides on chariots and is well versed in the use of weapons. The share of the Pāṇḍavas is known and fixed. It was lost by us to our enemies by chance. In the circumstances we must fight even if we may be slain. Recovery of one's ancestral property is preferable to accepting a kingdom belonging to another. You may explain these time-honoured precepts to the Kauravas in the royal court, O Sañjaya!"

"The Kurus with Bhīṣma at their head," Kṛṣṇa continued, "did not intercede when the illustrious and chaste Draupadī, the dearly beloved wife of the Pāṇḍavas, stood weeping in the clutches of that slave of lust. You did not then, in the council hall, utter one word of protest; but now you want to preach sense to the Pāṇḍavas. Draupadī, however, accomplished something pure and hard in that council. She saved herself and the Pāṇḍavas, as by a raft, from the ocean of misfortune. You are aware, O Sañjaya, of all the objectionable words that were said during the game of dice. I want to go to Dhṛtarāṣṭra's court myself to settle this difficult matter. If I can bring about peace without injury to the legitimate interests of the Pāṇḍavas, I shall have performed a virtuous act, resulting in great good, and at the same time I shall have freed the Kurus from the jaws of death. If it goes otherwise, know that the sons of Dhṛtarāṣṭra will be consumed by their own stupid deeds. They will be deprived of their prosperity by the car-warrior Arjuna and the great fighter Bhīma."

Sañjaya then said, "I bid you farewell, O divine ruler of men. I shall now leave. O son of Pāṇḍu, may all be well with you! I hope I have used no objectionable language, in the heat of the moment. If so, may I be forgiven!"

"I give you leave to depart, O Sañjaya," said Yudhiṣṭhira. "May you fare well! Do not ever think ill of us. We all know that, in the Kaurava court, you are a pure-souled man. O Sañjaya, you should make Duryodhana, the son of Dhṛstarāṣṭra, hear these words again: 'The desire which is tormenting your heart, to rule the kingdom of the Kurus without any rival, has no justification. We shall do nothing that will be disagreeable to you. Either restore to us the city of Indraprastha, or fight.' " He continued, "I am surely prepared for peace as well as for war, O Sañjaya. For acquiring wealth and earning virtuous merit I am ready for mild as well as harsh measures."

Then, by leave of Yudhiṣṭhira, Sañjaya departed, having carried out all the behests of the great-souled Dhṛtarāṣṭra. When he returned to Hāstinapura, Dhṛtarāṣṭra said to him, "Blessings be on you, O Sañjaya. Is the son of Pṛthā, he who has no enemies, happy? Is that king well, and also his sons, ministers, and younger brothers?"

Sañjaya replied: "Yudhiṣṭhira is well, as are his ministers. He who acquires virtue and wealth, and does no wrong deed, who is wise, learned, farsighted, and of good behaviour, desires to have again what was his previously. Now, following the vagaries of your son, you covet this doubtful property. This act has been loudly proclaimed to be wicked in this world, and is not worthy of you, O King!' O best of men, I am very tired from the speedy motion of the car and I seek your permission to retire to bed. In the morning the sons of Kuru, assembled in the council chamber, may listen to the message of Yudhiṣṭhira, who has made no enemies."

XXXIX

The next morning all the kings entered the council chamber with glad hearts, looking forward to seeing Sañjaya. Desirous of hearing the message of those sons of Pṛthā, full of virtue and worldly benefit, they all proceeded to the auspicious council chamber with Dhṛtarāṣṭra at their head.

Dhṛtarāṣṭra then said, "I ask you, O Sañjaya, in the midst of these kings, to tell us what the noble Arjuna of pure habits, leader in battles, destroyer of the lives of vicious men, said." Sañjaya replied, "Let Duryodhana listen to this speech which was made, with the permission of Yudhiṣṭhira and in the hearing of Kṛṣṇa, by Arjuna, who is eager to fight. Without the slightest fear, and conscious of the strength of his arms, the hero spoke to me in the presence of Kṛṣṇa. Arjuna said, 'Say this to the son of Dhṛtarāṣṭra in the midst of the Kurus. If the son of Dhṛtarāṣṭra does not surrender the kingdom of Yudhiṣṭhira, and if he thinks in terms of war with the Pāṇḍavas, then are all the objects of the Pāṇḍavas gained. Therefore do not suggest peace for the sake of the Pāṇḍavas; let there be war if you please.' "

When Sañjaya had delivered this message in the midst of all those kings, Bhīṣma spoke these words to Duryodhana, "Know that Arjuna and Kṛṣṇa are the gods Nara and Nārāyaṇa, whom the holy books declare to be the original gods. They are incapable of being vanquished by men in this world, or by Indra, or by the gods and asuras. Kṛṣṇa is Nārāyaṇa, and Arjuna is Nara. Nārāyaṇa and Nara are the same essence divided into two. If you do not accept my advice which is heeded by all the sons of Kuru, then you will hear of the slaying of numerous men of your army; you listen to the advice of only three persons: Karṇa, who was cursed by Paraśurāma, and who is a low-born fellow; Śakuni, the son of Subala; and your petty-minded, wicked brother Duḥśāsana."

Dhṛtarāṣṭra said, "The great tragedy of the Kurus beginning with the game of dice now works itself out; this wicked act has been done by that fool out of greed and desire for prosperity. I consider this to be the work of eternal time. Like the iron ring attached to the wheel, I am not able to run away from it. What shall I do, how shall I do it, and where shall I go, O Sañjaya? These foolish Kurus will be destroyed by fate."

"It is as you say, O Bhārata," agreed Sañjaya. "The destruction of the Kṣatriyas by the Gāṇḍīva bow in war seems certain. All this was predicted by me, and also by the wise Vidura at the time of the game of dice. These lamentations of yours for the sons of Pāṇḍu, O king, as if you had no hand in the matter, are all futile."

"There is nothing to fear, O great king," said Duryodhana, "nor should you grieve for us. We are capable of winning victory over our enemies in battle. Both the parties are of the same race. Why then do you foresee victory solely for the Pāṇḍavas? Our grandfather Bhīṣma, Droṇa, Kṛpa, the invincible Karṇa, Jayadratha, Somadatta, and Aśvatthāmā, are all on our side. Even Iṅdra along with the gods cannot defeat these wise and great bowmen. How can the Pāṇḍavas do it, O sire?"

Dhṛtarāṣṭra exclaimed, "My son raves like a madman, O Sañjaya; he is not capable of defeating in battle Yudhiṣṭhira the king of Dharma." "I do not wish war," he continued, "nor does Bhīṣma, nor Droṇa, nor Aśvatthāmā, nor Sañjaya. You do not act in this way of your own will; but Karṇa eggs you on to it, and Duḥśāsana, and the evil-souled Śakuni."

"I do not rely on Droṇa, or Aśvatthāmā, or Sañjaya, or Vikarṇa, or Kāṁboja, or Kṛpa, or Bāhlika," Duryodhana replied, "O sire, Karṇa and I will perform the sacrifice of war after preparing ourselves, making Yudhiṣthira the sacrificial animal. I myself, O sire, Karṇa, and my brother Duḥśāsana, we three will kill the sons of Pāṇḍu in battle. Either I shall rule this earth, having slain the sons of Pāṇḍu; or the sons of Pāṇḍu shall enjoy sovereignty over this earth after having slain me. I can sacrifice my life, my kingdom, my wealth; but I cannot live in peace with the sons of Pāṇḍu. O venerable sire, I shall not surrender to the sons of Pāṇḍu as much land as can be pierced by the point of a sharp needle."

Dhṛtarāṣṭra said, "I grieve for all of you, who are following that fool to the abode of the king of death; but I cast off Duryodhana forever. Like tigers among a herd of deer, these foremost of warriors, these Pāṇḍavas, assembled together, will kill the elite of the elite in battle. I apprehend a great disaster, if you do not make peace with the Pāṇḍavas. You will be killed by Bhīma with his mace, and then only will you attain peace.

"In this great battle," he continued, "I see that mighty bowman Arjuna, protected by Iṅdra and Upeṅdra, working havoc. Thinking of this day and night, O Bhārata, I am sleepless and unhappy through anxiety for the welfare of the Kurus. A terrible destruction of the Kurus is imminent if this quarrel should end otherwise than peacefully. Peace seems to me preferable to war with the Pāṇḍavas, O child! I have always been of the opinion that the Pāṇḍavas are possessed of greater strength than the Kurus."

Having heard these words of his father, the passionate Duryodhana became highly enraged and spoke again: "You think that because the Pāṇḍavas have the gods as their counsellors they are incapable of being withstood; let this fear of yours be dispelled, O king! You will in due course hear of my victory over the Pāṇḍavas, the Matsyas, the Pāñcālas, the Kekayas, and also over Sātyaki and Kṛṣṇa."

Disregarding Dhṛtarāṣṭra, who was about to make another inquiry about the strength of the Pāṇḍavas, Karṇa said these encouraging words to Duryodhana in that assemblage of Kauravas: "Let your grandfather stay near you, as well as Droṇa and those foremost among the rulers of men. Leading the main army, I shall kill the Pāṇḍavas. This is my responsibility."

Bhīṣma then said to Karṇa, "What are you saying, O Karṇa? Your intelligence has been dimmed at the near approach of death. Do you not know, O Karṇa, that when Duryodhana is killed, the other sons of

Dhṛtarāṣṭra will all be slain? You seem to rely on the weapon which that foremost of the gods, the great-souled and prosperous Indra, gave you. You will see it broken and turned into ashes, when struck by the cakra of Kṛṣṇa. You also cherish that arrow with a tip like the mouth of a serpent which is shining in your belt and which you ever worship with the best of garlands. When struck with the cluster of arrows by the sons of Pāṇḍu, this weapon too will go to ruin with you, O Karṇa!"

"Undoubtedly," said Karṇa, "the Lord Kṛṣṇa can do all that Bhīṣma says. Indeed he is even greater than that. The grandfather has said some harsh words. Let him hear my reply. I shall lay down my arms, and the grandfather will see me only in court and not in battle. When Bhīṣma has himself become quiet, then only will all the rulers of the earth see my prowess." So saying, the great bowman left the court and went to his own house; and, amidst those Kurus, Bhīṣma said to Duryodhana laughingly, "Karṇa keeps his promise well; now that he is gone, how will he discharge the responsibilities he undertook? Wait and see the havoc that Bhīma will work, breaking our heads and overcoming our military formations."

Duryodhana replied to Bhīṣma, "Why do you regard victory to be the sole monopoly of the Pāṇḍavas, who are similar to other men and of equal birth?" Vidura intervened, "Duryodhana desires a fight with Arjuna; but I do not see in him the strength or energy necessary for that purpose. Alone in his car, Arjuna brought the earth under his control. That hero is still willing to forgive, and looking to you to see what you will do. Like a fire urged on by the wind, the wrathful Drupada, Virāṭa, and Arjuna will leave no trace of your army. O Dhṛtarāṣṭra, treat King Yudhiṣṭhira fairly; for in a struggle between you two neither can win a complete victory."

Dhṛtarāṣṭra again pleaded with his son. He said, "O Duryodhana, reflect well on what I am telling you, my dear son. You imagine the wrong way to be the right one, like an inexperienced traveller. Abide by the words of your friends who advise you in your own interests. Accept the aged Bhīṣma, the son of Śantanu, who is your grandfather, as your guide."

When Duryodhana remained unmoved, Dhṛtarāṣṭra sent for Gāndhārī to talk to him. She too implored him to make peace, saying, "O you avaricious person, O you of wicked soul, you do not listen to the advice of your elders, and do not heed your father and me. You are giving up your wealth and your life, and enhancing the joy of your enemies as well as my grief. You will remember the words of your father only when you are slain by Bhīma."

XL

Meanwhile, at the Pāṇḍava camp, Yudhiṣṭhira said to Kṛṣṇa, "Relying on you, O Kṛṣṇa, we have without fear demanded our share of the kingdom from the son of Dhṛtarāṣṭra who is filled with vain pride, as are all his advisers. You have heard what Dhṛtarāṣṭra and his son intend to do. It is exactly as Sañjaya told me. He wants to make peace with us without restoring our kingdom to us; the greedy man, moved by his sinful heart, shows bias towards his own son. We said to him, 'Give us, O sire, five villages or towns where we may live together; for we do not desire the destruction of the Bhāratas.' Even this the wicked-souled son of Dhṛtarāṣṭra does not permit, thinking that he is the sole lord. What is more deplorable than this?"

"Wealth is said to be the best virtue," Yudhiṣṭhira continued. "Everything is established on wealth; and rich men live in this world, while poor men are practically dead. Poverty is a greater danger to a man than death; for it destroys his prosperity, which is the source of his virtue as well as his pleasures. A man who is born poor does not suffer so much as one who, after having enjoyed great prosperity and a life of great happiness, is deprived of it. We have many cousins, and our elders are our allies on both sides. Their slaughter would be extremely sinful. One may well ask: what then is the good of engaging in battle? A Kṣatriya kills another Kṣatriya; a fish lives on another fish; a dog kills another dog. See how each follows his rule of life, O Kṛṣṇa. In all cases war is evil. Who that strikes is not struck in return? Victory and defeat, O Kṛṣṇa, are the same to one who is killed. Defeat is not very much better than death, I think; but he whose side gains victory also surely suffers some loss."

Yudhiṣṭhira asked him, "What then do you think, O Kṛṣṇa, to be appropriate to the occasion? How shall I find a way out without deviating from virtue as well as from worldly good? In such a predicament, whom else but yourself is it proper for us to consult, O best among men?" In reply, Kṛṣṇa said to Yudhiṣṭhira, "For the good of both of you I shall go to the Kuru camp. If I succeed in ensuring peace without sacrificing your interests, then I shall have performed a virtuous and fruitful act."

"As it pleases you, O Kṛṣṇa!" said Yudhiṣṭhira. "May good come out of it! May I see you return from the Kurus with your object gained, and in good health!" Kṛṣṇa said, "Going to the Kurus, I shall seek to make peace without any sacrifice of your interests; and I shall also observe their intentions. After noting the conduct of the sons of Kuru and ascertained their preparations for war, I shall return to make victory yours, O Bhārata."

Having come to know through his spies of the departure of Kṛṣṇa, Dhṛtarāṣṭra said to Bhīṣma, after paying him due honour, "The powerful scion of the Dāśārha race is coming here for the sake of the Pāṇḍavas; he is at all times worthy of our respect and regard. Prepare for his worship and erect pavilions on the way, filled with all needed articles." Then at many places on the way, at spots of great beauty, pavilions were constructed and decked with all kinds of gems. The king sent there comfortable seats, girls, perfumes, ornaments, fine fabrics, excellent viands and drinks, and several kinds of fragrant garlands.

Vidura addressed Dhṛtarāṣṭra, "O king, the five Pāṇḍavas desire only five villages. If you do not give them even those, who will conclude peace? You wish to win over Kṛṣṇa by wealth; and by this means you want to separate him from the Pāṇḍavas. Let me tell you this: he cannot be separated from Arjuna by wealth, or by efforts, or by accusations and complaints against the Pāṇḍavas."

Duryodhana said, "What Vidura has said just now regarding Kṛṣṇa has been truly spoken; for he is firmly attached to the Pāṇḍavas and inseparable from them. Listen to this great idea which I am determined to carry out. I shall imprison Kṛṣṇa, the refuge of the Pāṇḍavas. On his imprisonment, the Vṛṣṇis and the Pāṇḍavas, in fact the whole world, will be at my disposal. Kṛṣṇa will be here tomorrow morning."

Hearing these words of terrible significance, the plan of making Kṛṣṇa a captive, Dhṛtarāṣṭra and his ministers were much pained. Dhṛtarāṣṭra then said to Duryodhana, "Do not say such foolish things, O my son. This is against eternal virtue. Kṛṣṇa is an ambassador, and he is also our kinsman. He has done no wrong to the Kurus. How then is it right that he should be made prisoner?"

Bhīṣma said, "This son of yours, Dhṛtarāṣṭra, has been seized by folly. He chooses evil rather than good, despite the entreaties of his well-wishers. I wish never to listen to the risk-laden words of this sinful and wicked wretch who has abandoned all virtue." Having said these words, the old chief of the Bhāratas, the truthful Bhīṣma, rose in a towering rage and left the court.

XLI

In honour of Kṛṣṇa the city was well decorated and the streets were adorned with various gems. The people, with their heads bowed low to the ground, were in the streets when Kṛṣṇa entered the city. That lotus-eyed hero entered the ash-coloured palace of Dhṛtarāṣṭra, graced with many buildings. He was duly honoured by Dhṛtarāṣṭra and then came out with the permission of the king. Having exchanged greetings with the Kurus in the assembly, Kṛṣṇa went to the enchanting abode of Vidura. The virtuous Vidura completed the rites of hospitality for Kṛṣṇa, and then asked him about the welfare of the Pāṇḍavas.

After his visit to Vidura, Kṛṣṇa went in the afternoon to visit his aunt Kuṅtī. Seeing Kṛṣṇa approach, shining like the radiant sun, Kuṅtī clasped his neck with her arms, and poured forth her lamentations, remembering her sons whom she had not seen for so long. Kṛṣṇa said to her, "Your sons, along with Draupadī, salute you. They are well and have asked me to inquire about your welfare. You will soon see the Pāṇḍavas, in good health, with all their objects gained, their enemies killed and themselves surrounded by prosperity." Bidding her farewell, and respectfully circumambulating her, the mighty-armed Kṛṣṇa then left for Duryodhana's mansion.

During the night, after he had dined and refreshed himself, Vidura said to him, "O Kṛṣṇa, this mission of yours is not a well-considered act. The sons of Dhṛtarāṣṭra and Karṇa are convinced that the Pāṇḍavas are not capable even of gazing at an army under the leadership of Bhīṣma and Droṇa. The idea of your going and speaking in the midst of all those misguided, impure, and evil-minded men does not please me. All the sons of Dhṛtarāṣṭra have come to the conclusion, O Kṛṣṇa, that they can give battle to Iṅdra himself along with the other gods. Your words, though wise in themselves, will be of no avail against those who are thus inclined, and who follow the dictates of desire and anger."

Kṛṣṇa said, "You have spoken wisely—you have spoken as a man of insight, and even as one friend to another. When there is a dispute between cousins, the wise men say that the friend who does not serve them as a mediator by all his efforts is not a true friend. If I can bring about peace with the Kurus without sacrificing the interests of the Pāṇḍavas, then my conduct will have been meritorious and very significant; and the Kurus will have been freed from the shackles of death."

In such talk the two wise men spent that starlit and beautiful night. At dawn many professional bards and singers endowed with good voices awakened Kṛṣṇa with the sound of conch and cymbal. Duryodhana and Śakuni came to Kṛṣṇa while he was still performing his morning rites, and said to him, "King Dhṛtarāṣṭra has come to the assembly hall, and so have the other Kurus, headed by Bhīṣma and all the rulers of the earth. They are waiting for you, O Kṛṣṇa, as the gods in heaven may await Iṅdra's arrival." Kṛṣṇa received them courteously, and in due course proceeded to the assembly hall.

When all the kings and courtiers had taken their seats and perfect stillness prevailed, Kṛṣṇa said in a voice like a drum, "I have come so that there may be peace between the Kurus and Pāṇḍavas, O Bhārata, without the slaughter[1] of heroes on either side. However, your sons, headed by Duryodhana, are acting impiously, putting behind them all considerations of morality and earthly good. As boys the Pāṇḍavas lost their father and were brought up by you; protect them in accordance with justice, as you would your own sons, O king. The Pāṇḍavas salute you, and have sent you this message: 'At your command our followers and we ourselves have suffered untold misery. We have spent twelve years in banishment in the forest and the thirteenth year in disguise. We did not break our word, truly believing that our father would not break his pledge towards us. The Brāhmaṇas who accompanied us know this. Therefore abide by your pledge as we have done by ours, O best of the Bhārata race. We have suffered long, and now we desire to get our share of the kingdom.' "

Having given this message, Kṛṣṇa continued, "Restore to the Pāṇḍavas their due share of the ancestral kingdom, and enjoy the blessings of life, along with your sons. As for me, O Bhārata, I desire your welfare as much as that of the others. In the interests of virtue, profit, and happiness, O king, I adjure you not to allow the destruction of your subjects. Restrain your sons, who regard evil as good and good as evil, and who, moved by greed, have gone too far. The Pāṇḍavas are as ready to serve you dutifully as to fight. O king, adopt that course which seems wisest to you."

XLII

Dhṛtarāṣṭra said to Kṛṣṇa, "O Kṛṣṇa, I agree with what you have said to me. It will lead to the attainment of heaven, besides being beneficial to the world, as well as virtuous and just. But I am not my own master and I cannot do what I would like to do. O Kṛṣṇa, try and persuade my wicked son Duryodhana, who disregards the injunctions of the scriptures. Then you will have discharged a great duty as a friend."

So Kṛṣṇa addressed himself to the wrathful Duryodhana, in sweet

[1] The expression used is "aprayatnena vīrāṇāṁ." Both Dutt and Roy have translated this "without the slaughter of heroes," which suits the context. The literal translation would be "without the exertion of heroes."

words pregnant with virtue and worldly profit, "O Duryodhana, listen to these words of mine, which are meant for your benefit and that of your followers. Born as you are in a family of very wise men, and endowed as you are with learning and good conduct and with all good qualities, it is right and proper that you should behave honourably. In this case your obstinacy is perverse and unrighteous, and it will result in great and terrible loss of life. O tiger among men, be reconciled with the Pāṇḍavas, who are wise, heroic, energetic, self-restrained, and greatly learned. It is beneficial to you, and will be appreciated by the wise Dhṛtarāṣṭra, as well as by the grandfather Bhīṣma, Droṇa, and the intelligent Vidura. Let there be some survivors of the Kuru race and let not the whole race be destroyed, and do not let yourself, O king, become notorious as the exterminator of the race."

Duryodhana became enraged on hearing the words of Kṛṣṇa. Bhīṣma said to him, "Kṛṣṇa has spoken as a friend wishing peace; listen to his words, my dear son, and do not follow the lead of anger." But Duryodhana did not heed Bhīṣma's advice. He remained under the influence of wrath, breathing hard. Then Droṇa told him, "Kṛṣṇa said words to you which are filled with virtue and profit, my dear son; so did Bhīṣma, the son of Śaṅtanu; heed them, O ruler of men." At the end of Droṇa's speech, Vidura spoke in similar terms to Duryodhana, the irate son of Dhṛtarāṣṭra. "Duryodhana," he said, "I do not grieve for you, but for these two old people, your father and Gāndhārī your mother." Dhṛtarāṣṭra then said to Duryodhana, who was seated along with his brothers and surrounded by other kings, "O Duryodhana, listen to this advice given by the great-souled Kṛṣṇa; accept his words which are beneficial, of eternal validity and conducive to our salvation."

So, among the assembled Kurus, Duryodhana had to listen to this counsel which he little liked. Finally he said in reply to Kṛṣṇa, "No doubt, as is proper, you have spoken to me after due consideration; but you find fault only with me. I have not committed the slightest fault, nor do I see even the smallest misconduct on my side after a searching examination. I may recall that the Pāṇḍavas were defeated at a game of dice in which they engaged of their own free will and in the course of which their kingdom was won by Śakuni; what misconduct was there on my part? Indeed, you will remember that I ordered at the time the return of the wealth which the Pāṇḍavas had lost. It is not our fault that the Pāṇḍavas were defeated at another game of dice and were then banished to the forest. The principal duty of a Kṣatriya is that he should lie down on a bed of arrows in the battlefield. I am ready to do so. I shall not, during my lifetime, allow the Pāṇḍavas to regain the share of the kingdom that was given them by our ancestors in early days."

After reflecting on Duryodhana's speech, Kṛṣṇa, his eyes red with anger, spoke these words to Duryodhana in that assembly of the Kurus: "It is your desire to get the bed of a hero, and it will be fulfilled; you and your advisers will not have to wait long. Soon there will be a great massacre. O fool, you think that there is nothing blameworthy in your conduct towards the Pāṇḍavas. All the kings here know the truth of what I am now going to say. Being jealous of the prosperity of the great Pāṇḍavas, you arranged for a game of dice in evil cabal with Śakuni. Who save yourself could have treated the wife of your brothers in the way you did? After dragging Draupadī to the council hall, who else could have spoken to her as you did? You went to great trouble to burn the Pāṇḍavas alive when they were mere boys, and were staying with their mother at Vāraṇāvata, but that attempt of yours did not succeed. By poison, by snake, and by rope, in fact by every means, you have attempted the destruction of the sons of Pāṇḍu, but you have not been successful. You have been urged again and again, by your mother and by your father and also by Bhīṣma, Droṇa, and Vidura, to make peace but you do not wish to do so."

When Kṣṛṇa had thus charged the wrathful Duryodhana, Duḥśāsana said these words in the assembly of the Kurus, "If you do not make peace of your own free will with the Pāṇḍavas, it looks as if the Kauravas will make you over to Yudhiṣṭhira bound hand and foot." Hearing these words of his brother, Duryodhana could no longer restrain himself. He got up from his seat hissing like a huge serpent. Disregarding all those present—Vidura, King Dhṛtarāṣṭra, Bāhlika,

Kṛpa, Somadatta, Bhīṣma, Droṇa, and Kṛṣṇa—that shameless and wicked prince walked out of the court.

XLIII

Dhṛtarāṣṭra then said to Vidura, "Go, my friend, to the wise Gāndhārī; get her here; along with her I shall try to persuade our son." In response to the request of Dhṛtarāṣṭra, Vidura brought the farsighted Gāndhārī. By command of Dhṛtarāṣṭra and also at the request of Gāndhārī, Vidura had the wrathful Duryodhana brought back. Seeing her son, who was following the wrong course, Gāndhārī spoke these significant words, "O Duryodhana, my dear son, listen to these words of mine which will be to your benefit and that of your followers, and which will bring you all happiness. It is my fond and earnest wish, as well as that of Bhīṣma, your father, and other well-wishers, the chief of whom is Droṇa, that you should make peace."

Disregarding those sensible words spoken by his mother, the obstinate Duryodhana again went to his own palace burning with rage. Then he consulted King Śakuni, the expert in the game of dice, as well as Karṇa and Duḥśāsana. The four, namely, Duryodhana, Karṇa, Śakuni, and Duḥśāsana, reached the following conclusion: "Kṛṣṇa means to waste no time, and wants to capture us first in concert with Dhṛtarāṣṭra and Bhīṣma. We shall, however, capture Kṛṣṇa by force, before he can carry out his plan."

Coming to know of this plan through Sātyaki, Vidura said to Dhṛtarāṣṭra, "O king, your sons are approaching the hour of doom, because they are ready to perpetrate an infamous act, even though they are incapable of doing it." He then informed the king of Duryodhana's nefarious plot. On hearing this, Dhṛtarāṣṭra said to Vidura, "Bring here again the sinful Duryodhana, who covets the kingdom." Therefore Vidura made the reluctant Duryodhana return once more to the council chamber, along with his brothers.

King Dhṛtarāṣṭra addressed Duryodhana, Karṇa, Duḥśāsana, and the kings who surrounded them, "O you of inhuman conduct, of exceeding sinfulness, having for your supporters only petty men, I know of your secret desire to commit a wicked deed. Kṛṣṇa cannot be captured by force, even as air cannot be held by the hand, as the moon cannot be touched, and as the earth cannot be supported on the head." Vidura's warning was: "If you try to use force on the mighty Kṛṣṇa, you, along with your advisers, will perish like an insect falling into the flame."

When Vidura had finished speaking, Kṛṣṇa said to Duryodhana, "O Duryodhana! since, out of your folly, you suppose me to be alone, you think you can effect my capture by overpowering me." So saying, he laughed aloud. And at his laughter the body of the great-souled one became like lightning. From his body issued forth gods only as big as the thumb but bright as rays of fire. Brahmā was found to be on his brow and Rudra on his breast. On his arms appeared the regents of the earth and from his mouth issued forth the god of fire. When Kṛṣṇa thus showed himself on the floor of the assembly hall, celestial drums were sounded and there was a shower of flowers. After a moment he discarded that celestial and wonderful form. Taking Sātyaki by the hand, Kṛṣṇa went out, with the permission of the sages present in the court.

As he was about to depart on the chariot which was ready for him, the great king Dhṛtarāṣṭra again said to Kṛṣṇa, "You have seen, O Kṛṣṇa, what little influence I wield over my sons; you have been a witness to that; nothing has happened behind your back." Then Kṛṣṇa said to Dhṛtarāṣṭra, and to Droṇa and the grandfather Bhīṣma, and to Vidura, and to Bāhlika and Kṛpa, "Your exalted selves are witnesses to what went on in the assembly of the Kurus; how today that fool, like an uneducated and unmannerly fellow, walked out. Now you have heard the ruler of the earth Dhṛtarāṣṭra say that he is powerless in the matter. With the permission of all of you I shall go to Yudhiṣṭhira."

Then in that large, white chariot, furnished with tinkling bells, Kṛṣṇa went first to see his aunt Kuntī. Entering her abode, he bowed at her feet, after which he briefly described to her what had happened in the assembly of the Kurus. Having completed his report he respectfully circumambulated her, and took leave of her.

When Kṛṣṇa had left, Bhīṣma and Droṇa said to Duryodhana, "The sons of Kuntī will do what Kṛṣṇa advises, and they will not be pacified without the restoration of the kingdom. The Pāṇḍavas and Draupadī too were persecuted by you in the assembly hall, but they were bound by the ties of virtue at that time. Now they have in Arjuna a master of all weapons and in Bhīma a giant of firm determination. They have the Gāṇḍīva bow and the two quivers and the chariot and the flag, and they have Kṛṣṇa as their ally. The Pāṇḍavas will not forgive the past."

XLIV

Before leaving Hāstinapura, Kṛṣṇa met Karṇa and said to him: "O Karṇa, you know the eternal instruction of the holy books and are fully conversant with all their subtleties. The two classes of sons called Kānīna and Sahoḍha who are borne by a girl before her marriage have for their father the man who marries their mother subsequently—so it is said by people conversant with the holy books. You were born in that way and you are therefore morally the son of Pāṇḍu; so come with me and be a king in your own right. Let us go together to the Pāṇḍava camp, and let the sons of Pāṇḍu know you to be the son of Kuntī born before Yudhiṣṭhira. The five Pāṇḍava brothers will clasp your feet, as will the five sons of Draupadī, and the invincible son of Subhadrā. Enjoy the kingdom in company with your brothers, the sons of Pāṇḍu, who are ever engaged in prayer and sacrifice and other auspicious ceremonies. Let your friends rejoice and in the same way let your enemies suffer; be reconciled today with your brothers, the sons of Pāṇḍu."

Karṇa replied: "I have no doubt, O Kṛṣṇa, that you have spoken these words out of good will, love, and friendship, and also out of the desire to do me good. Before her wedding with Pāṇḍu, Kuntī conceived me by the Sun-god, and at his command she abandoned me as soon as I was born. I know I was born in this way and I am therefore morally the son of Pāṇḍu. I was however left destitute at birth by Kuntī, who had no thought of my welfare. On the other hand, I have been practically a member of the family of Dhṛtarāṣṭra and, under the protection of Duryodhana, I have enjoyed sovereignty for thirteen years without let or hindrance. Relying on me, Duryodhana has made preparations for war with the Pāṇḍavas. At this stage, I cannot behave treacherously towards Duryodhana out of fear of being slain or captured, or from covetousness."

Kṛṣṇa said, "I fear that this world will surely come to an end, O Karṇa, since my advice does not seem acceptable to you." "O Kṛṣṇa," replied Karṇa, "I shall see you again if I survive this great battle which has come upon us. Otherwise we shall surely meet in heaven. I now feel that I shall meet you only there, O sinless one."

Having learnt of the failure of Kṛṣṇa's mission, Kuṅtī decided to make a personal appeal to Karṇa. Thus resolved, she went towards the river Gaṅgā for the attainment of her object. On the banks of the river she heard the sound of the chanting of hymns by her son, the kind and truthful Karṇa. That austere lady waited behind Karṇa, whose arms were raised and whose face was turned to the east, till the end of his devotions, which continued till his back had been scorched by the rays of the sun. Karṇa then turned and, seeing Kuṅtī, did her honour by saluting her and folding his hands before her, according to proper form.

Karṇa first introduced himself, by saying, "I am Karṇa, the son of Rādhā and of Adhiratha, and I salute you. Why are you come here? Tell me what I may do for you." Kuṅtī replied, "You are the son of Kuṅtī and not the son of Rādhā; nor is Adhiratha your father. O Karṇa, you are not born in the race of Sūta; know this word of mine to be true. I conceived you illegitimately when I was an unmarried girl and you were the first in my womb; you were born in the palace of Kuṅtibhoja, my dear son. The maker of brightness, the Sun-god, begot you on me, O Karṇa. O my son, you were born in my father's palace, wearing earrings, clad in a coat of mail, like a divine being. But, owing to ignorance of your true birth, you are now serving the sons of Dhṛtarāṣṭra, without recognizing your brothers. That is not proper, my son. Let the Kurus witness today the union between Karṇa and Arjuna; and seeing that true reconciliation among brothers let dishonest men bow down!"

Then Karṇa heard an affectionate voice issue from the solar disc from afar. It was Sūrya himself, speaking with the affection of a father. The voice said, "O Karna, Kuṅtī has spoken the truth. Act according to the advice of your mother; by doing so, you will benefit greatly." But in spite of this entreaty both by his mother and by his father, Karṇa's attitude did not waver.

"O Kṣatriya lady," he said, "I cannot heed the words you have spoken and I do not feel that the way to virtue lies in my doing as you urge me to do. What you did to me was sinful, and I have thereby suffered what is tantamount to the destruction of my fame. Though I was born as a Kṣatriya I did not get the baptismal rites of a Kṣatriya; it was all your sinful doing; what enemy can possibly do me a greater injury? Without having shown me any mercy at that time, you come today to urge me, who was deprived of the rites of my order as a Kṣatriya at birth, to be reconciled to my brothers. You did not think as a mother of my good and you have now come to me purely out of desire for your own good. Unknown as a brother before, and recognized as such now, by whom shall I be called a Kṣatriya if I go over to the side of the Pāṇḍavas on the eve of battle?

"This is the time for those who have obtained their living from Duryodhana to show their fidelity," Karṇa continued, "and I shall do so even at the risk of my life. I shall stay on the side of the sons of Dhṛtarāṣṭra, and I shall fight your sons with all my might and prowess; I do not speak falsely to you. I promise you this: it is with Arjuna alone, among all the forces of Yudhiṣṭhira, that I shall fight. Killing Arjuna in battle, I shall obtain great merit. Slain by him, I shall obtain great glory. O illustrious lady, you will thus always be left with five sons; with Arjuna dead and me alive, or with me slain and Arjuna alive."

When she heard Karṇa's words, Kuṅtī trembled with grief. Embracing her son, who was unmoved in his fortitude, she said, "Indeed, what you say is possible. As you say, fate is all-powerful." Before leaving him, Kuṅtī said to Karṇa, "May you be blessed and may all be well with you." Karṇa also saluted her, and the two went their own ways.

XLV

Kṛṣṇa returned to Yudhiṣṭhira and reported the failure of his mission. The virtuous and just Yudhiṣṭhira, after hearing Kṛṣṇa's account, said to his brothers, "You have heard what happened in that assemblage of the Kurus and you have no doubt understood what Kṛṣṇa has said. Therefore let us make a division of our army; here are the seven Akṣauhiṇis which are gathered for our victory. Listen to the names of those famous men who are to be their respective commanders. Drupada, Virāṭa, Dhṛṣṭadyamna and Śikhaṇḍī, Sātyaki, Cekitāna, and Bhīma endued with strength, these heroes, who are prepared to sacrifice their lives if necessary, will be the commanders of my army."

There was a speedy gathering of the soldiers and there was everywhere the trumpeting of elephants, the neighing of horses, and the clatter of chariot wheels, which mingled with the noise caused by the blare of the conch and the sound of the drum. The mobilization of that army caused a roar like that of the sea at high tide. Indeed, the tumult of those happy warriors seemed to reach the very heavens.

Forty thousand chariots, five times that number of horses, ten times that number of foot soldiers, and sixty thousand elephants were gathered there. Anādhṛṣṭi and Cekitāna, the king of Cedi, and Sātyaki surrounded Yudhiṣṭhira along with Kṛṣṇa and Arjuna. Finally, they reached Kurukshetra with their army ready for action and they then blew their conches. All the soldiers of the army became cheerful on hearing the thunderous sound of Kṛṣṇa's conch, the Pāñcajanya.

The next morning, King Duryodhana surveyed his forces, which consisted of eleven Akṣauhiṇis. Dividing his men, elephants, chariots, and horses into superior, inferior, and indifferent, he distributed them among his forces. He selected men who were wise and also heroic to be the leaders of his army. They were Kṛpa, Droṇa, Śalya, Jayadratha the king of the Siṁdhus, Sudakṣiṇa the king of the Kāṁbojas, Kṛtavarmā, Aśvatthāmā the son of Droṇa, Karṇa, Bhūriśravas, Śakuni the son of Subala, and Bāhlika the great car-warrior.

Then, with clasped hands, Duryodhana went to Bhīṣma along with the other kings, and said to him, "Without a commander in chief even a large army is broken up like a swarm of ants when engaged in battle. You are like the sun among the luminous bodies, the moon among deciduous herbs,[1] Kubera among the Yakṣas, Iṅdra among the gods. If you lead and protect us, we shall be like the gods protected by Iṅdra, and we shall surely be invincible even if faced by the denizens of heaven."

Bhīṣma replied, "I am at your disposal, O Duryodhana; but as you are dear to me, so are the Pāṇḍavas. It is my duty to look after their welfare too, but I shall fight on your side since I have promised to do so. In a moment I can make this world destitute of men, gods, asuras, and rākṣasas by the strength of my weapons. But I cannot kill these sons of Pāṇḍu. Instead, I shall slay ten thousand of the opposing warriors every day. In this way, I shall try to bring about their defeat, if indeed they do not kill me before I have time to carry out my plans in the battle."

"There is another condition," Bhīṣma continued, "on which I shall be commander in chief of your army; it is only fair that I should tell you about it now. Either let Karṇa fight first or I myself, but not both, since Karṇa always compares his prowess in battle with mine." Karṇa replied, "O king, I shall not fight as long as Bhīṣma the son of Gaṅgā lives. Should Bhīṣma be slain, I shall fight with Arjuna, the wielder of the Gāṇḍīva bow."

Meanwhile, in the Pāṇḍava camp, Yudhiṣṭhira summoned before him Drupada, Virāṭa, Sātyaki, Dhṛṣṭadyumna, Dhṛṣṭaketu, Śikhaṇḍī, and the king of Magadha, and made these heroes, who were eager for battle, the leaders of his army. Finally he installed Dhṛṣṭdyumna, who had emerged from the sacrificial fire for causing the death of Droṇa, as commander in chief. The curly-haired Arjuna was made supreme commander over all those great men, while Kṛṣṇa was chosen as the guide of Arjuna and the driver of his horses.

Seeing that a very destructive battle was about to take place, Balarāma, elder brother of Kṛṣṇa, entered the encampment of the royal Pāṇḍavas. He said, "There will be a very fierce massacre; it is

[1] The moon is often referred to in Sanskrit literature as "auṣadhī patiḥ," lord of the deciduous herbs.

surely ordained by fate and cannot be averted. Both these heroes, Bhīma and Duryodhana, well skilled in fighting with the mace, are my pupils and I bear the same affection for both of them. I shall now go on a pilgrimage to the sacred waters of the Sarasvatī for ablutions, for I cannot stay and look on with indifference while this destruction of the Kurus takes place."

XLVI

Meanwhile, in the Kaurava camp, Bhīṣma was making an assessment of the enemy's strength. He said, "That subjugator of hostile cities, Śikhaṇḍī, the son of the Pāñcāla king, is, in my opinion, one of the foremost of Yudhiṣṭhira's car-warriors. Having divested himself of his former state, he will fight in battle, and earn great fame among your troops. But I shall not slay Śikhaṇḍī, the prince of Pāñcāla, even though I see him advancing against me, ready to strike. The world knows that, out of a desire to do what was agreeable to my father, I renounced a kingdom and have observed the vow of celibacy. I installed Citrāṅgada on the throne of Kauravas and designated the infant Vicitravīrya as the heir presumptive. I have proclaimed among all the kings of the earth that I shall never slay a woman nor one who has been a woman. That Śikhaṇḍī was formerly a woman—perhaps you have heard of it; he afterwards became a male, and therefore I shall not fight with him. O king, except for Śikhaṇḍī, and the Pāṇḍavas, I shall slay all other rulers of the earth whom I meet in battle." "Tell us, O chief," asked Duryodhana, "why you will not slay Śikhaṇḍī, even though you see him ready to strike you in battle?" Bhīṣma replied, "Listen, O Duryodhana, along with these kings, and I shall tell you why I will not slay Śikhaṇḍī even if we come face to face in battle."

Bhīṣma then recounted the story of the svayaṁvara of the daughters of the king of Kāśī, the abduction of the three princesses, and Aṁbā's plea to be set free because of her love for the king of the Śālvas. He continued, "Then I submitted the matter to our advisers, Brāhmaṇas and priests, and also to Satyavatī. In accordance with their advice I permitted Aṁbā, who was the eldest among the sisters, to go away. Aṁbā proceeded to the capital of the king of the Śālvas, escorted by old Brāhmaṇas, and followed by her own nurse. When she finally reached the capital, she approached the king, and said, 'I have come to you.' The king of the Śālvas replied to her, 'O fair lady, I do not desire you as my wife, since you have been accepted by another. How can a king like myself, who is acquainted with all branches of knowledge, and who lays down the law for others, take a woman who has been wedded to another? O blessed lady, go where you will, and do not waste your time here.'

"Aṁbā, who was very much in love, said to the king, 'Do not speak thus, O monarch! You know I did not go willingly with Bhīṣma. Weeping, I was led away by force after he had vanquished the other kings. Therefore accept me, O lord of the Śālvas—a young girl who is innocent and devoted to you. No religion approves of the desertion of the devoted. Accept me, a maiden who has come of her own will desirous of your love, and who has never known another.' Śālva, however, abandoned the princess, like a serpent casting off its slough.

"As she sorrowfully left the Śālva capital Aṁbā thought, 'In this world there is no one in a more difficult situation than myself. All of us have our share of worldly happiness and misery; as for me, Bhīṣma is the prime cause of my sorrow. I want to have my revenge on Bhīṣma either by obtaining merit through austerities or by defeating him in battle. However, who will dare to fight with Bhīṣma on my behalf?'

"Thus ruminating, she went to a hermitage outside the city and she stayed there for the night surrounded by the anchorites. In the morning she told those hermits in the fullest detail of all that had happened to her—of her abduction, her release, and her rejection by Śālva.

"Then all the hermits considered what they should do for that lady. While they were thinking thus, the royal sage Hotravāhana came there. He asked Aṁbā about her wrongs and the cause of her sorrow and she informed him of everything as it had happened, and of her desire to return to Kāśī. Trembling, he said to the distressed and sorrowful girl, 'Do not go to your father's palace, gentle lady. I am the father of your mother. Paraśurāma will dispel your great grief by killing Bhīṣma in battle, if the latter does not heed his words.'

"Meanwhile the sage Akṛtavarṇa visited the hermitage, and the royal sage Hotravāhana asked him about Paraśurāma. Akṛtavarṇa replied, 'I think Paraśurāma will be here tomorrow. Since you desire to see him, he will surely appear.'

"Next morning, Paraśurāma came there, blazing with energy, and surrounded by his disciples. At the end of their discourse, the royal sage said to Paraśurāma, 'O Rāma, this is my granddaughter, the daughter of the king of Kāśī. Hear what she has to say and see what can be done for her.' Rāma bade her: 'Repeat your story'; thereupon she told it to him. At the end she said, 'When I was being abducted by Bhīṣma, I made this vow to myself, that I should cause Bhīṣma to be slain. I pray that you will fulfil my desire, O Rāma! Slay Bhīṣma, even as Iṅdra slew Vṛtra.'

"Then, accompanied by those best of Brāhmaṇas, Paraśurāma left for Kurukṣetra, taking Aṁbā with him. All the sages with Paraśurāma at their head reached the river Sarasvatī and encamped there. On the third day of their encampment Paraśurāma sent me word, 'I am come. Do what is agreeable to me.' Hearing that the mighty Paraśurāma had come to our kingdom, I hurried with a joyous heart to see that illustrious sage. He said to me, 'O Bhīṣma, when you did not desire her for yourself, what made you abduct the daughter of the king of Kāśī, and then let her go? Because of you, she was rejected by Śālva too. Therefore, I ask you to accept her yourself.' I replied, 'You know the vow of celibacy I have taken. I cannot break it, out of fear or pity, avarice or lust.' Then he said to me, his eyes dilated with wrath, 'If you do not respect my words, I shall slay you along with your ministers.' Again and again he repeated this threat. I entreated him with sweet words, but could not calm him."

Bhīṣma continued, "Then began that terrible battle between him and me, which made the hairs of all creatures stand on end. Filled with anger and vindictiveness, Paraśurāma brought forth a mighty weapon of Brahmā. On my part, I produced the same excellent weapon of Brahmā in order to counter the effect of his weapon. Those two weapons of Brahmā met each other in mid-air, without being able to reach either Rāma or myself. Around them a flame blazed forth, and all living things were greatly afflicted thereby.

"When all creatures, as well as the gods, the asuras, and the rākṣasas, began to utter exclamations of woe, I thought, 'This is the time,' and contemplated shooting my cherished weapon Prasvapa, according to the words of command of the Brāhmaṇas. I also remembered the spells for using that weapon. A mighty din of tumultuous voices then arose in the sky saying, 'O Bhīṣma, do not release the Prasvapa weapon.' Thereupon I withdrew it, and let the Brahmā weapon blaze forth according to the scriptures. Seeing that the Prasvapa weapon was withdrawn, Paraśurāma was greatly excited and said, 'Fool that I am, I am vanquished by Bhīṣma.'

"Then he said to Aṁbā, 'O maiden, in the very sight of the whole world, I have exerted my utmost and displayed all my prowess. I have not, however, been able to conquer in battle the foremost among warriors, Bhīṣma. Seek the protection of Bhīṣma himself. There is no other refuge for you. I have been vanquished by Bhīṣma.'

"Aṁbā replied to Paraśurāma; 'O holy one, it is as you have said. This Bhīṣma cannot be vanquished in battle, even by the celestials. You have not been able to conquer him. As for me, I shall never again go to him. I shall repair to the forest, where I shall myself try to obtain the means to fell Bhīṣma in battle.' "

XLVII

Bhīṣma continued, "Aṁbā then proceeded to a secluded spot on the banks of the Yamunā, and began practising austerities of superhuman endurance. In due course, Śiva appeared before that ascetic lady in his own form and promised her a boon. Thereupon she asked for my defeat. The god answered, 'You shall slay him.' Again she addressed Śiva: 'How can it happen that I shall win in battle, O god, woman as I am?' Śiva replied to her, 'My words cannot be false. They shall turn out to be true, O blessed one. You shall slay Bhīṣma in battle, and you shall also attain manhood. You will remember all this, when you enter another body. Born in the family of Drupada, you shall be a Mahāratha, a great car-warrior, quick in the use of weapons, skilled in various ways of fighting.' Having given her this boon, the Lord Śiva vanished."

"The beloved queen of King Drupada," Bhīṣma went on, "was childless at first. During this time King Drupada worshipped the god Śiva for the sake of offspring. Bent upon killing me, he engaged in the most severe penances, saying that he wanted a son by the favour of the great god, and not a daughter. 'O god,' he prayed, 'I desire a son, to revenge myself on Bhīṣma.' Then Śiva said, 'Your son shall be both male and female.' Though Drupada repeatedly begged for a son, Śiva said, 'It is decreed by destiny. It shall not be otherwise, but even as I have told you.'

"As ordained by destiny, in due time the wife of Drupada conceived and gave birth to a daughter of great beauty, who was named Śikhaṇḍinī. Thereupon King Drupada caused all the necessary rites to be performed, just as if the child were a son. The queen too protected the secret with all care, saying, 'It is a son indeed.' And no one else in that city knew the child to be a daughter.

"Drupada bestowed all possible attention on his child, teaching her writing, painting, and all the arts. She became a disciple of Droṇa in the practice of archery. When she grew up, the queen urged King Drupada to find a bride for her, as if she had been a son. After much hesitation, the royal couple made a decision and arranged for the marriage of their daughter Śikhaṇḍinī with the daughter of the king of Daśārṇa. The king of Daśārṇa, Hiraṇyavarmā, gave his daughter in marriage to Śikhaṇḍinī. When some time had passed, Hiraṇyavarmā's daughter became aware that Śikhaṇḍinī was a female, and bashfully informed her nurses and companions of this. When the news reached him, the king of the Daśārṇas became enraged and sent an emissary to the palace of Drupada, threatening vengence and demanding restitution.

"Seeing her parents in great distress, Śikhaṇḍinī was filled with shame, and thought, 'My father and mother are afflicted with grief because of me.' She made up her mind to take her own life. With this resolution, the grief-stricken Śikhaṇḍinī went to a lonely and uninhabited forest. The forest was ruled by a very rich and powerful yakṣa named Sthūṇakarṇa, and through fear of him all men avoided the place. Appearing before her, the yakṣa Sthūṇakarṇa asked, 'Why have you come here? What is the cause of your grief? Tell me, and I will find a remedy.' She said repeatedly, 'You cannot do so.' The yakṣa however replied, 'I shall accomplish it. O princess, I am an attendant of Kubera the god of wealth, and I can grant any boon, however difficult. So tell me what you desire.'

"Then Śikhaṇḍinī told Sthūṇakarṇa, the chief of the yakṣas, her whole story. At the end she said, 'You have promised to remove the cause of my grief. Let me become a man, O yakṣa, through your grace.' After considerable reflection, the yakṣa answered, 'O blessed one, I will accomplish your wish, but on one condition. I will bestow upon you my own manhood, for a certain period. At the end of that period, my manhood shall return to me.' Śikhaṇḍinī replied, 'O holy one, I will return your manhood to you. Bear my womanhood only for a certain period.' Thereupon by agreement the two exchanged their respective sexes.

"After some time, while making a journey through the earth, Kubera came to the abode of Sthūṇa. 'This mansion of Sthūṇa is well kept,' he said. 'But why does this fool not come to see me?' The yakṣas explained, 'O king, a daughter was born to King Drupada, by name Śikhaṇḍinī. For her sake, Sthūṇa has given away his manhood. Hence he is not appearing before you.' Then Kubera cursed him in his anger: 'Let this sinful one remain a woman.' The yakṣas began to pacify Kubera. For the sake of Sthūṇakarṇa, they pleaded, 'Set a limit on your curse,' Relenting, Kubera said, 'On the death of Śikhaṇḍī in battle, Sthūṇa shall regain his own form. Therefore let the yakṣa be free from anxiety.' "

Bhīṣma concluded, "Thus it happened that the eldest daughter of the king of Kāśī, known by the name of Aṁbā, was born in the family of Drupada as Śikhaṇḍī. I know these facts about the birth of Śikhaṇḍī, and hence I will not slay him in any battle, even though he advances weapon in hand." Hearing this story, Duryodhana reflected for a moment, and concluded that this was only proper for Bhīṣma.

Bhīṣma Parva

XLVIII

Before the fighting began, the Kurus, the Pāṇḍavas, and the Somakas entered into certain covenants regarding the different kinds of combat. Thus it was agreed that a car-warrior should fight only with a car-warrior. He who rode on an elephant could fight only with another such combatant. A horseman might fight with a horseman and a foot soldier with a foot soldier. It was also agreed that a combatant who was engaged in fighting with another, one seeking refuge, one retreating, one whose weapon was broken, and one who was not clad in armour should never be attacked. Likewise charioteers, animals, men engaged in carrying weapons, drummers, and conch-blowers should not be attacked.

When the two armies were ready for battle, the holy Vyāsa, foremost of all learned men, grandfather of the Pāṇḍavas and the Kurus, who was gifted with divine vision, spoke in private to Dhṛtarāṣṭra, who was distressed by the evil policy of his sons. "O king," said Vyāsa, "the last moments of your sons and of other kings have come. They have gathered to fight and they will kill one another. If you wish to witness the fighting, I shall bestow sight on you."

Dhṛtarāṣṭra replied, "O foremost of sages! I have no desire to see the slaughter of my kinsmen. Through your grace, however, I would like to hear a full account of this battle." Thereupon Vyāsa bestowed a boon on Sañjaya, saying, "O king, Sañjaya will give you an account of this great battle. He will be able to see everything that takes place over the entire battlefield."

Vyāsa then made a last appeal for peace. He said, "O king, Death himself has been born in the form of your son, Duryodhana. Slaughter is never praised in the Vedas. It can never produce any good. Save your good name and fame, and your virtue. Let the Pāṇḍavas have their kingdom and let the Kauravas have peace. You will thereby assure yourself of a place in heaven." Having made this final and fruitless appeal, Vyāsa went away, while Dhṛtarāṣṭra reflected in silence.

Meanwhile both sides prepared to give battle. When the troops were arrayed according to rule, Duryodhana said to Duḥśāsana, "O Duḥśāsana, let chariots be quickly directed so as to assure the protection of Bhīṣma. Make haste in urging all our troops to advance. What I have been wishing for a number of years has at last come to pass: the clash of the Pāṇḍavas and the Kurus at the head of their respective armies."

At sunrise the next day, the armies of the Kurus and the Pāṇḍavas completed all their arrangements. The eleventh division of the Kuru army stood in advance of all others; at the head of these troops stood Bhīṣma. On one side were the eleven splendid divisions of the Kaurava army. On the other side were the seven divisions of the Pāṇḍava army, protected by the foremost of men. The two armies facing each other looked like two mighty oceans agitated by fearful makaras.

Sañjaya reported to Dhṛtarāṣṭra: "When placed in battle array, the two armies, full of elephants, cars, and horses, looked like two woods in blossom. Both of them seemed as if they could conquer the very heavens. Both of them were commanded by excellent men. The Kaurava armies stood facing the west while the Pāṇḍavas stood facing the east—all ready for battle."

XLIX

Then Arjuna, whose flag bore the figure of an ape, looked at the Kauravas drawn up in battle array; as the fighting was about to begin, he took up his bow and said to Kṛṣṇa, "I wish to see my opponents who are eager for battle and whom I have to fight in the great struggle. Station my chariot, O Kṛṣṇa, between the two armies!" As requested by Arjuna, Kṛṣṇa drove the chariot to a position between the two armies.

Arjuna saw his closest kinsmen, related to him as father or grandfather, uncle or brother, son or grandson, preceptor as well as companion and friend, on both sides. Overcome by this sight, he said in sorrow and compassion, "O Kṛṣṇa, when I see my own people ready to fight and eager for battle, my limbs shudder, my mouth is dry, my body shivers, and my hair stands on end. Furthermore, I see evil portents, and I can see no good in killing my own kinsmen. It is not right and proper that we should kill our own kith and kin, the Kauravas. How can we be happy if we slay our own people?" Having said these words, Arjuna threw away his bow and arrows, and sat down sorrowfully on the seat of his car.

When he observed that Arjuna was overcome with compassion and that tears were welling up in his eyes, Kṛṣṇa said these words to him who was thus troubled and dejected: "O Arjuna, why have you become so depressed in this critical hour? Such dejection is unknown to noble men; it does not lead to the heavenly heights, and on earth it can only cause disgrace. Do not yield to cowardice, for it is not worthy of you. Cast away this faintness of heart and arise."

Arjuna said, "O Kṛṣṇa, how can I strike with my arrows people like the grandsire Bhīṣma and the preceptor Droṇa, who are worthy of my respect?" After such reflection, he finally told Kṛṣṇa, "I will not fight."

Kṛṣṇa smiled at Arjuna, so troubled in mind and dejected in spirit, and said, "You grieve for those for whom you should not grieve. The wise do not lament the dead or pine for the living. Anyone who believes that this kills, or thinks that this is killed, fails to understand that one neither kills nor is killed. The embodied soul merely casts off old bodies and enters new ones, just as a person discards used garments and puts on new clothes."

"The soul that lives in every human body is eternal and immortal," Kṛṣṇa went on to say. "Therefore do not grieve for any creature. As a Kṣatriya, your duty is to fight a righteous battle. This is the highest good for you, and you should not falter at this hour. Such a fight is an open door to heaven, and happy are they who engage in such a battle. Either you will win a victory and enjoy the earth, or be killed and go to heaven. Therefore arise, O Arjuna, and be determined to fight. Get ready for battle without thought of pleasure and pain, gain and loss, victory and defeat. In this way, you will not incur any sin. Remember that you have a right to action alone, but not to the fruits thereof. Be not motivated by the desire for the fruits of action. At the same time, do not pursue a policy of inaction."

"O Arjuna," he continued, "in this world I have taught a twofold way of life: the way of knowledge for men who engage in contemplation, and the way of works for men of action. One cannot maintain even one's physical life without action. Therefore, do your allotted work regardless of results, for men attain the highest good by doing work without attachment to its results. Resign yourself to me and fix your consciousness in the self, without desire or egoism, and then fight, freed from your fever."

Arjuna replied, "My confusion has been dispelled by this supreme discourse concerning the self, which you have given me out of your grace." Kṛṣṇa said, "I am Time itself, grown mature, capable of destroying the world, and now engaged in subduing it. Even without your effort, all the opposing warriors shall cease to exist. Therefore arise and win great glory, conquer your enemies, and enjoy a prosperous kingdom. They are already slain by me and you, O Arjuna, are merely the occasion. Kill Droṇa, Bhīṣma, Jayadratha, Karṇa, and all the other great warriors whom I have already doomed. Do not fear, but fight and conquer your enemies in battle."

"O Lord," said Arjuna, "I desire to know the true nature of 'renunciation' and of 'relinquishment.' " Kṛṣṇa replied, "The wise understand 'renunciation' to mean the giving up of those works which are prompted by desire. 'Relinquishment' means the abandonment of the fruits of all works. It is not right to renounce one's duty, but when one performs a prescribed duty, with detachment and without thought of the fruit thereof, that is 'relinquishment.' Courage, vigour, resourcefulness, steadfastness in battle, generosity, and leadership are the natural duties of a Kṣatriya.

"The Lord dwells in the hearts of all men and causes them to turn round by his power as if they were mounted on a machine," Kṛṣṇa concluded. "Seek shelter in him with your whole being, and you shall attain supreme peace and the eternal station by his grace." "My bewilderment is gone," said Arjuna. "By your grace, O Kṛṣṇa, I have been made to realize my true duties. My doubts have been dispelled and I stand ready to do your bidding."

L

When the two armies, which resembled two oceans, were ready for battle and surging continuously, the brave King Yudhiṣṭhira doffed his armour and cast aside his excellent weapon. Quickly alighting from his chariot, he proceeded on foot, with joined hands and with restrained speech, in the direction of the hostile host, towards his grandfather, Bhīṣma, whom he addressed thus: "O invincible one, I salute you. We shall fight with you. Give us your permission and your blessings." Bhīṣma replied, "O son, I am pleased with you. Fight and triumph. Whatever else you may have desired, may you obtain it in this battle! O king, man is the slave of wealth, though wealth is no one's slave. And I am bound to the Kurus by wealth." To this, Yudhiṣṭhira answered, "O wise one, I pray that, desiring my welfare from day to day, you may keep my interests in mind, while you fight for the Kurus."

Then, in the midst of the army, Yudhiṣṭhira loudly proclaimed, "Whoever will choose us, him I shall accept as our ally." Thereupon Yuyutsu said with a cheerful heart to Yudhiṣṭhira, "I shall fight against the Kauravas in this battle, O king! I shall fight on your side, if you will accept me." So, abandoning the Kurus, Yuyutsu went over to the Pāṇḍava army to the accompaniment of kettledrums.

On the forenoon of that awful day the terrible battle began. The Kurus and the Sṛñjayas, both desirous of victory in battle, roared like lions and made both the sky and the earth resound with their war cries. In that general melee thousands of single combats took place between car-warriors, horsemen, and foot soldiers. Just for a short while that engagement was a beautiful sight. Soon, however, the fighting became confused and fierce in the extreme, with heroes rushing against each other in the melee.

In the afternoon Durmukha, Kṛtavarmā, Kṛpa, Śalya, and Viviṁśati surrounded Bhīṣma and began to protect him. Thus sheltered by those five mighty car-warriors, Bhīṣma penetrated the Pāṇḍava host. With his bow stretched to a circle, he shot therefrom blazing arrows that resembled virulent poison. Creating continuous lines of arrows in all directions, that hero slew many Pāṇḍava car-warriors, naming each victim beforehand. When the troops of the Pāṇḍavas were routed and crushed all over the field, the sun set and nothing could be seen. Then, while Bhīṣma proudly stood surveying the battlefield, the Pāṇḍavas withdrew their forces for the night.

LI

On the second day Yudhiṣṭhira said to the commander of his army, Drupada, "Form the array known by the name of Krauñcāruṇa. It is destructive of all foes and was suggested by Bṛhaspati to Indra in days of old when the gods and the asuras fought." Then Bhīṣma and Droṇa formed a mighty array to resist that of the Pāṇḍavas. Surrounded by a large body of troops Bhīṣma advanced, like the chief of the celestials himself.

There was, however, no man in the Kaurava army who could advance against the heroic Arjuna in battle. Whoever tried to do so was pierced by Arjuna's sharp shafts and dispatched to the other world. Bhīṣma, seeing the Kaurava host thus routed, smilingly said to Droṇa, "This mighty and heroic Arjuna, accompanied by Kṛṣṇa, is dealing with our troops as he alone can deal with them. He is incapable of being vanquished in battle today by any means; he is like the Destroyer himself at the end of the Yuga!" Bhīṣma then caused the Kaurava army to be withdrawn. About the same time the sun set, and the withdrawal of both armies took place in the twilight.

When the night had passed and the dawn brought the third day of fighting Bhīṣma gave the order for the Kaurava army to prepare for battle. Desirous of victory, he formed the mighty array known as Garuḍa. The beak of that Garuḍa was Bhīṣma himself, and its two eyes were Droṇa and Kṛtavarmā. In opposition to the Garuḍa array Yudhiṣṭhira formed the fierce array in the shape of the half-moon.

In the afternoon, when the tide of battle was running in favour of the Pāṇḍavas, Bhīṣma rushed towards the Pāṇḍava host. Displaying his extreme lightness of touch, as if he were dancing along the track of his car, he seemed to be present everywhere like a circle of fire. In consequence of the speed of his movements, the embattled Pāṇḍavas saw that hero multiplied a thousandfold. Everyone regarded Bhīṣma as having made counterparts of himself by illusion because, having seen him now in the east, the next moment they saw him in the west; and having seen him in the north, the next moment they saw him in the south. There was no one amongst the Pāṇḍavas capable of even looking at Bhīṣma. What they saw were only the countless shafts shot from his bow. The vast host of the just King Yudhiṣṭhira, thus slaughtered by Bhīṣma, gave way in a thousand directions.

Beholding the Pāṇḍava army thus routed, Kṛṣṇa said unto Arjuna, "The hour is now come, O Pārtha, which you desired all along! Strike Bhīṣma, O tiger among men!" Kṛṣṇa urged those steeds of silvery hue towards the dazzling car of Bhīṣma. Taking up his celestial bow, whose twang resembled the roar of the clouds, Arjuna caused Bhīṣma's bow to drop, cutting it off with his keen shafts. In the twinkling of an eye, Bhīṣma took up another bow and struck both Kṛṣṇa and Arjuna with keen shafts all over their bodies.

Then the mighty Kṛṣṇa, beholding the prowess of Bhīṣma in battle, as well as the mildness with which Arjuna fought, abandoned the reins of the steeds. He jumped down from the car, whirling on his right arm his cakra which was sharp as a razor, bright as the sun, and powerful as a thousand heavenly bolts. And making the earth tremble under his tread, the high-souled Kṛṣṇa ran impetuously towards Bhīṣma, like a lion blinded with fury rushing upon an elephant.

Beholding that foremost of men, the divine Kṛṣṇa, advancing against him armed with the cakra, Bhīṣma fearlessly said, "Come, O

Lord, the universe is your abode! I bow to you, who are armed with mace, sword, and bow! O Lord of the universe, who are the refuge of all creatures in this battle, throw me down from this car! Slain here by you, O Kṛṣṇa, great will be my good fortune both in this world and the next! Great is the honour you show me, O lord! My fame will be celebrated in the three worlds!"

Meanwhile, jumping down from his car, Arjuna quickly ran on foot after Kṛṣṇa and seized him by his two hands. And when Kṛṣṇa, decked as he was with a beautiful garland of gold, stopped, Arjuna bowed to him and said, "Control this wrath of yours, O lord! You are the refuge of the Pāṇḍavas. I swear to you, by my sons and brothers, that I will not withdraw from the action to which I have pledged myself! At your command I will certainly annihilate the Kurus!"

Hearing that promise, Kṛṣṇa was gratified. And ever bent as he was on doing what was agreeable to Arjuna, he once more mounted his car, cakra on arm. Arjuna drew his beautiful bow Gāṇḍīva, of immeasurable energy, with great force and invoked with proper maṅtras the wonderful and terrible Maheṅdra weapon, causing it to appear in the sky. That mighty weapon produced a great shower of arrows and Arjuna was thus able to check the entire Kaurava host.

LII

On the morning of the fourth day the high-souled Bhīṣma, supported by a large force, stationed himself at the head of the Bhārata army, and proceeded against the foe. Then the mighty Bhīma saw Duryodhana in the battlefield. Desirous of ending the strife, he took up his mace and proceeded against Duryodhana. The terrible mace of Bhīma resembled the fierce bludgeon of Death and was bright as Iṅdra's bolt. Indeed, that mace dealing death at every turn looked like the club of the Destroyer himself at the time of the universal dissolution. Seeing him thus routing that large army and advancing like Death himself, all the warriors despaired.

Then fourteen sons of Dhṛtarāṣṭra, namely Senāpati, Suṣeṇa, Jalasaṅdha, Sulocana, Ugra, Bhīmaratha, Bhīma, Bhīmabāhu, Alolupa, Durmukha, Duṣpradharṣa, Vivitsu, Vikaṭa, and Sāma engaged Bhīma in battle. In a body they rushed against him. Their eyes were red with wrath as they showered countless arrows upon him, piercing him deeply. The heroic and mighty Bhīma licked the corners of his mouth like a wolf in the midst of sheep, and fell upon them with great impetuosity. He first cut off the head of Senāpati with a shaft having a head like a horseshoe. He then pierced Jalasaṅdha with three arrows, and dispatched him to Yama's abode. His next victim was Suṣeṇa. And thereafter, in that great battle, in the very sight of all the troops, Bhīma also dispatched Sulocana to the realm of Death with another arrow having a head like a horseshoe. The rest of Dhṛtarāṣṭra's sons fled from fear of Bhīma.

At this point Bhagadatta suddenly rushed on his elephant to where Bhīma was stationed. Excited with rage, that tiger among men struck Bhīma in the middle of his chest with a straight shaft. Deeply pierced by that shaft, the mighty Bhīma sat down on his car, his limbs deprived of sensation, and was on the point of swooning.

Then the terrible rākṣasa Ghaṭotkaca, beholding Bhīma in that state, became excited with rage. He first made himself invisible. Creating a terrible illusion, he reappeared in a moment, assuming a fierce form, frightening the timid. When that prince of rākṣasas saw a division of the enemy advance, he uttered a fierce and thunderous roar. Hearing that roar, Bhīṣma said to Droṇa, "I do not like to fight today with the wicked Ghaṭotkaca. He is incapable of being vanquished now by Indra himself. He is sure of aim, and endowed with great strength and energy, besides being well supported. As for ourselves, our animals are tired today. We have also been badly mangled by the Pāñcālas and the Pāṇḍavas. I do not want a fresh encounter with the victorious Pāṇḍavas at this stage. Let the withdrawal of our army, therefore, be proclaimed for the day. Tomorrow we will fight with the foe."

Hearing these words of Bhīṣma, the Kauravas, afraid as they were of Ghaṭotkaca, used the advent of night as a pretext, and gladly withdrew as the grandsire desired. Thereupon the Pāṇḍavas, crowned with victory, roared like lions, their shouts of joy mingling with the blare of conches and the shrilling of pipes.

Beholding his brothers, all mighty car-warriors, vanquished in battle, Duryodhana's heart was confounded with grief. He repaired with humility during the night to Bhīṣma's tent and asked him this question: "Droṇa, yourself, Śalya, Kṛpa, Aśvatthāmā, Kṛtavarmā, Sudakṣina, Bhūriśravas, Vikarṇa, and Bhagadatta are all regarded as mighty car-warriors. All are highborn, and prepared to lose their lives in battle. These heroes are a match for even the three worlds. All the warriors of the Pāṇḍava army cannot match their prowess. And yet, how is it that the Pāṇḍavas are defeating us repeatedly? On whom do they rely for victory? Please explain this to me."

Bhīṣma replied, "Listen, O king, to the words that I will say to you now. In the past, I have often told you this, but you never heeded my advice. Let peace be made with the Pāṇḍavas! I regard this to be of benefit both to the world and to you. O king, enjoy this earth with your brothers and be happy, pleasing all your well-wishers and delighting your kinsfold! Although I cried myself hoarse ere now you would not listen to me. Today you see the consequence of your ill treatment of the Pāṇḍavas."

Bhīṣma then reminded him that Arjuna and Kṛṣṇa were Nara and Nārāyaṇa, and said, "You have heard of the glory of the high-souled Kṛṣṇa and Arjuna, and have been told why both Nara and Nārāyaṇa have been born among men. You have also been told why those heroes are invincible and have never been vanquished in battle, and why the Pāṇḍavas are incapable of being slain in battle by anybody. Kṛṣṇa bears great love for the illustrious Pāṇḍavas. It is for this, O king of kings, that I say: 'Let peace be made with the Pāṇḍavas!' Restraining your passions, enjoy the earth with your mighty brothers around you! If you disregard the divine Nara and Nārāyaṇa, you will certainly be destroyed!"

Having said these words, Bhīṣma became silent and, dismissing the king, entered his tent. And Duryodhana also came back to his own tent, and went to bed.

LIII

The fifth day of the battle dawned and the two armies faced each other for battle. On the Kaurava side, Bhīṣma ordered the formation of an array in the shape of a makara. And beholding the Kaurava array prepared for battle, the illustrious Pāṇḍavas drew up their troops in that invincible array called the śyena.

Then Bhīṣma fought fiercely, desirous of protecting the Kauravas from Bhīma, whom they feared. On the Pāṇḍava side, the mighty Sātyaki, invincible in battle, approached Bhūriśravas. Meanwhile Bhūriśravas, beholding the ranks of the sons of Dhṛtarāṣṭra laid low by Sātyaki, rushed in wrath against him.

Thereupon the mighty sons of Sātyaki, all famous and mighty car-warriors, challenged that great bowman, Bhūriśravas, to battle. It was towards the afternoon that the dreadful battle took place between Bhūriśravas alone on one side and the many sons of Sātyaki on the other. Excited with rage, Bhūriśravas cut off their bows, and then their heads, with sharp shafts. Thus slain, they fell down like giant trees struck by lightning.

Seeing his mighty sons thus slain in battle, Sātyaki uttered a loud roar and rushed against Bhūriśravas. Those great warriors pressed their cars against each other, each of them in that combat slaying the steeds of the other's car. Thus deprived of their chariots, the two mighty warriors jumped to the ground, and engaged in a sword duel. Then Bhīma quickly came up to Sātyaki and took him up on his own car. And Duryodhana, too, speedily took up Bhūriśravas on his car.

Just at that time the sun disappeared, and all the combatants seemed to be deprived of their senses. And the troops of both the Pāṇḍavas and the Kurus, filled with fear and anxiety, proceeded to their respective camps and rested for the night.

Having rested, both the Kurus and the Pāṇḍavas once more went out for battle on the sixth day. Then King Yudhiṣṭhira said to Dhṛṣṭa-dyumna, "O mighty hero! dispose the troops in the array called makara." Thus addressed by Yudhiṣṭhira, Dhṛṣṭadyumna issued the order to the car-warriors to form the makara array. Then Bhīṣma placed his army in counter-array after the form of a huge crane.

Soon the heroic Bhīma penetrated into the mighty Kaurava array that was protected by Bhīṣma. At the same time Dhṛṣṭadyumna, forsaking Droṇa with whom he had been engaged, hastened to the spot where Śakuni was stationed. He saw Bhīma consuming the hostile ranks and felling Kṣatriya warriors like a storm laying low rows of trees. Then the Kaurava warriors surrounded Bhīma on all sides, and fearlessly poured upon him their showers of arrows. Thereupon that mighty car-warrior, the youthful Dhṛṣṭadyumna, applied the fierce weapon called Pramohana, which had the effect of depriving the opposing foe of their senses. The energetic Droṇa, foremost of all wielders of weapons, heard that the Kauravas were being deprived of their senses by the Pramohana weapon. Discharging the weapon called Prajña, he neutralized the Pramohana weapon which Dhṛṣṭadyumna had shot.

Thus ended the day's fighting. Yudhiṣṭhira applauded the feats of both Dhṛṣṭadyumna and Bhīma. Filled with joy, they retired to their tents for the night.

LIV

On the dawn of the seventh day, when the sky was clear, the valiant Bhīṣma disposed his troops in the array that was known as the maṇḍala, bristling with weapons, and abounding in leading warriors, tuskers, and foot soldiers. Beholding the fierce maṇḍala array of the enemy, King Yudhiṣṭhira placed his troops in the array called vajra.

During the progress of that fierce and dreadful battle, there was great confusion among all the troops. In consequence of that confusion the arrays of both armies were broken. Then the Kṣatriyas summoned one another individually, with a view to engaging in single combat. And while they were thus battling and achieving difficult feats, the sun retired behind the western hill, while on the battlefield flowed an awful river whose current and waves were made up of blood.

Having passed the night in sound sleep, on the eighth day the Kauravas and the Pāṇḍavas once more proceeded to battle. Bhīṣma formed a mighty array fierce as the ocean and appeared in the van of the whole army, supported by the Mālavas, the inhabitants of the southern countries, and the Avantis. Seeing that powerful array, the great car-warrior Yudhiṣṭhira said to the commander of his forces, Dhṛṣṭadyumna, "Behold, O great bowman, the Kaurava array resembling the ocean! Form without pause a counter-array!" Dhṛṣṭadyumna then prepared the terrible array called śṛṅgāṭaka that is destructive to all hostile arrays.

The Pāṇḍavas were incapable of even looking at Bhīṣma, who was excited with rage and scorching everything around him like the Sun himself. All the Pāṇḍava troops rushed at Bhīṣma, who delighted in felling the mightiest of bowmen amongst the Sṛñjayas and the Pāñcālas with his shafts. Though many of them were thus slaughtered by him, the Pāñcālas along with the Somakas still rushed impetuously at him, without fear of death.

On another part of the battlefield, King Duryodhana rushed against Ghaṭotkaca, his bow ready for action, and repeatedly roaring like a lion. Beholding Duryodhana thus advancing, surrounded by an elephant division, that ranger of the night[1] Ghaṭotkaca was inflamed with rage. Then commenced a fierce battle between the formidable rākṣasa and the troops of Duryodhana.

In that battle Ghaṭotkaca first vanquished all the warriors supporting Duryodhana and then rushed at Duryodhana himself, desirous of slaying him. He created an illusion, in consequence of which all the troops turned their backs upon the field. They saw one another cut down and lying prostrate on the earth, writhing convulsively, helpless and bathed in blood. This broke their morale, and the entire Kaurava army, routed by Ghaṭotkaca, fled in all directions as the hour of sunset approached.

That night Duryodhana, Śakuni, Duḥśāsana, and the invincible Karṇa met together in earnest consultation. They asked themselves

[1] "Ranger of the night" is a literal translation of nisācara, which means rākṣasa: the rākṣasas were supposed to become more powerful at night.

how the sons of Pāṇḍu, with their followers, could be vanquished in battle. Karṇa said, "Do not grieve, O chief of the Bhāratas! I will do what is agreeable to you. After Bhīṣma has withdrawn from the fight and laid aside his weapons, I will slay Arjuna along with all the Somakas, in the very sight of Bhīṣma! I pledge myself to do so, O king! Bhīṣma always shows leniency towards the Pāṇḍavas. Besides, he is incapable of vanquishing those mighty car-warriors."

Duryodhana then decided to ask Bhīṣma to relinquish command of the Kaurava forces. He proceeded to Bhīṣma's tent, alighted from his horse, and, after greeting him, said, "O slayer of foes! Depending on your protection, we would have dared to challenge the very gods with Iṅdra at their head. We are, however, making no progress against our enemy. If you are sparing the Pāṇḍavas out of kindness for them, or because of your dislike for my unfortunate self, then permit Karṇa, that ornament of battle, to fight! He will vanquish the Pāṇḍavas with all their friends and kinsmen!"

These words pierced the high-souled Bhīṣma as if they were daggers and he was filled with grief. But he uttered not a single disagreeable word in reply. Instead he said, "O mighty hero, the same son of Pāṇḍu rescued you while you were being led away a captive by the Gaṅdharvas. On that occasion, your brave brothers had all fled, as had Karṇa. Again, in Virāṭa's city, singlehanded, Arjuna attacked all of us united together! He defeated in battle the Nivātakavacas who were incapable of defeat by Iṅdra himself. These are sufficient indications of his prowess. Who, indeed, is capable of vanquishing Arjuna in battle?

"In consequence of your folly, O Duryodhana," continued Bhīṣma, "you know not what should and what should not be said. You were responsible for provoking this fierce hostility with the Pāṇḍavas and the Sṛñjayas. Fight with them in battle! Let us see you act like a man! As for myself, I will slay all the Somakas and the Pāñcālas, with the sole exception of Śikhaṇḍī. Now you can go to bed, and pass the night in happy sleep. Tomorrow I will fight a fierce battle about which men will speak as long as the world lasts!" Thus addressed by Bhīṣma, Duryodhana bowed to the grandsire and returned to his own tent.

LV

On the ninth day Bhīṣma disposed his own troops in a mighty array called sarvatobhadra. Then King Yudhiṣṭhira, Bhīma, Nakula, and Sahadeva, clad in mail, took up their position in the van of the Pāṇḍava array, at the very head of all their troops.

At midday, a fierce battle raged between Bhīṣma and the Somakas, resulting in terrible carnage. That foremost of car-warriors, Bhīṣma, began to consume the ranks of the Pāṇḍavas by hundreds and thousands. Then Dhṛṣṭadyumna, Śikhaṇḍī, Virāṭa, and Drupada fell upon Bhīṣma and discharged numberless arrows at him. Even though Śikhaṇḍī pierced the grandsire with many shafts, Bhīṣma of unfading glory, regarding his foe as a female, did not strike back.

Surrounded on all sides, yet unvanquished by that large body of car-warriors, Bhīṣma blazed like a fire in the midst of a forest. His car was his hearth; his bow constituted the flames, his swords, darts, and his maces, the fuel; his shafts were the sparks of that fire. He took the lives of the opposing warriors like the sun sucking the energies of all things with his rays during summer. He broke the Pāṇḍava ranks, and the routed soldiers, helpless and fainthearted, unable even to look at him in battle, were slaughtered in their thousands by Bhīṣma.

While they were thus battling, the sun set, and there came the dreadful hour of twilight when the fighting could no longer be seen. Then King Yudhiṣṭhira, seeing how his own troops had been decimated by Bhīṣma, and how the mighty car-warriors of the Somakas had been vanquished, despaired and ordered the troops to be withdrawn for the day.

Late that night the Pāṇḍavas, the Vṛṣṇis, and the invincible Sṛñjayas sat down for a consultation. Yudhiṣṭhira said, "Even before this conflict began, I made an agreement with Bhīṣma. He said, 'I will give you counsel, but I cannot fight for you, since I shall have to fight for Duryodhana.' Therefore, O Kṛṣṇa, all of us, together with you, will once more go to Bhīṣma, and ask him about the means of his own death."

Having thus deliberated, the heroic Pāṇḍavas and the valiant Kṛṣṇa proceeded together to Bhīṣma's quarters, casting aside their armour and weapons. Entering his tent, they all bowed low to him, and sought his protection. The mighty Bhīṣma, grandsire of the Kurus, greeted them and said, "Welcome, O Kṛṣṇa, welcome O Arjuna. Welcome to you, O King Yudhiṣṭhira the Just, and to you, O Bhīma. Welcome to you also, twins. What can I do now to make you happy? However difficult of achievement, I will yet do it with all my heart."

Unto Bhīṣma, who spoke to them with such affection, King Yudhiṣṭhira, with love in his heart, said these words, "You are conversant with everything. Tell us how we may obtain victory and acquire sovereignty. Tell us also how this destruction may be stopped. Tell us, O lord, the means of your own death. How can we cope with you in battle?"

Bhīṣma replied, "O son of Pāṇḍu, as you say, I am invincible. When I take my weapons and my large bow in hand, I am incapable of being defeated in battle by the very gods with Indra at their head. If, however, I lay aside my weapons, almost any car-warrior can slay me. That mighty car-warrior, the son of Drupada, who fights on your side, and who is known by the name of Śikhaṇḍī, was once a woman but subsequently obtained manhood. You may know how all this took place. I therefore suggest this: let Arjuna, brave in battle and clad in mail, keep Śikhaṇḍī before him, and attack me from behind with his sharp shafts. When I see that inauspicious omen, in the form of one who was a woman before, I will never seek to strike back. Taking advantage of that opportunity, let Arjuna quickly pierce me on all sides with his shafts. Except the blessed Kṛṣṇa and Arjuna, I do not see anyone in the three worlds who is capable of killing me in battle."

After Bhīṣma had blessed them again, the Pāṇḍavas saluted their high-souled grandsire and returned to their own tents.

LVI

The tenth day of the battle dawned. Soon afterwards the Pāṇḍavas, to the sound of drums and cymbals and the blare of conches, set forth to give battle, placing Śikhaṇḍī in front. But the Pāṇḍava army was torn into pieces by Bhīṣma who let loose his shafts by hundreds and thousands. The Pāṇḍavas seemed incapable of defeating in battle the great bowman Bhīṣma who resembled the Destroyer himself.

Beholding the prowess of Bhīṣma in battle, Arjuna said to Śikhaṇḍī, "Proceed towards the grandsire! Do not entertain the slightest fear of Bhīṣma today. I shall dislodge him from his excellent car by means of my sharp arrows." Thus urged by Pārtha, Śikhaṇḍī rushed at Bhīṣma.

Approaching Bhīṣma, Śikhaṇḍī struck him in the centre of the chest with ten broad-headed arrows. Bhīṣma did not retaliate but looked at Śikhaṇḍī with wrath, as if he would consume the Pāñcāla prince with that look.

Then all the Pāṇḍavas, placing themselves behind Śikhaṇḍī, attacked Bhīṣma in that battle repeatedly from all sides. Śikhaṇḍī himself, protected as he was by the diadem-decked Arjuna, pierced Bhīṣma with ten shafts. And he struck Bhīṣma's charioteer with other arrows and cut off his standard with one well-aimed shaft. Then Bhīṣma took up another bow that was tougher, which was cut off by Arjuna with three sharp shafts. Indeed, the ambidextrous Arjuna, excited with rage, cut off one by one all the bows that Bhīṣma took up.

When his bows were thus cut off, Bhīṣma, excited with rage, took up a dart that was capable of riving a hill, and hurled it at Arjuna's car. Seeing it coursing towards him like the blazing bolt of heaven, Arjuna fixed five sharp broad-headed arrows on his bowstring. And with those five arrows he cut into five fragments that dart hurled by Bhīṣma, which fell down like a flash of lightning separated from a mass of clouds.

Beholding his dart cut off, Bhīṣma became filled with rage. Soon he calmed down a little, and began to reflect. And he said to himself, "With only a single bow I could slay all the Pāṇḍavas, if the mighty Viṣṇu himself were not their protector. Moreover, I will not fight with the Pāṇḍavas because of the femininity of Śikhaṇḍī. Formerly, when my father married Satyavatī, he gave me two boons, that I should be incapable of being slain in battle and that my death should depend on my own choice. I think this is the proper hour for me to wish my own death."

Ascertaining this to be the resolve of the great Bhīṣma, the Ṛṣis and the Vasus stationed in the firmament said, "O son, we approve of your resolve. Act accordingly and withdraw from battle!" When they had said these words, a fragrant and auspicious breeze began to blow. The celestial cymbals were sounded, and a shower of flowers fell upon Bhīṣma.

Then Arjuna, drawing his Gāṇḍīva bow, pierced the son of Gaṅgā with twenty-five arrows. Once more he drew closer to Bhīṣma and cut off his bow. Bhīṣma took up another bow that was stronger. However, within the twinkling of an eye, Arjuna cut that bow into three fragments with three broad-headed shafts.

After that, Bhīṣma, the son of Śaṅtanu, no longer desired to battle with Arjuna. Deeply pierced by Arjuna with keen shafts, Bhīṣma addressed Duḥśāsana with a smile, saying, "These arrows coursing towards me in one continuous line are surely not Śikhaṇḍī's. Except for Arjuna, all other kings united together cannot cause me pain!"

Bhīṣma had slain ten thousand warriors on that day, the tenth day of the battle, and now he stood on the field with his vitals pierced. There was not a space even two fingers wide in all his body that was free from arrow wounds. A little before sunset the heroic Bhīṣma fell down from his car on the field, with his head towards the east, in the very sight of the Kauravas. When he fell, loud lamentations of "Alas!" and "Oh!" were heard everywhere, among the kings and among the celestials in heaven. The heroic combatants of both armies laid down their weapons and withdrew from battle. Meanwhile Bhīṣma betook himself to yoga as taught in the great Upaniṣads and remained quiet, engaged in prayer.

LVII

When Bhīṣma was overthrown from his car and fell, he lay on a bed of arrows so that his body did not touch the earth. Informed by Duḥśāsana of the fall of Bhīṣma, Droṇa immediately fell down from his car in a faint. But he soon regained consciousness and ordered his own troops to stop fighting. Thereupon the Pāṇḍavas, sending out messengers riding fleet horses, ordered their own armies to stop fighting.

When the troops of both armies had ceased fighting everywhere, all the kings took off their armour and went to see Bhīṣma. The virtuous Bhīṣma spoke these words to the Pāṇḍavas and the Kauravas who, after saluting him, were standing at the head of the various kings. He said, "Hail, O great heroes, hail, O mighty car-warriors. I am indeed pleased to see you."

Having thus greeted them, he said, "My head needs support; give me a pillow." Thereupon the kings fetched many soft pillows made of delicate fabrics. But the grandsire did not like them. Smiling, he said to the kings, "These pillows do not suit a hero's bed." Then seeing Arjuna, Bhīṣma said to him, "O mighty Arjuna, my head needs support; give me a suitable pillow!" Arjuna said, "So be it." Determined to do Bhīṣma's bidding, he took up the Gāṇḍiva bow and some fine shafts, which he purified with mantras. He then discharged three sharp arrows with great velocity into the earth, so that they supported Bhīṣma's head.

Seeing that Arjuna had rightly divined his thoughts, Bhīṣma became greatly pleased. He praised Arjuna, foremost of warriors, for having given him a warrior's pillow, after which he spoke these words to all the kings and princes assembled there, along with the Pāṇḍavas, "I shall lie on this bed until the sun rolls back. When the maker of the day, the resplendent illuminator of the world, mounted on his brilliant chariot, proceeds towards the point of the compass occupied by Vaiśravaṇa, then I shall yield up my vital breath, like one bidding adieu to his dear friends.

"My body is burning," Bhīṣma continued, "and I feel faint because of the wounds caused by the arrows. I need something to drink." Then the kings came with excellent viands and several pitchers of cold water. Seeing what they had brought, Bhīṣma said, "It is not possible for me to partake of any article of human enjoyment." In a weak voice, he addressed the mighty Arjuna, "My body is burning, and

I am covered with arrows. I am in great pain all over and my mouth is dry. Give me water, O Arjuna, for the refreshment of my body. You alone are capable of providing me with water which is ritually clean."

Thereupon the heroic Arjuna mounted on his chariot. He first circumambulated that prostrate chief of the Bhāratas, Bhīṣma. Then he fixed on his bowstring an effulgent arrow inspired with mantras for the Parjanya weapon. Before the eyes of all the people present he penetrated the earth a little to the south of the spot where Bhīṣma lay. Thereupon there gushed out a pure jet of water, cool and nectar-like and filled with celestial fragrance and taste. Thus Arjuna quenched Bhīṣma's thirst. Seeing this feat of Arjuna's, which resembled that of Indra himself, all the kings were struck with wonder.

Bhīṣma then observed, "You have seen, even now, O Duryodhana, how the intelligent Arjuna created that jet of water, cool and fragrant as nectar. No one else in the universe could achieve such a feat. The weapons of which the presiding deities respectively are Agni, Varuṇa, Soma, Vāyu, Viṣṇu, Indra, Paśupati, Parameṣṭhi, Prajāpati, Dhātā, Tvaṣṭā, and Savitā, all these celestial weapons are known among all men only to Arjuna and to Kṛṣṇa, the son of Devakī, and to no one else. You can therefore never hope to win a victory against them in battle, my son. Renounce your anger. Make peace with the Pāṇḍavas. Let friendship be restored with the death of Bhīṣma. Give half of your kingdom to the Pāṇḍavas. Let Yudhiṣṭhira rule over Indraprastha. Do not create internal dissensions among the rulers of the earth." But Duryodhana was deaf even to this last appeal of Bhīṣma.

LVIII

Then Karṇa approached that hero lying with his eyes closed, and fell at his feet. His voice choked with weeping as he said, "I am Rādhā's son, O foremost of the Kurus. Whenever I became the object of your sight, you looked upon me with enmity." Bhīṣma replied, "You are the son of Kuntī, and not of Rādhā; there is no doubt about this; I have heard all this from Nārada, as well as from Vyāsa and Kṛṣṇa.

I tell you in all truth that I bear you no malice, but used harsh words against you only to curb your impetuosity. I know your prowess in battle, your devotion to the Brāhmaṇas, your bravery, and your great capacity for charity. Among men there is none to rival you, and indeed you resemble an immortal. I spoke to you harshly only in the hope of avoiding internal dissensions. You know the Pāṇḍavas are your brothers. If you desire to do what is agreeable to me, then be reconciled to them. O Karṇa, let hostilities end with my fall, and let all the kings of the earth be freed of danger."

Karṇa replied, "I know all this to be true, O hero! As you say, I am Kuṅtī's son, and not the son of a charioteer. I was, however, disowned by Kuṅtī, and brought up by a charioteer. Having enjoyed Duryodhana's bounty for so long, I cannot disappoint his hopes at this stage. O sire, with your full heart permit me to fight. I intend to fight only with your permission. I also pray you to forgive me for any unworthy expression I may have uttered against you at any time, and also for any act injurious to you that I may have done through malice or fickleness."

"If you cannot renounce the fierce hostility you have against the Pāṇḍavas," said Bhīṣma, "then, O Karṇa, I give you my permission. Be actuated by a desire to attain heaven. Free from wrath and malice, carry out the commissions of the king to the best of your ability and energy. Be observant of the conduct of the righteous. Engage in fighting without arrogance, depending on your prowess and strength. There is nothing more desirable to a Kṣatriya than a righteous battle."

Bhīṣma concluded, "Long and strenuously I strove to bring about peace, but I failed to accomplish the task. Where justice is, there victory shall be!" After Bhīṣma had spoken thus, Karṇa saluted him, mounted his chariot, and proceeded towards the camp of Duryodhana.

Droṇa Parva

LIX

Having lost Bhīṣma, the Kauravas were filled with great anxiety, and resembled a herd of sheep without a shepherd, in a forest teeming with beasts of prey. The frightened kings as well as the common soldiers lost confidence and seemed to sink into the depths of gloom. Then the Kauravas remembered Karṇa, who indeed was the peer of Bhīṣma himself. For his part, Karṇa began to console the Dhārtarāṣṭras, though his own heart was cheerless, and his eyes filled with tears.

Duryodhana said, "Bhīṣma was our natural commander, endowed as he was with age, prowess, and learning and supported as he was by all our warriors. But now that he is about to ascend to heaven, O Karṇa, who do you think is fit to succeed him as our commander?" "All these kings are high-souled persons," said Karṇa. "Every one of them deserves to be our leader. All, however, cannot be leaders at the same time. Only one who has special merit should be chosen to be our chief. Droṇa is the preceptor of all these warriors, venerable in years, and worthy of respect. Therefore Droṇa, foremost of all wielders of weapons, should be made our leader."

With Droṇa's consent, Duryodhana made him the commander in chief of his forces according to the prescribed rites. As the fighting was about to begin on the eleventh day, King Duryodhana consulted with Karṇa and Duḥśāsana and others, and said to Droṇa, that invincible warrior, "If you would do me a favour, seize that foremost of car-warriors, Yudhiṣṭhira, and bring him alive to me here!"

When the fighting started, the mighty Droṇa cut off with a couple of arrows the heads of both Simhasena and Vyāghradatta. Then he rained arrows on the other mighty car-warriors among the Pāṇḍavas, and stood in front of Yudhiṣṭhira's car, like all-destroying Death himself, while among the warriors of Yudhiṣṭhira's army loud cries of lamentation arose that the king was taken.

Hearing these cries, the diadem-decked Arjuna suddenly came upon Droṇa's division, and covered it with a thick network of arrows which confounded the very senses. He was so quick in placing his arrows on the bowstring and shooting them that none could notice any lapse of time between these two acts of the renowned Arjuna. Neither the four cardinal directions, nor the sky above, nor the earth, could be seen, as everything became one dense mass of arrows.

Just then the sun also set, and neither friend nor foe could any longer be distinguished. Then Droṇa and Duryodhana ordered the withdrawal of their troops. Arjuna too caused his troops to be withdrawn slowly. The Pāṇḍavas and Sṛñjayas and Pāñcālas, filled with joy, praised Arjuna.

Thus on the eleventh day the Kaurava ranks were broken by Arjuna and Droṇa could not keep his vow, in consequence of Yudhiṣṭhira's being well protected. The Kaurava warriors knew they were defeated, and all of them, with coats of mail torn and covered with dust, cast anxious glances around them.

On the twelfth day Droṇa said to Duryodhana, "I tell you truly: today, I will slay a mighty car-warrior, one of the foremost heroes of the Pāṇḍavas. Today I will also form an array that is impenetrable by the very gods. I wish, however, that by some means Arjuna should be drawn away from the field." After Droṇa had spoken these words, the Saṃśaptakas challenged Arjuna to battle and diverted him to the southern side of the battlefield.

The preceptor then formed the great circular array. In it were placed all the kings on the Kaurava side, determined bowmen all, numbering ten thousand, with Dhṛtarāṣṭra's grandson, Lakṣmaṇa, at their head. All of them sympathized with one another in joy and grief, emulated one another in daring, desired to excel one another in valour, and were devoted to one another's good. Duryodhana was surrounded by the mighty car-warriors, Karṇa, Duḥśāsana, and Kṛpa.

With a white umbrella over his head he looked like Iṅdra, the king of the celestials. At the head of this army was stationed the commander Droṇa. And there also stood the king of the Siṅdhus, Jayadratha, immovable like the Meru mountain. He was flanked by those mighty car-warriors, namely, Śakuni, Śalya, and Bhūriśravas.

LX

Seeing Droṇa advancing in rage against him, Yudhiṣṭhira thought of diverse means for checking his progress. At last, convinced that Droṇa could not be resisted by anyone else, he placed that heavy and unbearable burden on Abhimanyu. Addressing Abhimanyu, the king said, "O child, act in such a way that Arjuna, returning from the Samśaptakas, may not reproach us! We do not know how to break the circular array."

Abhimanyu replied, "I shall soon penetrate the circular array formed by Droṇa. My father has taught me how to break this kind of array. I shall not be able, however, to come out of it if any kind of danger should overtake me."

"Break this array, O foremost of warriors," said Yudhiṣṭhira, "and make a passage for us! All of us will follow in your wake. In battle, you are equal to Arjuna himself. When you enter, we shall follow you and protect you on all sides."

Thereupon, wearing golden armour and flying an excellent standard that bore the device of a Karṇikāra tree, Abhimanyu fearlessly attacked the mighty car-warriors headed by Droṇa, like a lion cub assailing a herd of elephants. The battle between those heroes became fierce and terrible. And in the course of that awful battle, in the very sight of Droṇa, Abhimanyu broke the array and penetrated into it. Single-handed he achieved this most difficult feat.

No car-warrior succeeded in obstructing Abhimanyu's progress towards Droṇa. Karṇa, most honoured of all bowmen, pierced Abhimanyu with hundreds of arrows, displaying his best weapons. Despite the shower of arrows let loose by Karṇa, Abhimanyu, splendid as a celestial, did not yield. Seeing that vast Kaurava army turning away from the fight, Jayadratha rushed to rally the warriors, attacking the Pāṇḍavas and their followers, who were anxious to rescue Abhimanyu. By the strength of his celestial weapons, Jayadratha, singlehanded, held in check the entire army of the Pāṇḍavas.

Later on, Droṇa, Kṛpa, Karṇa, Aśvatthāmā, Bṛhadbalā, and Kṛtavarmā, these six car-warriors, surrounded Abhimanyu, and put his chariot out of action. Without his car, with his bow broken, but still with an eye to his duty as a warrior, Abhimanyu took up a sword and shield and leaped forward. Then Droṇa cut off the gem-decked hilt of Abhimanyu's sword, while Karṇa cut off his excellent shield with sharp arrows.

At this point Lakṣmaṇa, the irate son of Duḥśāsana, took up his mace and rushed at Abhimanyu. Those two heroes, who were cousins, attacked each other with upraised maces, like the three-eyed Mahādeva and the asura Aṅdhaka in days of old. As Abhimanyu was on the point of rising, Lakṣmaṇa struck him with the mace on the crown of his head. Stunned by the violence of that tremendous blow as well as by fatigue, Abhimanyu fell senseless on the ground.

Thus was one killed by many in battle. Abhimanyu had laid waste a whole army, like an elephant destroying a tankful of lotuses. Finally he fell, like a wild elephant slain by the hunters.

LXI

After the slaughter of the hero Abhimanyu, the Pāṇḍava warriors left their cars and took off their armour. They all sat round King Yudhiṣṭhira, brooding over their grief and thinking of the deceased Abhimanyu.

At the end of that terrible day the sun set and the beautiful twilight spread over the horizon. The armies on both sides retired. Then Arjuna, who had in the course of the day slain a large number of Samśaptakas by means of his celestial weapons, proceeded towards his tent, mounted on his victorious car.

As he went, he inquired of Kṛṣṇa, in a thin voice, "Why is my heart so agitated, O Kṛṣṇa, and why does my speech falter so? I see evil omens and my body is weak!" Thus conversing, Kṛṣṇa and Arjuna entered their own camp. And they saw the Pāṇḍavas, without cheer, plunged in great grief. Seeing his brothers and sons in this plight, Arjuna himself became very depressed. Not seeing Abhimanyu there, he said, "I see your pale and cheerless faces! I do not see Abhimanyu; I also observe that no one greets me. I had heard that Droṇa had today formed the circular array. None amongst you, save Abhimanyu, could break that array. However, I had not taught him how to come out of that array, after having pierced it. Did you ask Abhimanyu, a mere boy, to enter that array? Having pierced that array, and being outnumbered in battle, has Abhimanyu fallen at last in the fight?"

Yudhiṣṭhira confirmed Arjuna's fears and gave an account of Abhimanyu's heroic stand. Then Kṛṣṇa consoled Arjuna who was afflicted with grief on account of his son's death, saying, "Be not depressed. This is the way of all brave, unretreating heroes, and especially of Kṣatriyas, who live to fight. Death is certain for heroes that do not retreat. There is no doubt that Abhimanyu has ascended to those regions that are reserved for righteous persons. This fate is coveted by all brave warriors, that they may die in battle, facing their foes."

"O mighty Arjuna," said Yudhiṣṭhira, "after you had gone towards the army of the Saṃśaptakas, the preceptor Droṇa made a fierce effort to seize me. We succeeded, however, in resisting Droṇa and disposed our vigorous car divisions in counter-array. Though he was thus held in check, and though I myself was well protected, Droṇa began to attack with great energy, hitting us with his sharp shafts. We could not face his army, far less break it in battle."

Yudhiṣṭhira continued, "All of us then addressed your son by Subhadrā, who was equal to you in prowess, saying to him, 'O son, pierce this array of Droṇa!' Thus urged by us, Abhimanyu sought, like a good horse, to take that burden on himself, however heavy it might have been for him. Endowed as he was with your energy, and with the knowledge of weapons he had learnt from you, the child penetrated that array, like Garuḍa penetrating the ocean. As for us, we followed the hero Abhimanyu in the path which he had taken. Then the wretched king of the Sindhus, Jayadratha, in consequence of the boon granted to him by Rudra, checked all of us. Droṇa, Kṛpa, Karṇa, Aśvatthāmā, Bṛhadbala, and Kṛtavarmā, these six car-warriors, surrounded the son of Subhadrā and deprived him of his car. After Abhimanyu's car had been put out of action, Duḥśāsana's son succeeded by a fluke in slaying him."

After hearing this account, Arjuna said, "Truly I swear that tomorrow I will slay Jayadratha! If from fear of death he does not forsake the Dhārtarāṣṭras and implore our protection or that of Kṛṣṇa, that foremost of men, or yours, O king, I shall slay him tomorrow! I swear that if tomorrow's sun should set without my destroying that wretch, then even here I shall enter the blazing fire!"

After Arjuna had vowed the death of Jayadratha, Kṛṣṇa said to him, "You have vowed that you would slay the ruler of the Sindhus. This is an act of great rashness on your part. You have done so without consulting me, and thus taken upon yourself a great burden. How shall we now avoid the ridicule of the whole world? You should know that, following a piteous appeal by King Duryodhana to the preceptor, precautions have been taken. Chariots and horses have been arranged. Karṇa, Bhūriśravas, Aśvatthāmā, the invincible Vṛṣasena, Kṛpa, and Śalya, these six will be in front. Droṇa will form an array, half of which will be a waggon and half a lotus. In the centre of the leaves of that lotus will be a needle-mouthed array, where Jayadratha will take his stand, protected by heroes. Consider the strength of each of those six defenders of Jayadratha. Those tigers among men, when united, cannot be easily overcome."

Arjuna replied, "The united strength of these six car-warriors whom you regard to be so strong, is not, I think, equal to even half of mine. O Kṛṣṇa, you shall see me shattering the weapons of all these heroes, anxious as I am to kill Jayadratha. In the very sight of Droṇa, I shall make the head of the ruler of the Sindhus fall on the earth, while all his men grieve for him."

Then Arjuna said to Kṛṣṇa, "Comfort your sister Subhadrā, along with her daughter-in-law, and her companions. O lord, console them with soothing words fraught with truth!" Thus requested,

Kṛṣṇa went sad in heart to Arjuna's abode, and began to comfort his sorrowing sister.

LXII

There was none in the Pāṇḍava camp who slept that night. When the thirteenth day dawned Durmarṣaṇa, accompanied by a thousand cars, a hundred elephants, three thousand horses, and ten thousand foot soldiers, covering a piece of ground fifteen hundred bows long, took up his position at the very van of all the Kaurava troops. Arjuna said, "Take me, O Kṛṣṇa, to where Durmarṣaṇa is stationed! Breaking through that elephant division, I will penetrate into the hostile army!" So saying, he covered his foes with showers of arrows, like clouds pouring rain over the mountain.

When Arjuna thus began to break and slay the Kaurava force, many heroes were either slain or, losing spirit, fled away. Then Duḥśāsana became filled with wrath and rushed against Arjuna, eager for battle. Disregarding him, like a makara penetrating the ocean, Arjuna pierced that elephant host. Duḥśāsana's forces, thus slaughtered by Arjuna, fled. Duḥśāsana himself, greatly afflicted by Arjuna's shafts, and overcome by fear, with his division entered the śakaṭa array, seeking Droṇa's protection.

After defeating the forces of Duḥśāsana, the ambidextrous Arjuna proceeded against the division of Droṇa, with the object of getting at Jayadratha. And while he penetrated the Kaurava army, those high-souled princes of Pāñcāla, Yudhāmanyu and Uttamaujas, followed him on either flank. Jaya, Kṛtavarmā, the ruler of the Kāṁbojas, and Śrutāyus, began to oppose Arjuna's progress.

Held in check by them, Arjuna, foremost of car-warriors, was pursued by Droṇa from behind. The son of Pāṇḍu, however, blasted that army, scattering his sharp shafts like the sun scattering countless rays of light.

Then the Aṅgas surrounded Arjuna with their elephant force. Urged by Duryodhana, many kings of the west and the south, and many others headed by the ruler of the Kaliṅgas, with their huge elephants, also surrounded Arjuna. But Arjuna careered over the field, slaying steeds and car-warriors and elephants. As a fire, urged by the wind, consumes a dense forest of trees, even so did that Pāṇḍava fire Arjuna, having shafts for its flames and urged on by Kṛṣṇa as by the wind, angrily consume the forest of Kaurava warriors.

Meanwhile, the rest of the Pāṇḍavas advanced against the three divisions of the Kauravas. Bhīma dashed against the mighty-armed Jalasaṅdha, while Yudhiṣṭhira with his troops engaged Kṛtavarmā, and Dhṛṣṭadyumna rushed against Droṇa. On the afternoon of that day, in the hair-raising battle that took place between the Pāñcālas and the Kurus, Droṇa became as it were the stake.

Seeing the Kuru army slaughtered by Sātyaki, Droṇa himself rushed towards that warrior of true prowess. Meanwhile, Yudhiṣṭhira suddenly heard the blare of Kṛṣṇa's conch Pāñcajanya. At the same time, while the heroic protectors of Jayadratha were fighting Arjuna, and while the sons of Dhṛarāṣṭra were roaring in front of Arjuna's car, the twang of the Gāṇḍīva bow could not be heard. As a result Yudhiṣṭhira became anxious and prone to dejection. He thought, "Without doubt, all is not well with Arjuna since that prince of conches Pāñchajanya is blowing and since the joyful Kauravas are shouting so repeatedly."

Thinking thus, with an anxious heart, Yudhiṣṭhira said to Sātyaki, his voice choked with weeping, "As Kṛṣṇa is ever the refuge of the Pāṇḍavas, even so are you, O Sātyaki, who are the equal of Kṛṣṇa in prowess. I will, therefore, lay a burden on you which you are fit to bear. Arjuna is your brother, friend, and preceptor. Go now to his aid, in this hour of distress. You are devoted to virtue. You are a hero. You are the refuge of your friends. Because of your acts you are famous in the world as one who speaks the truth."

After saying this, the king had quivers full of shafts and diverse weapons placed on Sātyaki's car. Then Sātyaki, joyful in every limb, said to Bhīma, "O Bhīma, protect the king! This is your foremost duty. Meanwhile, I shall proceed to break through this host whose hour has come."

After Sātyaki's departure, Droṇa rushed at Bhīma. The battle between Droṇa and the high-souled Bhīma was furious and terrible, and resembled the encounter between the gods and the asuras of old. Bhīma was able to hold his own in that encounter. Passing through the Bhoja division and that of the Kāṁbojas, and countless tribes of Mlecchas too, who were all accomplished in fighting, he proceeded resolutely and with great speed, desirous of seeing Arjuna.

Thus pressing forward, overtaking all the Kaurava warriors, Bhīma saw Arjuna fighting, striving to kill Jayadratha. Having seen him, Bhīma shouted aloud. Both Kṛṣṇa and Arjuna, when they heard that shout, repeatedly shouted back. Hearing the roar of Bhīma, as well as that of Arjuna, Yudhiṣṭhira became highly gratified; his grief was dispelled. And the lord Yudhiṣṭhira wished Arjuna success in battle.

LXIII

While the mighty Bhīma was uttering those roars, Karṇa, unable to bear them, rushed at him with a loud shout, his bow stretched for action. Seeing that encounter between Bhīma and Karṇa, all the struggling combatants, car-warriors, and horsemen began to tremble. The valiant Bhīma, however, vanquished Karṇa in battle, and uttered a loud shout of victory deep as the roar of the clouds. Hearing that roar, Yudhiṣṭhira was greatly pleased, knowing that Karṇa had been vanquished by Bhīma.

When they saw that Karṇa had been defeated by Bhīma, five of Dhṛtarāṣṭra's sons, Durmarṣana, Duḥsaha, Durmada, Durdhara, and Jaya, clad in beautiful mail, together attacked Bhīma. Surrounding him on all sides, they covered all the points of the compass with their shafts looking like flights of locusts. Bhīma almost smilingly received those princes of celestial beauty thus rushing suddenly against him. With five and twenty arrows discharged from his formidable bow, Bhīma dispatched all those princes to Yama's abode along with their horses and charioteers. Fallen from their cars beside their charioteers, their lifeless forms looked like large trees uprooted by a tempest.

Then the great bowmen of the Trigarta country, whose standards were adorned with gold, surrounded on all sides the mighty Sātyaki who was rushing against Duḥśāsana's car. Beholding Sātyaki, invincible in battle, coming to help Arjuna, Bhūriśravas suddenly advanced against him. And the two heroes poured upon each other dense showers of arrows like masses of clouds. Those two foremost of warriors fought on while Kṛṣṇa and Arjuna watched their encounter.

Then Kṛṣṇa said to Arjuna, "Behold, that tiger among the Vṛṣṇis and the Aṅdhakas has fallen to Somadatta's son! Sātyaki is exhausted with exertion, and has lost his car! O Arjuna, protect Sātyaki, your heroic disciple! See that Sātyaki does not, for your sake, fall to Bhūriśravas."

Meanwhile loud cries of "Oh, Oh!" arose among the troops as the mighty-armed Bhūriśravas struck Sātyaki and brought him to the ground. Like a lion dragging an elephant, Bhūriśravas dragged that leader of the Sātvatas. Looking splendid in his triumph, Bhūriśravas seized Sātyaki by the hair of his head and struck him on the chest with his feet.

Seeing Sātyaki thus dragged in battle, Kṛṣṇa again said to Arjuna, "Behold, mighty Arjuna, that tiger among the Vṛṣṇis and the Aṅdhakas, who is your disciple and who is not inferior to you in archery, has succumbed to Somadatta's son Bhūriśravas." Arjuna replied, "My eyes were concentrated upon the king of the Siṅdhus, Jayadratha, and I could not see Sātyaki. I shall, however, for his sake, now achieve a most difficult feat." So saying, Arjuna discharged an arrow and cut off the arm of the Kuru warrior Bhūriśravas, even with the sword in its hand.

Thereupon, releasing his hold of Sātyaki, Bhūriśravas wrathfully reproved Arjuna. He said, "You have done a cruel and heartless deed, by cutting off my arm from a concealed position when you were not engaged in a duel with me." After these words, the illustrious Bhūriśravas entered Prāya in the battlefield. Distinguished as he was for many righteous deeds, he spread with his left hand a bed of arrows and, desirous of proceeding to the region of Brahmā, he committed his senses to the care of the deities presiding over them. Fixing his gaze on the sun, his mind pure and cleansed, and thinking of the great Upaniṣad, Bhūriśravas betook himself to yoga.

Set free of Bhuriśravas, Sātyaki arose. He drew his sword, desiring to cut off the head of the high-souled Bhūriśravas, who had already lost his arm, and who resembled a trunkless elephant. All the warriors loudly censured him for his evil intention. But, though checked by Kṛṣṇa and the high-souled Arjuna, Bhīma, Yudhāmanyu, Uttamaujas, Aśvatthāmā, Kṛpa, Karṇa, Vṛṣasena, and Jayadratha too, and even while the soldiers were uttering shouts of disapproval, Sātyaki with his sword cut off the head of Bhūriśravas who had been deprived of his arm by Arjuna and who was then sitting in Prāya.

LXIV

After Bhūriśravas had gone to the other world, the mighty-armed Arjuna said to Kṛṣṇa, "Urge the steeds, O Kṛṣṇa, to greater speed and take me to where King Jayadratha is! We have no time to lose, as the sun is hastening towards the western mountain."

Arjuna overcame all obstacles and got close to Jayadratha, whom he pierced with four and sixty arrows. Thus wounded by Arjuna, Jayadratha, who bore the device of the boar on his banner, became filled with rage like a goaded elephant, and quickly discharged at the ambidextrous Arjuna many straight shafts equipped with feathers of vultures, which looked like angry snakes of virulent poison.

Meanwhile, the sun was setting, and Kṛṣṇa once more addressed Arjuna. He said, "O Arjuna, quickly cut off the head of the wicked-souled ruler of the Sindhus! The sun is about to set behind the excellent mountain of Asta. Listen, however, to the words I have to say about the slaughter of Jayadratha. His father is Vṛddhakṣatra, famous all over the world. It was after long waiting that he got Jayadratha for his son. On the birth of Jayadratha, an aerial voice said to the king, 'O lord, this son of yours will become a leader among the two races[1] by his birth, conduct, and other attributes. But while he fights with enemies in the battlefield some prominent foeman will cut off his head.' Hearing these words and overwhelmed with affection for his

[1] The solar and the lunar.

son, the king of the Siṅdhus summoned all his kinsmen and told them: 'If any man causes the head of my son to fall on the earth while struggling in battle, I say that without fail the head of that man will crack into a hundred pieces!'

"Having spoken these words and having installed Jayadratha on the throne," Kṛṣṇa continued, "Vṛddhakṣatra repaired to the woods, and devoted himself to penance. He is still engaged in the observance of the most austere of penances outside this very Samaṅtapañcaka. Therefore, O Arjuna, when you cut off Jayadratha's head in this dreadful battle, you should use your fierce celestial weapon capable of wonderful feats, so that Jayadratha's head may fall upon the lap of Vṛddhakṣatra himself. If you let Jayadratha's head fall on the earth your own head will then, without fail, crack into a hundred fragments. Aided by your celestial weapon, O Arjuna, do the deed in such a way that Vṛddhakṣatra may not know of it!"

Hearing these words of Kṛṣṇa, Arjuna quickly shot the arrow which he had taken up to kill Jayadratha. That shaft, sped from Gāṇḍīva, snatched Jayadratha's head away, like a hawk snatching away a smaller bird from the top of a tree. By shooting his shafts repeatedly after it Arjuna sent the head along in the sky without allowing it to fall down.

Meanwhile, King Vṛddhakṣatra was engaged in his evening prayers. While he was thus occupied, the head of Jayadratha, decked with black locks and adorned with earrings, fell upon his lap. Vṛddhakṣatra was so absorbed in his prayer that he did not know what had happened. As he stood up after finishing his prayers, Jayadratha's head abruptly fell down on the earth. At the same moment, Vṛddhakṣatra's head cracked into a hundred pieces. All who saw this were filled with wonder. And Kṛṣṇa applauded the mighty car-warrior Arjuna.

Having slain Jayadratha in the evening, Arjuna met the great bowman, Sātyaki, and together they went to meet Droṇa. Meanwhile the night became pitch dark, heightening the terrors of the timid. That night was inauspicious for warriors, propelling them towards their death, as well as many elephants, horses, and men. And during the progress of that fierce and dreadful battle in the night, the Pāṇḍavas and the Sṛñjayas, united together, rushed angrily against Droṇa.

However, all those who set forth against the illustrious Droṇa were either obliged to turn back or dispatched to the abode of Yama.

LXV

The next day was the fourteenth day of battle. In the course of the day's fighting, Aśvatthāmā, filled with rage, rushed furiously against Sātyaki. Thereupon Bhīma's son Ghaṭotkaca rushed at him. He rode on a huge car made of black iron covered with bearskins, and drawn neither by horses nor by elephants, but by bearers resplendent as elephants. He was surrounded by an akṣauhiṇi of fierce-looking rākṣasas armed with lances, heavy clubs, rocks, and trunks of trees. Seeing him advance with uplifted bow, resembling the mace-armed Destroyer himself in the hour of universal dissolution, the opposing kings were struck with fear. As the evening advanced, the rākṣasas became more powerful and threw on the field of battle a thick shower of stones.

Duryodhana said to Karṇa, "O you who are devoted to friends, the hour has come when your help is most needed. O Karṇa, save in battle all my warriors!" Karṇa replied, "If Indra himself were to come hither to save Arjuna, I should quickly vanquish even him, and then slay that son of Pāṇḍu." When Karṇa spoke thus, Kṛpa, the mighty-armed son of Śāradvata, smiling the while, addressed him in these words: "Your speech is fair, O Karṇa! If words alone could achieve success, then Duryodhana would be well protected. You boast much, but your prowess or strength is seldom witnessed."

Karṇa replied, "It is true that the Pāṇḍavas cannot be vanquished by the very gods with Indra at their head, nor by the Daityas, the yakṣas, and the rākṣasas. Even so, I will vanquish them with the help of the weapon given me by Indra. You know, O Brāhman, that the dart given by Indra is invincible. With that I will slay the ambidextrous Arjuna in battle."

Meanwhile, in another part of the battle, Somadatta fearlessly attacked Sātyaki, scattering showers of arrows like the clouds pouring torrents of rain. Then Sātyaki let loose a terrible shaft of fiery effulgence, whetted on stone, and fitted with wings of gold. It struck Somadatta on his chest, and pierced him deeply, so that the great car-warrior Somadatta fell down from his car and expired.

Kṛṣṇa said, "I behold Karṇa, O Arjuna, careering in battle like the chief of the celestials himself. There is none else capable of advancing against him in battle, save you and the rākṣasa Ghaṭotkaca. I do not, however, think that the time has come for you to face Karṇa in battle. The blazing dart, resembling a mighty meteor, given him by Iṅdra, and intended for you, is still with him. Let the mighty Ghaṭotkaca proceed against Karṇa, the son of Rādhā. He is the offspring of Bhīma and is equal to a celestial in strength."

Hearing those words of Kṛṣṇa, Arjuna said to the rākṣasa Ghaṭotkaca, "O Ghaṭotkaca, yourself, the long-armed Sātyaki, and Bhīma, the son of Pāṇḍu, these three, in my judgment, are the foremost among all our warriors. Go and attack Karṇa in single combat tonight. The mighty car-warrior Sātyaki will protect your rear." Ghaṭotkaca said, "I am a match for Karṇa, as well as for Droṇa, O Bhārata, or for any illustrious Kṣatriya, however accomplished in weapons. This night I shall fight a battle with Karṇa that will be talked about as long as the world lasts." Having said these words, Ghaṭotkaca rushed against Karṇa in that dreadful fight.

When he saw that frightful rākṣasa advancing against him, Karṇa withstood him smilingly. The clash between Karṇa and the rākṣasa became terrible, resembling that between Iṅdra and the demon Śaṁbara. The air was filled with the sound of twanging bowstrings. Despite his best efforts Karṇa could not prevail over Ghaṭotkaca.

Then Karṇa, seeing the rākṣasa still alive at dead of night, and the Kuru army struck with fear, decided to hurl his dart. Inflamed with rage like a wrathful lion and unable to brook the assaults of Ghaṭotkaca, Karṇa in his desire to kill Ghaṭotkaca took up that foremost of victory-giving and invincible darts, the Śakti weapon. That dart which for years he had kept to kill Arjuna in battle, that foremost of darts which Iṅdra himself had given to Karṇa in exchange for the latter's earrings, that blazing and terrible missile twined with strings and seeming to thirst for blood, that fierce weapon which looked like the very tongue of the Destroyer or the sister of Death himself, that terrible and effulgent dart, Karṇa hurled at the rākṣasa.

Destroying the blazing illusion created by Ghaṭotkaca and piercing right through his breast, that resplendent dart soared aloft in the night and entered a starry constellation in the sky. Ghaṭotkaca, who had fought using diverse weapons against many heroic rākṣasa and human warriors, uttered a terrible roar and fell, deprived of his life by the dart of Iṅdra.

When Ghaṭotkaca was thus killed and lay like a riven mountain, all the Pāṇḍavas were filled with grief and began to shed copious tears. Only Kṛṣṇa was in transports of delight as he embraced Arjuna. He said, "Great is the joy I feel! Listen to me, O Arjuna! This will immediately dispel your sorrow and give you cheer. You know that Karṇa, having shot his Śakti bolt at Ghaṭotkaca, is already slain in battle. The man does not exist in this world that could withstand Karṇa armed with that dart and looking like Kārtikeya in battle. By good luck, his natural armour and his earrings were taken away. By good luck, he has now been deprived also of his infallible dart through Ghaṭotkaca. With his divine weapon, Karṇa was like a bountiful evening cloud, pouring showers of arrows. Without the dart given him by Iṅdra, Karṇa has now become a mere human. There will arise one opportunity for his slaughter, when his car wheels sink in the earth. Availing yourself of that opportunity, and warned by a sign which I will make beforehand, you should slay him when he is in that difficult situation."

LXVI

As fighting began on the fifteenth day, Yudhiṣṭhira said to Dhṛṣṭadyumna, "Attack Droṇa today. Remember you were born out of the sacrificial fire, clad in mail, and armed with bow and arrows and sword, for the destruction of Droṇa. Cheerfully give him battle, and have no fear."

Meanwhile the Pāñcālas, though suffering great pain, continued to contend in battle against Droṇa. Then Drupada and Virāṭa proceeded against Droṇa, that invincible warrior, who was dominating the field. The three grandsons of Drupada, and those mighty bowmen, the Cedis, also proceeded against Droṇa in that encounter. With three sharp shafts, Droṇa killed the three grandsons of Drupada, who fell lifeless on the ground.

Next Droṇa discharged a couple of well-tempered and broad-headed shafts which dispatched both Drupada and Virāṭa to the abode of Yama. Upon the fall of Virāṭa and Drupada, and the slaughter of the Kekayas, the Cedis, the Matsyas, and the Pāñcālas, as well as those three heroes, the three grandsons of Drupada, the high-souled Dhṛṣṭa-dyumna was filled with rage and grief, and swore in the midst of all the car-warriors: "Let me lose the merits of all my religious acts if Droṇa should escape alive, or if he should succeed in vanquishing me!"

Meanwhile Droṇa caused great carnage among the Pāñcālas. Seeing the Pāṇḍavas thus afflicted by the shafts of Droṇa and overcome by fear, the wise Kṛṣṇa who was ever devoted to their welfare said to Arjuna, "This foremost of all car-warriors cannot be vanquished in battle, not even by the very gods with Iṅdra at their head! Hence you must put aside fair means, and adopt some contrivance for gaining victory, so that Droṇa may not slay us all in battle. I think he will cease to fight if his son Aśvatthāmā should fall. Let some man, therefore, tell him that Aśvatthāmā has been slain in battle."

Arjuna did not relish this suggestion of Kṛṣṇa's, though others approved of it. Yudhiṣṭhira himself accepted it very reluctantly. Then the mighty Bhīma, having slain with a mace a huge elephant, named Aśvatthāmā, approached Droṇa on the battlefield, and—not without some embarrassment—exclaimed aloud, "Aśvatthāmā has been slain!"

Meanwhile, Kṛṣṇa grew seriously concerned because Droṇa, foremost of warriors, was capable of sweeping all the Pāṇḍavas off the face of the earth. He said to King Yudhiṣṭhira, "If Droṇa, roused to anger, fights for even half a day, I tell you truly, your army will be annihilated. Save us then from Droṇa! Under such circumstances, falsehood is preferable to truth. By telling a lie to save a life, one is not touched by sin."

Bhīma supported Kṛṣṇa's argument. He said, "Droṇa did not believe my words. To ensure our victory, accept Kṛṣṇa's advice. Tell Droṇa that his son is no more. If you say so, Droṇa will believe you and will never fight thereafter, since you are famed for your truthfulness in the three worlds."

Urged thus by Bhīma and induced by the counsels of Kṛṣṇa, and also because of the inevitability of destiny, Yudhiṣṭhira gave in. Fearing to tell a downright lie, but earnestly desirous of victory, Yudhiṣṭhira added indistinctly that the elephant was slain. Before this, Yudhiṣṭhira's car had stayed at a height of four fingers above the surface of the earth; after he had uttered that lie, his vehicle and animals touched the earth.

Hearing those words of Yudhiṣṭhira's, the mighty car-warrior Droṇa was afflicted with grief for the reported death of his son, and lost all desire to live. Already he was feeling a sense of guilt for fighting against the high-souled Pāṇḍavas. Hearing now of the death of his son, he became deeply depressed and filled with anxiety. Thus, when Dhṛṣṭadyumna approached him, Droṇa had no mind to fight as before.

Seeing that Droṇa was filled with great anxiety and almost deprived of his senses by grief, Dhṛṣṭadyumna, the hero who had been obtained by King Drupada at a great sacrifice from the bearer of sacrifical libations expressly for Droṇa's destruction, rushed at him. He took up a formidable bow and fixed on it a fierce and fiery arrow, resembling a snake of virulent poison, intent on killing Droṇa. But the invincible Droṇa cut off all the weapons, and all the bows of his antagonist, with the sole exception of his mace and sword.

Then Bhīma, in a great rage, approached Droṇa's chariot and deliberately said these words to him: "Wretched are the Brāhmaṇas who, not content with the avocations of their own order, have become well versed in arms, and taken to fighting. But for them the Kṣatriya order would not have been thus exterminated. Nonviolence to all creatures is said to be the highest of all virtues. The Brāhmaṇa is the root of all virtue. You, Droṇa, are supposed to be the best of Brāhmaṇas. And yet you fight, while your son lies dead on the field of battle, unknown to you and behind your back. Yudhiṣṭhira the just has told you this. It behoves you not to doubt this fact."

Thus addressed by Bhīma, Droṇa laid aside his bow. Deciding to give up all his weapons, the virtuous man called for Karṇa, Kṛpa, and Duryodhana. He repeated his son's name loudly. Laying aside his weapons, he sat down on the platform of his car, and devoted himself to yoga. Seizing this opportunity, Dhṛṣṭadyuma took up his sword and, jumping down from his vehicle, rushed quickly against Droṇa, among loud exclamations of woe from all sides.

Droṇa himself remained in a supremely tranquil state. Arjuna pleaded with Dhṛṣṭadyumna, saying, "O son of Drupada, seize the preceptor alive, do not slay him!" All the troops also cried out, "He should not be slain!" Arjuna, in particular, moved by pity, pleaded repeatedly that his life should be spared. Disregarding, however, the protests of Arjuna as well as those of all the kings, Dhṛṣṭadyumna slew Droṇa on the platform of his car.

Upon the fall of Droṇa, the Kaurava warriors, already sorely afflicted by the enemy's arrows, became leaderless. Broken and routed, and filled with grief, they gathered listlessly around Duryodhana, bewailing their loss.

Karṇa Parva

LXVII

When the mighty bowman Droṇa was slain, the Kaurava host became pale-faced and gloomy. Seeing his own forces standing as if paralysed and lifeless, King Duryodhana said to them, "Relying on the strength of your arms, I have challenged the Pāṇḍavas to this battle. Victory or death is the lot of all warriors. Why wonder then at the fall of Droṇa? Let us resume the fighting in all directions, encouraged by the sight of the lofty-minded Karṇa, the son of Vikartana, mighty bowman and wielder of celestial weapons, who is roving about in the field of battle. Permit me to remind you that it was he who slew Ghaṭotkaca, that creator of illusions, with the indomitable Śakti weapon." Then all those kings, headed by Duryodhana, quickly installed Karṇa as commander in chief, and bathed him according to rites with golden and earthen pitchers of holy water.

As the sixteenth day dawned, Karṇa summoned the Kaurava forces to battle with loud blasts on his conch. He arranged his army in the form of a makara, and proceeded to attack the Pāṇḍavas, desirous of victory. On the Pāṇḍava side, Arjuna, whose car was drawn by white horses, formed a counter-array in the shape of a half-moon.

The day's fighting was marked by many duels, between Bhīma and Aśvatthāmā, Sahadeva and Duḥśāsana, Nakula and Karṇa, Ulūka and Yuyutsu, Kṛpa and Dhṛṣṭadyumna, and Śikhaṇḍī and Kṛtavarmā. While they were thus engaged, the sun disappeared behind the western mountains. Then both sides retired from the field and proceeded to their own encampments.

Before the fighting began on the seventeenth day, Karṇa said to

Duryodhana, "Today, O king, I will go forth and battle with the famous Pāṇḍava, Arjuna. Either I shall slay that hero, or he shall slay me. You are aware of his energy, weapons, and resources. My bow, known by the name of Vijaya, is the greatest of all weapons. It was made by Viśvakarmā in accordance with Indra's wishes, and is a celestial and excellent weapon. On this count I believe I am superior to Arjuna."

"Now you must know," continued Karṇa, "in what respect Arjuna is superior to me. Kṛṣṇa, born of the Dāśārha race, who is revered by all people, is the holder of the reins of his horses. He who is verily the creator of the universe thus guards Arjuna's car. On our side Śalya, who is the ornament of all assemblies, is of equal heroism. Should he take over the duties of my charioteer, then victory will surely be yours. Let the irresistible Śalya, therefore, act as my charioteer."

Duryodhana thereupon went to see Śalya. Humbly approaching the Madra prince, he affectionately spoke these words to him: "You have heard what Karṇa has said, namely that he chooses you, foremost of princes, as his charioteer. Therefore, for the destruction of the Pāṇḍavas, and for my own good, be pleased to become Karṇa's charioteer. As that foremost of charioteers, Kṛṣṇa, counsels and protects Arjuna, so should you support Karṇa at all times."

Śalya replied, "You are insulting me, O Duryodhana, or surely you must doubt my loyalty, since you so readily request me to do the work of a charioteer. You praise Karṇa and consider that he is superior to us. But I do not consider him to be my equal in the field of battle. Knowing that I can strike down the enemy, why do you wish to employ me in the office of charioteer to the lowborn Karṇa?"

Duryodhana replied to Śalya with great affection and high respect. Desirous of achieving his main objective, he addressed him in a friendly manner, saying sweetly, "O Śalya, what you say is doubtless true. However, in making this request I have a certain purpose. Even as Karṇa is reckoned to be superior to Arjuna in many ways so are you, in the opinion of the whole world, superior to Kṛṣṇa. As the high-souled Kṛṣṇa is expert in the handling of horses, even so, O Śalya, are you doubly skilled. There is no doubt about it."

Thus flattered, Śalya said, "O Duryodhana! As you tell me that amongst all these troops there is none but myself who is more accomplished than Kṛṣṇa, I am pleased with you. I therefore agree to act as the charioteer of the famous Karṇa while he is engaged in battle with Arjuna, foremost of the Pāṇḍavas. But there is one condition on which I accept your proposal: that I shall give vent in Karṇa's presence to such expressions as I may wish." Duryodhana, who was accompanied by Karṇa, readily accepted this condition, saying, "So be it."

LXVIII

After Śalya had taken over as his charioteer, Karṇa said to him, "Today I shall fearlessly fight Kṛṣṇa and Arjuna, foremcst among all wielders of weapons. My mind is, however, troubled by the curse of Paraśurāma, that best of Brāhmaṇas. In my early days, desirous of obtaining a celestial weapon, I lived with him in the disguise of a Brāhmaṇa. But, O Śalya, in order to benefit Arjuna, Iṅdra, the king of the gods, took on the horrible form of an insect and stung my thigh. Even so, I remained motionless for fear of disturbing my preceptor. When he woke up, he saw what had happened. He subsequently learnt the deception I had practised on him, and cursed me, that the invocation for the weapon I had obtained by such trickery would not come to my memory at the time of dire need."

"Once while wandering in the forest," Karṇa continued, "I accidentally killed the sacrificial cow of a Brāhmaṇa. Although I offered him seven hundred elephants with large tusks, and many hundreds of male and female slaves, the best of Brāhmaṇas was still not pleased, and although I begged for forgiveness, he said: 'O sūta, what I have prophesied will happen. It cannot be otherwise.' He had said, 'Your wheel shall fall into a hole.' In this battle, while I am fighting, that will be my only fear."

During the fighting on that day there was a dreadful and thrilling battle between Karṇa and the Pāṇḍavas which increased the domain of the god of Death. After that terrible and gory combat only a few of the brave Saṁśaptakas survived. Then Dhṛṣṭadyumna and the rest of the Pāṇḍavas rushed towards Karṇa and attacked him. As a mountain receives heavy rainfall, so Karṇa received those warriors in battle. Elsewhere on the battlefield Duḥśāsana boldly went up to Bhīma and shot many arrows at him. Bhīma leapt like a lion attacking a deer, and hurried towards him. The struggle that took place between those two, incensed against each other and careless of life, was truly superhuman.

Fighting fiercely, Prince Duḥśāsana achieved many difficult feats in that duel. With a single shaft he cut off Bhīma's bow; with six shafts he pierced Bhīma's driver. Then, without losing a moment, he pierced Bhīma himself with many shafts discharged with great speed and power, while Bhīma hurled his mace at the prince. With that weapon, from a distance of ten bow-lengths, Bhīma forcibly dislodged Duḥśāsana from his car. Struck by the mace, and thrown to the ground, Duḥśāsana began to tremble. His charioteer and all his steeds were slain, and his car too was smashed to pieces by Bhīma's weapon.

Then Bhīma remembered all the hostile acts of Duḥśāsana towards the Pāṇḍavas. Jumping down from his car, he stood on the ground, looking steadily on his fallen foe. Drawing his keen-edged sword, and trembling with rage, he placed his foot upon the throat of Duḥśāsana and, ripping open the breast of his enemy, drank his warm lifeblood, little by little. Then, looking at him with wrathful eyes, he said, "I consider the taste of this blood superior to that of my mother's milk, or honey, or ghee, or wine, or excellent water, or milk, or curds, or buttermilk."

All those who stood around Bhīma and saw him drink the blood of Duḥśāsana fled in terror, saying to each other, "This one is no human being!" Bhīma then said, in the hearing of all those heroes, "O wretch among men, here I drink your lifeblood. Abuse us once more now, 'Beast, beast,' as you did before!"

Having spoken these words, the victorious Bhīma turned to Kṛṣṇa and Arjuna, and said, "O you heroes, I have accomplished today what I had vowed in respect of Duḥśāsana! I will soon fulfil my other vow by slaying that second sacrificial beast, Duryodhana! I shall kick the head of that evil one with my foot in the presence of the Kauravas, and I shall then obtain peace!" After this speech, Bhīma, drenched with blood, uttered loud shouts and roared with joy, even as the mighty Iṅdra of a thousand eyes after slaying Vṛtra.

LXIX

Fleeing in the face of Arjuna's onslaught, the broken divisions of the Kauravas saw Arjuna's weapon swelling with energy and careering like lightning. But Karṇa destroyed that fiery weapon of Arjuna with his own weapon of great power which he had obtained from Paraśurāma. The encounter between Arjuna and Karṇa became very fierce. They attacked each other with arrows like two fierce elephants attacking each other with their tusks.

Karṇa then fixed on his bowstring the keen, blazing, and fierce shaft which he had long polished and preserved with the object of destroying Arjuna. Placing in position that shaft of fierce energy and blazing splendour, that venomous weapon which had its origin in the family of Airāvata and which lay within a golden quiver covered by sandal dust, Karṇa aimed it at Arjuna's head. When he saw Karṇa aim that arrow, Śalya said, "O Karṇa, this arrow will not succeed in hitting Arjuna's neck! Aim carefully, and discharge another arrow that may succeed in striking the head of your enemy!" His eyes burning in wrath, Karṇa replied, "O Śalya, Karṇa never aims an arrow twice!"

Thereupon Karṇa carefully let loose that mighty snake in the form of an arrow, which he had worshipped for many long years, saying, "You are slain, O Arjuna!" Seeing the snake aimed by Karṇa, Kṛṣṇa, strongest among the mighty, exerted his whole strength and pressed down Arjuna's chariot with his feet into the earth. When the car itself had sunk into the ground the steeds, too, bent their knees and laid themselves down upon the earth. The arrow then struck and dislodged Arjuna's diadem, that excellent ornament celebrated throughout the earth and the heavens.

The snake said, "O Kṛṣṇa! Know me as one who has been wronged by Arjuna. My enmity towards him stems from his having slain my mother!"

Then Kṛṣṇa said to Arjuna, "Slay that great snake which is your enemy." Thus urged by Kṛṣṇa, Arjuna asked, "Who is this snake that advances of his own accord against me, as if right against the mouth of Garuḍa?"[1] Kṛṣṇa replied, "While you were worshipping the fire-god at the Khāndava forest, this snake was ensconced within his mother's body, which was shattered by your arrows." As the snake took a slanting course across the sky, Arjuna cut it to pieces with six keen shafts, so that it fell down on the earth.

Then, because of the curse of the Brāhmaṇa, Karṇa's chariot wheel fell off, and his car began to reel. At the same time, he forgot the invocation for the weapon he had obtained from Paraśurāma. Unable to endure these calamities, Karṇa waved his arms and began to rail at righteousness, saying, "They that are conversant with virtue say that righteousness protects the righteous! But today righteousness does not save me."

Speaking thus, he shed tears of wrath, and said to Arjuna, "O Pāṇḍava! Spare me for a moment while I extricate my wheel from the earth! You are on your car while I am standing weak and languid on the ground. It is not fair that you should slay me now! You are born in the Kṣatriya order. You are the scion of a high race. Recollect the teachings of righteousness, and give me a moment's time!"

Then, from Arjuna's chariot, Kṛṣṇa said, "It is fortunate, O Karṇa, that you now remember virtue. It is generally true that those who are mean rail at Providence when they are afflicted by distress, but forget their own misdeeds. You and Duryodhana and Duḥśāsana and Śakuni caused Draupadī, clad in a single garment, to be brought into the midst of the assembly. On that occasion, O Karṇa, this virtue of yours was not in evidence! When Śakuni, skilled in dicing, vanquished Yudhiṣṭhira who was unacquainted with it, where was this virtue of yours? Out of covetousness, and relying on Śakuni, you

[1] The traditional enemy of snakes.

again summoned the Pāṇḍavas to a game of dice. Whither then had this virtue of yours gone?"

When Kṛṣṇa thus taunted Karṇa, Arjuna became filled with rage. Remembering the incidents to which Kṛṣṇa alluded, he blazed with fury and, bent upon Karṇa's speedy destruction, took out of his quiver an excellent weapon. He then fixed on his bow that unrivalled arrow, and charged it with mantras. Drawing his bow Gāṇḍīva, he quickly said, "Let this shaft of mine be a mighty weapon capable of speedily destroying the body and heart of my enemy. If I have ever practised ascetic austerities, gratified my preceptors, and listened to the counsels of well-wishers, let this sharp shaft, so long worshipped by me, slay my enemy Karṇa by that Truth!"

Having uttered these words, Arjuna discharged for the destruction of Karṇa, that terrible shaft, that blazing arrow fierce and efficacious as a rite prescribed in the Atharva of Añgiras, and invincible against the god of Death himself in battle. Thus sped by that mighty warrior, the shaft endowed with the energy of the Sun caused all the points of the compass to blaze with light. The head of the commander of the Kaurava army, splendid as the Sun, fell like the Sun disappearing in the blood-red sunset behind the western hills. Cut off by Arjuna's arrow and deprived of life, the tall trunk of Karṇa, with blood gushing from every wound, fell down like the thunder-riven summit of a mountain of red chalk with crimson streams running down its sides after a shower of rain.

Then from the body of the fallen Karṇa a light, passing through the atmosphere, illumined the sky. This wonderful sight was seen by all the warriors on the battlefield. After the heroic Karṇa was thus thrown down and stretched on the earth, pierced with arrows and bathed in blood, Śalya, the king of the Madras, withdrew with Karṇa's car. The Kauravas, afflicted with fear, fled from the field, frequently looking back on Arjuna's lofty standard which blazed in splendour.

Śalya Parva

LXX

After Karṇa's death the Kaurava forces were again without a leader. Then Aśvatthāmā said to Duryodhana, "Let Śalya become the commander of our army. In birth, in prowess, in energy, in fame, in beauty, and in every other accomplishment, he is qualified to lead us. He has joined us out of gratitude, having abandoned his own nephews. He has a large army of his own, and in personal valour he is without a rival. With Śalya as our commander, O king, we will be able to gain victory, as did the celestials after they made the invincible Skanda their commander."

Duryodhana, alighting from his car, respectfully folded his hands and, approaching Śalya, who was on his car, he said, "O brave hero! Become our commander in chief! When you go to battle, the Pāṇḍavas and their counsellors will lose heart, and the Pāñcālas will be depressed." Śalya answered, "O king of the Kurus, I will do as you desire. My life, my kingdom, my wealth, and everything else that belongs to me are at your disposal."

On the eighteenth day, the Kaurava soldiers led by Śalya once more rushed with great impetuosity into battle against the Pāṇḍavas. Śalya performed a wonderful feat in fighting the whole Pāṇḍava army singlehanded and slaying the opposing forces on all sides. When he saw his soldiers thus being killed by the king of the Madras, Yudhiṣṭhira was seized with rage. He swore: "Either Śalya shall kill me in battle today or I shall kill him."

Having made that vow, Yudhiṣṭhira proceeded against the king of the Madras. He took up a shining dart whose handle was made of gold and set with gems, and having inspired it with terrible mantras, and charged it with tremendous velocity by the exercise of great power and care, he hurled it along the best trajectory for the destruction of Śalya. The dart cut through his very vitals to penetrate his fair and broad chest, and then entered the earth as easily as if it were diving into water. Slain by Yudhiṣṭhira in fair fight, Śalya appeared like the dying embers of a sacrificial fire.

In the course of that day's battle Śakuni proceeded against Sahadeva. As Śakuni rushed quickly towards him, the valiant Sahadeva discharged at him veritable showers of quick-coursing arrows like a swarm of insects. Ulūka struck Bhīma with ten arrows. Meanwhile Śakuni gave Sahadeva a mighty blow on the head with a lance. Stunned, Sahadeva sat down on the platform of his car.

Desirous of rescuing his father, Ulūka again attacked Bhīma with seven arrows and Sahadeva with seventy. Bhīma retaliated by hitting Ulūka with many keen arrows and Śakuni with sixty-four. At this stage the heroic and brave Sahadeva cut off Ulūka's head with a broad-headed arrow.

Seeing his son slain, Śakuni's voice was choked with tears. Sighing heavily, he recollected the words of Vidura. Filled with anger, he rushed, singlehanded, against Sahadeva and, eager to kill him, attacked him with a lance ornamented with gold. Sahadeva aimed at him a broad-headed arrow made of hard iron, adorned with wings of gold, capable of penetrating every armour. Shot with great force and care, the arrow cut off Śakuni's head from his trunk. Thereupon the Pāṇḍava forces were filled with joy. Rejoicing with Kṛṣṇa, they blew their conches. All of them praised Sahadeva and said, "By good luck, O hero, you have killed the wicked Śakuni of evil ways, along with his son."

LXXI

After the fall of Ulūka and Śakuni, their followers were enraged. Prepared to sacrifice their lives in that fierce encounter, they began to oppose the Pāṇḍavas. Duryodhana too was filled with rage. Collecting his remaining chariots, still many hundreds in number, as well as his elephants, horses, and foot soldiers, he said these words to those warriors: "Kill the Pāṇḍavas with their friends and allies in this battle, and also the Pāñcāla prince with his own army. Then you may turn back from the field."

Respectfully obeying that mandate, the invincible warriors proceeded once more against the Pāṇḍavas. But because it had no leader, that army was destroyed in an instant by those great warriors the Pāṇḍavas. Thus all the eleven akṣauhiṇis of troops which had been collected by Duryodhana were killed by the Pāṇḍavas and the Sṛñjayas.

Looking on all sides, Duryodhana saw the field empty, and himself deprived of all his troops. Meanwhile the Pāṇḍavas, greatly pleased at having attained all their objects, were roaring aloud in joy. Overcome by despair, and bereft of troops and animals, Duryodhana decided to flee from the field. Taking up his mace, he fled on foot towards a lake.

In Duryodhana's army, which had consisted of many hundreds of thousands of warriors, not one single car-warrior was alive, save Aśvatthāmā the heroic son of Droṇa, Kṛtavarmā, Kṛpa, and Duryodhana himself. Duryodhana said to Sañjaya, "Tell the blind king that his son Duryodhana has entered into a lake." He then entered the waters of the lake, which he charmed by his power of wizardry.

Then the old men, who had been engaged to look after the ladies of the royal household, started for the city, followed by the princesses, who wept aloud when they heard of the destruction of the whole army. After the flight of the royal ladies the Kaurava camp was entirely empty, except for the three car-warriors. Filled with anxiety, and hoping to rescue Duryodhana, they too proceeded towards the lake.

Meanwhile Yudhiṣṭhira and his brothers felt happy, and ranged over the field with the desire to kill Duryodhana. Though they searched carefully for him everywhere, they could not discover the Kuru king who, mace in hand, had fled quickly from the field of battle, entered the lake, and solidified the water by his magic.

Not seeing Duryodhana who had thus concealed himself, and

wishing to put an end to that sinful man's evil courses, the Pāṇḍavas sent spies in all directions on the field of battle. Some hunters brought news of Duryodhana's whereabouts to Bhīma. Rewarding them with immense wealth, Bhīma disclosed this news to the righteous King Yudhiṣṭhira, saying, "Duryodhana, O king, has been found by the hunters who supply me with meat. He for whom you feel sorry now lies within a lake whose waters have been turned solid by him."

Thereupon, with Kṛṣṇa in the lead, Yudhiṣṭhira proceeded toward that lake, accompanied by Arjuna, the twins, Dhṛṣṭadyumna, the invincible Śikhaṇḍī, Uttamaujas, Yudhāmanyu, the great car-warrior Sātyaki, the five sons of Draupadī, and those amongst the Pāñcālas who had survived, with all their elephants, and infantry by the hundreds.

LXXII

Having arrived at the banks of the Dvaipāyana lake, they saw the reservoir enchanted by Duryodhana. Then Yudhiṣṭhira said to Kṛṣṇa, "Behold, the son of Dhṛtarāṣṭra has charmed these waters by his power of wizardry, and lives within them, without fear of injury." Kṛṣṇa replied, "With your own power of wizardry, O Bhārata, destroy this illusion of Duryodhana."

Then Yudhiṣṭhira derisively said to Duryodhana, who was still within the waters of the lake, "Why, O Duryodhana, have you charmed these waters, after having caused the death of all the Kṣatriyas, as well as your own family? Why have you entered this lake today, in order to save your own life? Arise and fight us, O Suyodhana!"

From the depths of the lake, Duryodhana replied, "It was not for the sake of saving my life, nor from fear, nor from grief, that I entered this lake. It was only out of fatigue that I did so. The Kurus for whose sake I desired sovereignty, those brothers of mine, all lie dead on the battlefield. This empty earth is now yours. Who could wish to rule a kingdom bereft of allies? As for myself, clad in deerskins I shall retire to the forest. Friendless as I am, I have no desire to live."

"You may now be willing, O Suyodhana," said Yudhiṣṭhira, "to make a gift of the earth to me. However, I do not wish to rule the earth as a gift from you. Before this, you would not agree to give me even so much of the earth as could be covered by the point of a needle. Either rule the earth after having defeated us, or go to the celestial regions after being slain by us."

Duryodhana said, "You Pāṇḍavas have friends, cars, and animals. I, however, am alone now, without a car or a mount. Alone as I am, and devoid of weapons, how can I venture to fight on foot against countless foes, all well armed and having cars? O Yudhiṣṭhira, fight one at a time with me. It is not fair that one should be called upon to fight with many, especially when that one is without armour, tired and wounded, and devoid of both animals and troops."

Thus challenged, Yudhiṣṭhira replied, "Fight any one of us, choosing whatever weapon you like. The rest of us will remain spectators. I grant you also this other wish of yours, that if you kill any one of us, you shall then become king. Otherwise, you shall be killed, and go to heaven."

"Brave as you are," answered Duryodhana, "if you allow me the option of fighting only one of you, I choose to fight with this mace that I have in my hand. Let any of you who thinks that he is a match for me come forward and fight me on foot, armed with mace." So saying, Duryodhana emerged from the water and stood there, mace in hand, his limbs covered with blood.

At the conclusion of this parley Kṛṣṇa, worked up with wrath, said to Yudhiṣṭhira, "Planning to kill Bhīma, O king, Duryodhana has practised with the mace upon a statue of iron for thirteen years. Except for Bhīma, I do not at this moment see any match for Duryodhana. However, Bhīma has not practised as hard as Duryodhana. I do not see any man in the world today, nor even a god, who can defeat the mace-armed Duryodhana in battle. In a fair fight between Duryodhana and Bhīma, our victory will be in doubt because Duryodhana is powerful, practised, and skilful."

Bhīma was, however, more confident. He said, "I shall surely kill Duryodhana in battle. I feel that the victory of the righteous Yudhiṣṭhira is certain. This mace of mine is one and a half times as heavy as Duryodhana's. Do not give way to anxiety. I dare to fight him, selecting the mace as the weapon. All of you, O Kṛṣṇa, witness this encounter!"

After Bhīma had said these words, Kṛṣṇa joyfully applauded him and said, "Thanks to you, O mighty Bhīma, the righteous King Yudhiṣṭhira will regain prosperity after achieving the destruction of all his foes. You should, however, always fight with care against Duryodhana. He is endowed with skill and strength and loves to fight."

When the fierce duel was about to start, and when all the great Pāṇḍavas had taken their seats, Balarāma came there, having heard that a battle between those two heroes, both of whom were his disciples, was about to start. Seeing him, the Pāṇḍavas and Kṛṣṇa were filled with joy. They greeted him and saluted him with due rites. They then said to him, "Witness, O Rāma, the skill in battle of your two disciples."

LXXIII

The duel then began. Duryodhana and Bhīma fought like two bulls attacking each other with their horns. The clash of their maces produced loud peals like those of thunderbolts. After the fierce and terrible battle had lasted for some time, both contenders were exhausted. They rested for some time and then, taking up their maces, they once again began to ward off each other's attacks.

While the fight was thus raging between those two heroes, Arjuna said to Kṛṣṇa, "Who, in your opinion, is the better of these two? What is their respective merit? Tell me this, O Kṛṣṇa!"

Kṛṣṇa replied, "They are equally well instructed. Bhīma is possessed of greater strength while Duryodhana has greater skill and has practised harder. If he fights fairly, Bhīma will never succeed in gaining victory. If, however, he fights unfairly, he will surely be able to kill Duryodhana. At the time of the gambling Bhīma promised to break the thighs of Duryodhana with his mace in battle. Let him now fulfil his vow. Let him, by deception, kill the Kuru king who is the master of deception! If Bhīma does not kill him by unfair means, the son of Dhṛtarāṣṭra will surely retain the kingdom!"

Thereupon Arjuna, before Bhīma's sight, struck his own left thigh. Understanding that sign, Bhīma began to move about with his mace raised, making many kinds of manoeuvres. Seeing the energetic and angry Bhīma rushing towards him and desiring to thwart his blow, Duryodhana thought of the manoeuvre called avasthāna, and prepared to jump upwards.

Bhīma fully understood the object of his opponent. Rushing at him, with a loud roar, he fiercely hurled his mace at Duryodhana's thighs, as the latter jumped into the air. The mace, hurled by Bhīma, broke the thighs of Duryodhana, and he fell down, so that the earth resounded.

Having struck Duryodhana down, Bhīma approached the Kuru chief and said, "O wretch, formerly you laughed at Draupadī who had only one bit of cloth in the midst of the assembly, and you called us cows. Bear now the consequences of that insult." Saying this, he kicked the head of his fallen foe with his left foot.

Balarāma became highly incensed when he saw Duryodhana thus brought down by a blow aimed at his thighs. Raising his arms, he sorrowfully said in the midst of those kings, "Oh, fie on Bhīma, that in such a fair fight a blow should have been inflicted below the navel! Never before has such a foul blow been seen in an encounter with the mace!

"Having unfairly killed the righteous King Duryodhana," Balarāma continued, "Bhīma shall be known in the world as an unfair fighter! The righteous Duryodhana, on the other hand, shall acquire eternal blessedness!"

Kṛṣṇa then said to Yudhiṣṭhira, "O king of virtue, why do you permit such a wrong act? Why do you suffer the head of the insensible and fallen Duryodhana to be thus kicked by Bhīma with his foot? Conversant as you are with the rules of morality, why do you look on this deed with indifference?"

Yudhiṣṭhira said, "O Kṛṣṇa, Bhīma's action in angrily touching the head of the fallen king with his foot does not please me, nor am I glad at this extermination of my race! But remember how we were cheated by the sons of Dhṛtarāṣṭra! Remember too the many harsh words they addressed to us, and how they sent us in exile into the forest. On account of all those things Bhīma has been nursing a great grief in his heart! Bearing all this in mind, O Kṛṣṇa, I looked on his actions with indifference!"

LXXIV

Having regained consciousness, and forgetting his poignant and unbearable pain, Duryodhana began to assail Kṛṣṇa with sharp and bitter words. He said, "O son of Kamsa's slave, it seems to me that you have no shame, for you have forgotten that I was struck down most unfairly in violation of the rules of mace-fighting. You were responsible for this foul play, by reminding Bhīma by a hint about the breaking of my thighs. Do you think I did not mark it when Arjuna under your instructions suggested it by sign to Bhīma?

"You caused the grandsire to be slain by placing Śikhaṇḍī in front. Too, by having an elephant of the name of Aśvatthāmā killed, you made the preceptor Droṇa lay aside his weapons. Do you think that all this is not known to me? Again, when the brave Droṇa was about to be killed by the cruel Dhṛṣṭadyumna, you did not dissuade Dhṛṣṭadyumna!

"The Śakti dart that Karṇa had obtained from Indra as a boon for the destruction of Arjuna was thwarted by you through Ghaṭotkaca. Likewise you caused the powerful Bhūriśravas, with one of his arms cut off, to be slain by Sātyaki while observing the Prāya vow. When Karṇa released the snake for killing Arjuna, you frustrated the object of Aśvasena, the son of Takṣaka, that prince of snakes. Again, when the wheel of Karṇa's car sank in the mire and Karṇa was afflicted by grief and almost defeated, and when he was struggling to free his wheel, you caused Karṇa then to be slain! If your side had fought me and Karṇa, Bhīṣma, and Droṇa by fair means, victory would never have been yours.

"I have obtained that end which Kṣatriyas observant of the duties of their own order look forward to, death in battle. Who then is so fortunate as myself? I have enjoyed pleasures, such as were worthy of the very gods, which could only with difficulty be gained by other kings. I have reached the highest prosperity. Who then is so fortunate as myself? With all my well-wishers, and my younger brothers, I am going to heaven! As for yourselves, with your purposes unfulfilled, and racked with grief, live in this unhappy world!"

After Duryodhana had said these words, a shower of fragrant flowers dropped from the sky. The Gandharvas played on many charming musical instruments. The Apsaras in chorus sang his glory. The Siddhas cried, "Praise be to King Duryodhana!" Sweet and fragrant breezes mildly blew on all sides. All the quarters became clear and the sky looked azure blue. Beholding these auspicious signs and this worship offered to Duryodhana, the Pāṇḍavas, with Kṛṣṇa at their head, were put to shame. Remembering that Bhīṣma, Droṇa, Karṇa, and Bhūriśraves were killed unfairly, they were afflicted with remorse and wept in grief.

Kṛṣṇa, seeing the Pāṇḍavas stricken with remorse, said, "Those four were very great warriors and regarded as atirathas in the world. The very Regents of the Universe could not have killed them in fair fight. Duryodhana too could never have been killed in a fair fight! The same is the case with all those powerful car-warriors led by Bhīṣma. Out of the desire to do you good, I repeatedly applied my illusory powers and caused them to be killed by various means in battle. If I had not adopted such deceitful ways, you would never have been victorious, nor could you have regained your kingdom or your wealth."

He continued, "You should not mind the fact that your enemy has been killed deceitfully. When one is outnumbered by his enemies, then destruction should be brought about by stratagem. The gods themselves, in killing the asuras, have followed the same methods. The way that was followed by the celestials may be followed by all. We have been crowned with success. It is evening, and we had better retire to our tents. O kings, let us all take rest, with our horses and elephants and cars!"

LXXV

Messengers brought news of Duryodhana's defeat in the duel with

Bhīma to the remnant of the Kaurava army—Aśvatthāmā, Kṛpa, and Kṛtavarmā. Those powerful car-warriors, though wounded by arrows and other weapons, rode at breakneck pace on their swift chargers to the field of battle. There they found the high-souled Duryodhana lying on the ground like a gigantic tree in the forest felled by a storm. They saw him suffering from his wounds and covered with blood, like an elephant in the forest laid low by a hunter.

Duryodhana wiped his eyes with his hands and shed tears of grief. He said to those heroes, headed by Kṛpa, "Death has been ordained by the Creator himself, and comes to all in course of time. Though you love me, do not therefore grieve for my death. If the scriptures are to be believed, I have certainly gained eternity."

On hearing this, Aśvatthāmā burned in anger like the fire at the universal dissolution. Beside himself with rage, he wrung his hands, and said to the king in a voice choked with sobs, "My father was killed by deceit by those wretches. His death, however, does not pain me so much as the condition to which you have been reduced. Listen to these words of mine which I swear by truth itself and by all my acts of piety. I shall today, in the very presence of Kṛṣṇa, dispatch all the Pāñcālas, by all means in my power, to the abode of the god of Death. O king, grant me permission to do so."

Duryodhana was well pleased with these words of Aśvatthāmā. He said to Kṛpa, "O preceptor, bring me a pot full of water." That foremost of Brāhmaṇas at once brought a vessel full of water. Duryodhana then said to Kṛpa, "O Brāhmaṇa, may you be blessed! If you wish me well, let Aśvatthāmā be anointed as our commander in chief. At the command of the king, a Brāhmaṇa may fight, especially one who has adopted Kṣatriya ways. Those learned in the scriptures say so."

Thereupon, in accordance with the king's wishes, Kṛpa installed Aśvatthāmā as the supreme commander. After the ceremony Aṣvatthāmā embraced Duryodhana and departed, making the ten cardinal points resound with his war cry. Meanwhile the anguished Duryodhana, bathed in blood, prepared to endure that dreadful night.

LXXVI

After the fall of Duryodhana, Kṛṣṇa proceeded on his chariot to Hāstinapura and entered that city. There he saw that best of sages, Vyāsa, who had arrived before him. He respectfully saluted Vyāsa and Dhṛtarāṣṭra, as well as Gāndhārī. Holding Dhṛtarāṣṭra by the hand, Kṛṣṇa wept softly. After a while he washed his eyes and his face with water according to rules.

He then said sweetly to Dhṛtarāṣṭra, "O Bhārata, you are aware of the past and the future. You are also well acquainted with the course of time. Out of respect for you the Pāṇḍavas tried to prevent the destruction of their family and the extermination of the Kṣatriyas. On the eve of battle I myself came to you, and in the presence of all I begged of you only five villages. Out of avarice, and as destiny would have it, you did not grant my request. As a result of this transgression all the Kṣatriyas have been exterminated.

"Everyone, it seems," Kṛṣṇa continued, "loses his sense under the influence of destiny, and that perhaps is why even you acted so foolishly in regard to this matter. Knowing all this to be the fruit of your own folly, you should not now harbour any ill feeling towards the Pāṇḍavas. For both Gāndhārī and yourself the perpetuity of the race, the offering of the funeral cake, and everything else that has to be performed by one's offspring now depend on the Pāṇḍavas. I therefore plead that you and Gāndhārī should not entertain any malice towards them. You know King Yudhiṣṭhira's devotion and affection towards you. Though he has gained a victory in battle, he grieves for you and for the illustrious Gāndhārī, and does not enjoy any happiness."

Kṛṣṇa then turned to the queen and said, "You remember, O queen, those just and fair words which you yourself uttered in the assembly before me, words that were beneficial to both parties, but that your sons did not heed. Let not your heart be bent on the destruction of the Pāṇḍavas. I know that, because of the power of your penance, an angry look by you can consume the whole Earth."

Hearing these words of Kṛṣṇa, Gāndhārī said, "O Kṛṣṇa, what you say is true! I was deeply disturbed because my heart was burning with grief. After hearing your words of solace my heart has been calmed. As for the blind old king, who has now become childless, you and the Pāṇḍavas are his only refuge!" Saying so, Gāndhārī, mourning the death of her sons, covered her face with a fold of her garment and began to weep aloud.

Kṛṣṇa comforted the grief-stricken queen as well as the old king, with sweet words. At the same time, his supernatural knowledge made him aware of the evil design of Aśvatthāmā. Rising up quickly after touching Vyāsa's feet with his head, Kṛṣṇa said to Dhṛtarāṣṭra, "I take leave of you, O king! Do not grieve. I must leave you so suddenly because I have come to know that Aśvatthāmā has formed a plan for destroying the Pāṇḍavas during the night."

Hearing these words, Dhṛtarāṣṭra said to Kṛṣṇa, "Go quickly, O mighty Kṛṣṇa, and protect the Pāṇḍavas. But come back and see us again soon." After Kṛṣṇa had gone, Vyāsa, worshipped of the whole world, also comforted King Dhṛtarāṣṭra.

Having achieved his mission, the virtuous Kṛṣṇa left Hāstinapura along with Dāruka and proceeded to the Pāṇḍava camp where he met the Pāṇḍavas, took his seat with them, and told them everything.

Sauptika Parva

LXXVII

Aśvatthāmā, Kṛpa, and Kṛtavarmā left Duryodhana, and had not proceeded far when they entered a dense forest, full of trees and creepers. Feeling sleepy, and being very tired as well as being wounded, they laid themselves down on the bare earth. Kṛpa and Kṛtavarmā soon fell asleep. But Aśvatthāmā, possessed by wrath and revenge, could not sleep. He lay awake, breathing heavily.

As he surveyed that forest filled with various creatures, he beheld a large banyan tree full of crows. While those birds were sleeping peacefully, Aśvatthāmā saw a terrible owl suddenly appear there. Alighting on one of the branches of the banyan tree, the owl killed a large number of the sleeping crows.

Droṇa's son began to reflect on the massacre of the crows, desirous of guiding his own conduct by the example of the owl. He said to himself, "This owl teaches me a lesson in battle. Bent as I am upon the destruction of the enemy, the time for action has come. Normally I cannot hope to kill the victorious Pāṇḍavas. They are powerful and persevering, sure of aim and skilled in attack. If I were to fight fairly with them I should surely have to lay down my life! By deceit, however, I may yet obtain success and cause great destruction to my enemies."

He then mused: "Concerning this, certain ancient verses, full of truth, and sung by righteous persons, come to my mind. They are: 'The enemy's forces should be attacked even if they are fatigued, or are wounded, or are eating, or retreating, or resting within their camp. They should be treated in the same way when sleeping at dead of night, or when bereft of commanders, or when routed, or when labouring under an error.' "

Thereupon the valiant Aśvatthāmā resolved to kill the sleeping Pāṇḍavas and Pāñcālas that very night. Having formed this wicked resolution and pledged himself repeatedly to execute it, he awoke both his uncle Kṛpa and the chief of the Bhojas Kṛtavarmā. Aroused from sleep, those two illustrious men heard Aśvatthāmā's plans. At first they both recoiled in horror from this foul scheme, but they were ultimately persuaded to participate in it.

LXXVIII

Having entered the Pāṇḍava camp, Aśvatthāmā proceeded very softly towards Dhṛṣṭadyumna's quarters. Entering his tent, he saw the prince of the Pāñcālas sleeping on his bed. Aśvatthāmā awoke him with a kick and, as he was rising from his bed, caught him by the hair of his head, pressed him down on the earth with both hands, and killed him after a struggle.

After killing Dhṛṣṭadyumna and all his followers, he saw Uttamaujas asleep on his bed. Pressing his foot on that great hero's throat and chest, Aśvatthāmā killed him while he writhed in agony. Proceeding along the various roads of the camp, Aśvatthāmā, expert in the use of the sword, saw a number of tents and killed in no time the unarmed and tired warriors sleeping within them.

Terrible to behold, he moved about in the camp like the god of death himself, and at last he saw the sons of Draupadī and the remnant of the Somakas. Remembering the death of his father, Aśvatthāmā became furious with rage. He got down from his car and made a desperate rush against his enemies. First he struck Prativindhya in the abdomen and felled him, lifeless, on the earth. Then the brave Sutasoma rushed at him with his uplifted sword. But Aśvatthāmā cut off Sutasoma's hand holding the sword, and struck him in the flank, so that Sutasoma dropped down dead.

Taking up a car wheel, the brave Śatānīka, the son of Nakula, attacked Aśvatthāmā and violently struck him on the chest. Aśvatthāmā hit back with vigour, and Śatānīka fell down, whereupon Aśvatthāmā cut off his head. Then, seizing a spiked bludgeon, Śrutakarmā attacked Aśvatthāmā, and struck him violently on his forehead. Aśvatthāmā struck back with his sword. Senseless and disfigured, Śrutakarmā fell dead on the earth.

Awakened by the noise, the heroic Śrutakīrti came up and discharged a shower of arrows on Aśvatthāmā. Defending himself with his shield, Aśvatthāmā severed his enemy's beautiful head bedecked with earrings. Then Śikhaṇḍī, along with all the Prabhadrakas, assailed Aśvatthāmā from all sides with various weapons. Śikhaṇḍī himself struck Aśvatthāmā with an arrow between his two eyebrows. Worked up with anger at this, the powerful Aśvatthāmā closed in on Śikhaṇḍī and killed him with his sword.

Aśvatthāmā then rushed furiously against the other Prabhadrakas, and the residue of Virāṭa's forces. Those that tried to flee the camp to save their lives were killed by Kṛtavarmā and Kṛpa, who were stationed at the gate. At this stage, those two set fire to the Pāṇḍava camp in three places, so that the whole encampment was in flames. Thus, before half the night was over, Aśvatthāmā had sent the large army of the Pāṇḍavas to their death.

Having killed all the Pāñcālas and the sons of Draupadī, the three Kuru heroes together came to report to Duryodhana. Speaking to Duryodhana, who, with his thighs broken, was lying almost senseless, Aśvatthāmā said, "O Duryodhana, if you are still alive, listen to these agreeable tidings. On the side of the Pāṇḍavas, only seven are alive, and among the Dhārtarāṣṭras, only we three survive. The seven on their side are the five brothers, Kṛṣṇa, and Sātyaki; on our side, the three are myself, Kṛpa, and Kṛtavarmā. All the sons of Draupadī and all the sons of Dhṛṣṭadyumna have been killed, as well as the Pāñcālas and the remnant of the Matsyas. Mark the vengeance I have taken: the Pāṇḍavas are now childless!"

On hearing these words, so pleasing to his heart, Duryodhana regained full consciousness and replied, "That which neither Bhīṣma nor Karṇa nor your father could accomplish, you have done today, with the help of Kṛpa and Kṛtavarmā. You have killed that mean wretch, Dhṛṣṭadyumna, the commander of the Pāṇḍava forces, as well as Śikhaṇḍī. For this I regard myself to be equal to Iṅdra himself. Goodbye to you all! May you prosper! All of us will meet again in the kingdom of the gods." Having said this, the great king of the Kurus breathed his last, and his soul went to heaven.

LXXIX

In the morning, Dhṛṣṭadyumna's charioteer reported to King Yudhiṣṭhira the great slaughter caused by Aśvatthāmā during the night. On hearing the terrible news, the brave Yudhiṣṭhira fainted with grief at the loss of his sons.

Soon Nakula joined Yudhiṣṭhira, accompanied by the princess Draupadī. She had been living at Upaplavya, and had heard the heart-rending news of the destruction of all her sons. Trembling like a plantain tree shaken by the wind, the princess appeared before Yudhiṣṭhira and said sadly, "O son of Kuṅtī, hearing of the slaughter of those sleeping heroes by the sinful Aśvatthāmā, grief burns me as if I were in the midst of fire. If you do not kill that wicked wretch, along with his followers, and if he is not compelled to reap the fruit of his evil deed, then I shall sit here in Prāya. I have heard that Aśvatthāmā was born with a gem on his head. I want that gem brought to me after his death in battle. Placing it on your head, O king, I shall live. This is my vow."

Having said these words to Yudhiṣṭhira, the beautiful Draupadī approached Bhīma and said to him, "Remember the duties of a Kṣatriya, O Bhīma, and protect me. Kill that sinful wretch as Iṅdra slew Śaṁbara." The brave and energetic Bhīma immediately left the Pāṇḍava camp and proceeded quickly along the track of Aśvatthāmā's car.

Then Kṛṣṇa, foremost of all bowmen, got upon his car, and set out after Bhīma, accompanied by Arjuna and Yudhiṣṭhira. Proceeding very quickly, they soon overtook the mighty Bhīma. They could not, however, stop Bhīma who, filled with anger, hotly pursued Aśvatthāmā.

Soon they reached the hermitage of the illustrious Vyāsa, who was sitting near the water's edge surrounded by many sages. There too sat Aśvatthāmā, covered with dust, clad in a piece of cloth made of Kuśa grass, and smeared all over with clarified butter. Taking up his bow and arrows, the mighty Bhīma, the son of Kuntī, rushed towards Aśvatthāmā and challenged him.

When he saw the terrible Bhīma coming towards him bow in hand, and his two brothers on Kṛṣṇa's car, Aśvatthāmā became alarmed and thought his end was near. However, being of an indomitable nature, he remembered the mighty weapon which he had obtained from his father. He took up a blade of grass with his left hand, inspired it with the proper mantras, and then released it, crying, "For the destruction of the Pāṇḍavas!" A fire was generated by that blade of grass, which appeared capable of destroying the three worlds like the all-destroying Yama at the end of the Yuga.

LXXX

From the very beginning, Kṛṣṇa had understood from signs the evil intention of Aśvatthāmā. He said to Arjuna, "The time has come for the use of the celestial weapon which was taught to you by Droṇa. For your own protection, as well as that of your brothers, discharge that weapon which is capable of counteracting all other weapons."

Thus adjured by Kṛṣṇa, Arjuna quickly got down from the car, taking with him his bow, with an arrow fixed on the string. He first wished good to his preceptor's son, and then to himself, and to all his brothers. Then he bowed to all the gods and all his superiors and finally discharged his weapon, having in mind the well-being of all the worlds and saying, "Let this weapon neutralise Aśvatthāmā's weapon."

Seeing those two weapons consuming the three worlds, two great sages came there, namely Nārada, who is the soul of every creature, and Vyāsa, the grandfather of all the Bhārata princes. They tried to pacify the two heroes, Aśvatthāmā and Arjuna. Desirous of ensuring the well-being of all creatures, the two sages took up their position between those two blazing weapons.

In response to the appeal of the two sages, Arjuna quickly resolved to withdraw his celestial arrow. Truthful, heroic, celibate, and ever obedient to his superiors as he was, Arjuna could withdraw his weapon. But, despite his desire to respond to those two sages standing before him, Aśvatthāmā could not by his own power withdraw his own dreadful weapon.

Vyāsa said to Aśvatthāmā, "Arjuna too knew the use of the weapon called Brahmaśiras. He discharged it neither from anger, nor for your destruction in battle, but only for counteracting your weapon. He has now withdrawn it. For the welfare of the Pāṇḍavas and of the kingdom, as well as for your own good, withdraw your celestial weapon. Give the Pāṇḍavas the gem which is on your head. In return, the Pāṇḍavas will grant your life."

Aśvatthāmā replied, "O holy one, whatever you command me, I shall do. Here is this gem! The arrow will, however, find its mark, for it cannot be thwarted. I am unable to withdraw it, having once discharged it. I will instead direct this weapon into the wombs of the Pāṇḍava women. As to your other commands, O sage, I will obey them"

Vyāsa appealed again to Aśvatthāmā, saying, "O pure one! Do not let this weapon enter the wombs of the Pāṇḍava women." Notwithstanding these words of the sage Vyāsa, the son of Droṇa aimed that weapon there.

Knowing that the weapon had been thus directed by the wicked Aśvatthāmā, Kṛṣṇa said with a cheerful heart, "While she was at Upaplavya, a certain pious Brāhmaṇa said to the princess Uttarā, Virāta's daughter and Arjuna's daughter-in-law, 'While the Kuru line will become extinct, a son will be born to you. This your son will for that reason be called by the name of Parikṣit.' The words of that pious man shall be fulfilled. These Pāṇḍavas shall have a son called Parikṣit for the continuance of their race. The impact of this mighty weapon will not be in vain, for the foetus will die. But it will revive and have a long life."

Then, turning to Aśvatthāmā, Kṛṣṇa said, "As for yourself, all wise men know you to be a coward and a sinful wretch. You are the slayer of children. Therefore, you must bear the fruit of your sinful deeds. For three thousand years you shall wander over this earth, without a companion and without being able to talk to anyone."

Thus cursed by Kṛṣṇa, Aśvatthāmā gave his gem to the Pāṇḍavas and cheerlessly proceeded to the forest. Led by Kṛṣṇa, the sage Vyāsa, and the great ascetic Nārada, and taking the gem that was born with Aśvatthāmā, the Pāṇḍavas quickly returned to Draupadī, who was observing Prāya.

Then,. as desired by Yudhiṣṭhira, the mighty Bhīma gave that celestial jewel to her, saying, "This gem, O blessed lady, is yours. The slayer of your sons has been defeated. Rise and shake off your sorrow, remembering the duties of a Kṣatriya lady!" Draupadī said, "I desired only revenge. The preceptor's son deserves my respect even as the preceptor himself. Let the king put this gem on his head." Taking the gem, Yudhiṣṭhira placed it on his head, as wished by Draupadī, treating it as a gift from the preceptor.

Strī Parva

LXXXI

Having lost all his sons, King Dhṛtarāṣṭra was grief-stricken. Looking like a tree shorn of its branches, he was overcome by depression and lost his power of speech. The wise Sañjaya approached the king and said to him, "Why do you grieve, O monarch? Forget your sorrow, and arrange for the due performance of the obsequial rites of your fathers, sons, grandsons, kinsmen, preceptors, and friends."

Dhṛtarāṣṭra lamented, "Deprived as I am of sons and counsellors and all my friends, I shall have to wander in sorrow over the earth. In the midst of the assembly, Kṛṣṇa told me what was for my good. He said, 'Let us end hostilities, O king! Let your son take the entire kingdom, except for five villages.' Foolishly I disregarded that advice, and I am now forced to repent. I must have committed great sins in my previous births, and hence the Creator has made me suffer such grief in this life. Ask the Pāṇḍavas to come and see me this very day, determined as I am upon following the long way that leads to the regions of Brahmā."

Though he too was grief-stricken because of the death of his own sons, Yudhiṣṭhira, accompanied by his brothers, set out to see Dhṛtarāṣṭra. He was followed by Kṛṣṇa and Sātyaki, and by Yuyutsu. The grieving princess Draupadī too, accompanied by the Pāñcāla ladies, sorrowfully followed.

Having duly saluted their sire, the Pāṇḍavas announced themselves to him, each uttering his own name.[1] Dhṛtarāṣṭra first greeted the eldest son of Pāṇḍu, Yudhiṣṭhira, who was the cause of the slaughter of all his sons. Having embraced Yudhiṣṭhira and spoken a few

[1] Since, being blind, he could not see them.

comforting words to him, the wicked Dhṛtarāṣṭra sought Bhīma, like a fire ready to burn everything that would approach it. Understanding his wicked intentions towards Bhīma, Kṛṣṇa dragged away the real Bhīma, and presented an iron statue of the second son of Pāṇḍu to the old king. Grasping with his two arms that iron statue, the powerful king broke it into pieces, taking it for the real Bhīma.

His passion gone, the king then cast off his anger and became normal. Overcome by grief, he began to weep aloud, "Alas, O Bhīma! Alas!" Knowing that he was no longer under the influence of anger, and that he was truly sorry for having, as he believed, slain Bhīma, Kṛṣṇa said, "Do not grieve, O Dhṛtarāṣṭra, for you have not killed Bhīma. What you broke was only an iron statue."

LXXXII

Then, at the request of Dhṛtarāṣṭra, the Pāṇḍava brothers, accompanied by Kṛṣṇa, went to see Gāndhārī. The innocent Gāndhārī was grief-stricken at the death of her hundred sons. Recalling that Yudhiṣṭhira had killed all his enemies, she wished to curse him. Knowing her evil intentions, Vyāsa prepared to keep them from being fulfilled.

He said to her, "Do not be angry with the Pāṇḍavas, O Gāndhārī! May you have peace! Control the words you are about to say! Listen to my counsel." Gāndhārī said, "Thanks to the folly of Duryodhana and Śakuni, of Karṇa and Duḥśāsana, this extinction of the Kurus has taken place. But in the very presence of Kṛṣṇa, Bhīma did something that excites my anger. Having challenged Duryodhana to a deadly duel with the mace, and knowing that my son was superior to him in skill, he struck him below the navel. It is this that provokes my wrath. Why should heroes forget their duties to save their lives?"

Hearing these words of Gāndhārī, Bhīma was afraid, and tried to soothe her. He said, "Whether the deed was fair or unfair, I did it through fear and to protect my own self! Please forgive me now! Your son was incapable of being killed by anybody in a fair fight. And therefore I did what was unfair."

Gāndhārī then said, "When Vṛṣasena had deprived Nakula of his horses, you drank Duḥśāsana's blood in battle. That was an act of cruelty which is censured by the good, becoming only to an unworthy person. It was an evil act, O Bhīma!"

"It is wrong to drink the blood of even a stranger," Bhīma replied. "One's brother is like one's own self, and there is no difference between them. The blood, however, did not pass my lips and teeth, as Karṇa knew well. Only my hands were covered with Duḥśāsana's blood. When Draupadī was seized by the hair after the gambling match, in my anger I gave vent to certain words which I still remember. For all the years to come I would have been deemed to have neglected the duties of a Kṣatriya if I had left that promise unfulfilled. It was for this reason, O queen, that I committed that act." Gāndhārī wailed, "You have killed a hundred sons of this old man [Dhṛtarāṣṭra]! Why did you not spare even one son of this old couple, deprived of their kingdom, who had committed only a minor offence?"

LXXXIII

Filled with anger at the slaughter of all her sons and grandsons, Gāndhārī then inquired after Yudhiṣṭhira, saying, "Where is the king?" After she had asked for him, Yudhiṣṭhira approached her, trembling and with joined hands, and said these soft words, "Here is Yudhiṣṭhira, O queen, that cruel destroyer of your sons! I deserve your curses, for I am the real cause of this universal destruction! Curse me! I do not care for life, for kingdom, or for wealth, having killed such friends."

Sighing heavily, Gāndhārī could say nothing to Yudhiṣṭhira as, overcome with fear, he stood in her presence. When Yudhiṣṭhira, with body bent, was about to prostrate himself at her feet, the far-sighted Kuru queen, conversant as she was with righteousness, directed her eyes from within the folds of the cloth that covered them to the tip of Yudhiṣṭhira's toe. Thereupon, the king whose nails had till then been perfect came to have a scorched nail on his toe.

Seeing this, Arjuna moved behind Kṛṣṇa, and the other Pāṇḍavas too became restless. Meanwhile Gāṅdhārī shook off her anger, and comforted the Pāṇḍavas as a mother should. With her permission those heroes then proceeded to see their mother.

Seeing her sons after a long time, Kuṅtī, who had been filled with anxiety for them, covered her face with a fold of her garment and shed copious tears. She then repeatedly embraced and patted each of her sons. Next she consoled Draupadī who had lost all her children and who was lying on the bare earth, wailing piteously. Raising the grief-stricken princess of Pāñcāla who was weeping thus, Kuṅtī began to comfort her.

Accompanied by Draupadī, and followed by her sons, Kuṅtī then proceeded towards the sorrowful Gāṅdhārī, though she herself was in greater sorrow. Seeing that illustrious lady with her daughter-in-law, Gāṅdhāṛī said, "Do not grieve thus, O daughter. I too am much afflicted with grief. I think this universal destruction has been caused by the irresistible course of Time. Since it was not brought about by human agency, this dreadful slaughter was inevitable. What the wise Vidura foretold, after Kṛṣṇa's supplication for peace had failed, has now come to pass!"

Gāṅdhārī then said to Kṛṣṇa, "The Pāṇḍavas and the sons of Dhṛtarāṣṭra have destroyed each other. Why did you look on while they were thus exterminating each other? Because you were deliberately indifferent to their destruction, you shall obtain the fruit of this act. O Kṛṣṇa, by constant service to my husband I have acquired a little merit. By that merit, which was so difficult to obtain, I now curse you. Since you remained indifferent while the Kauravas and Pāṇḍavas slew each other, O Kṛṣṇa, you shall be the slayer of your own kinsmen. Thirty-six years hence you shall, after causing the death of your kinsmen, friends, and son, perish by ignoble means in the wilderness."

Śānti Parva

LXXXIV

Along with Vidura, Dhṛtarāṣṭra, and all the Bhārata ladies, the Pāṇḍavas offered oblations of water to all their departed kinsmen and friends. The noble descendants of the Kurus then passed a month of purification outside the city. Many famous sages came there to see the virtuous King Yudhiṣṭhira. Among them were Vyāsa, Nārada, the great sage Devala, Devasthāna, and Kaṇva, and their worthy disciples.

Yudhiṣṭhira said, "I am haunted by grief because of the death in battle of young Abhimanyu, the sons of Draupadī, Dhṛṣṭadyumna, Virāṭa, King Drupada, Vasuṣeṇa, King Dhṛṣṭaketu, and other kings coming from various countries. I feel that, through my desire to recover my kingdom, I caused the destruction of my kinsmen and the extermination of my own race. I am an evil-doer and a sinner and the cause of the destruction of the earth. Seated as I am now, I shall starve myself to death."

Vyāsa consoled Yudhiṣṭhira, saying, "You should not, O king, grieve so. I shall repeat what I have once said. All this is Destiny. Do what you have been created to do by your Maker. That is your fulfilment. Remember, O king, you are not your own master.

"O king, do not indulge in grief!" Vyāsa continued. "Remember the duties of a Kṣatriya, All those fighters were killed while performing their legitimate duties. You too have performed the duties of a Kṣatriya and obtained the kingdom blamelessly. Do your duty now, O son of Kuntī, and you shall obtain happiness in the next world." Thus was Yudhiṣṭhira comforted, and persuaded to return to his kingdom.

When the Pāṇḍavas reentered the city, many thousands of citizens came out to greet them. Entering the interior of the palace, the illustrious Yudhiṣṭhira approached the deities and worshipped them with offerings of gems and incense and garlands of all kinds.

Freed of his grief and his sickness of heart, Yudhiṣṭhira cheerfully sat facing eastward on an excellent seat made of gold. Those two heroes, Sātyaki and Kṛṣṇa, sat facing him on a seat covered by a rich carpet. On either side of the king sat the great-minded Bhīma and Arjuna upon two soft seats set with gems. Upon a white ivory couch, decked with gold, sat Kuntī with Sahadeva and Nakula.

Then by Kṛṣṇa's leave the priest Dhaumya consecrated, according to rule, an altar facing the east and the north. He next seated the great Yudhiṣṭhira and Draupadī upon a soft seat covered with a tiger-skin, called Sarvatobhadra. Thereafter he began to pour libations of clarified butter upon the sacrificial fire while chanting the prescribed incantations. King Dhṛtarāṣṭra was first to anoint Yudhiṣṭhira and all the others followed him. Thus worshipped by those pious men, Yudhiṣṭhira the king of virtue, with his friends, was restored to his kingdom.

Accepting the greetings of his subjects, King Yudhiṣṭhira answered them, saying: "Blessed are the sons of Pāṇḍu, whose merits, deservedly or otherwise, are thus recited in this world by the foremost of Brāhmaṇas assembled together. King Dhṛtarāṣṭra, however, is our father and supreme deity. Those who wish to please me should obey his commands and respect his every wish. The whole world is his, as are the Pāṇḍavas, and everybody else. These words of mine should be borne in mind by all of you."

Having given the citizens and the villagers leave to depart, the Kuru king appointed his brother Bhīma as yuvarāja. He gladly appointed the highly intelligent Vidura to help him with advice and to look after the sixfold requirements[1] of the state. The venerable Sañjaya, wise and thoughtful and endued with every accomplishment, was designated as the superintendent of finances.

Nakula was placed in charge of the forces, to give them food and

[1] Peace, war, marching, halting, sowing dissensions among opponents, and strengthening the defence of the kingdom by seeking alliances and constructing forts.

pay and to look after the other affairs of the army. Yudhiṣṭhira made Arjuna responsible for resisting hostile forces and punishing the wicked. Dhaumya, the foremost of priests, was asked to attend to the Brāhmaṇas and to perform all Vedic rites and all other rites. Sahadeva was always to remain by Yudhiṣṭhira's side, as his protector.

Anuśāsana Parva

LXXXV

Meanwhile Bhīṣma, foremost among the Kauravas, was lying on a bed of arrows—a bed worthy of heroes. The Pāṇḍavas gathered around him, and the wise Yudhiṣṭhira heard from him many expositions on the subject of duty which removed all his doubts.

Then Vyāsa said to Bhīṣma, "O king, Yudhiṣṭhira has been restored to his own, along with his brothers and the kings who followed him. With Kṛṣṇa by his side he salutes you, O tiger among men! Give him leave to return to the city."

Thereupon Bhīṣma permitted Yudhiṣṭhira and his counsellors to leave. Addressing his grandson in a sweet voice, the royal son of Śantanu added, "When my time comes, and when the Sun, stopping in his southward course, begins to return northward, then you may return here, O king!"

Bhīṣma, when it was time for him to leave this world, remained silent for a while. He then held his life breath according to rites. By means of yoga, the parts of Bhīṣma's body became whole one after another. Within a short time, in the very sight of the assembled kings, the entire body of Bhīṣma became free of wounds and whole. On seeing this, all the great personages, headed by Kṛṣṇa, and all the sages, including Vyāsa, were filled with wonder.

The life breath, restrained and unable to escape, at last broke through the crown of Bhīṣma's head and ascended to heaven, as the celestial kettledrums began to play and there was a rain of flowers. The holy men assembled were filled with delight and exclaimed, "Excellent, excellent!" Thus did Bhīṣma, that pillar of Bharata's race, unite with eternity.

Then the great Pāṇḍavas and Vidura collected a large quantity of wood and various kinds of fragrant scents, and made a funeral pyre. They cremated Bhīṣma's body and proceeded to the sacred river Gaṅgā, accompanied by the sages. Arrived at the sacred river, they duly offered oblations of water to the great son of Gaṅgā.

Then the goddess Gaṅgā herself emerged from the river, weeping and distracted by sorrow. In the midst of her lamentations; she said, "O kings! Listen to me as I tell you all that took place. My son Bhīṣma was of regal bearing, and endowed with wisdom and high birth. He was the benefactor of all the elders of his family. He was devoted to his father and was a strict observer of vows. He could not be defeated even by Paraśurāma, son of Jamadagni. Alas, that such a hero was killed by Śikhaṇḍī. Truly, my heart must be made of adamant, since it does not break even on the disappearance of that son from my view. At the svayaṁvara at Kāśī, single-handed he defeated the assembled Kṣatriyas and carried away the princesses. There was no one on earth who equalled my son in prowess; alas, that my heart does not break upon hearing of his slaughter by Śikhaṇḍī."

Listening to the goddess of the great river bewail her son's death, Kṛṣṇa consoled her with many soothing words. He said, "O Gaṅgā, be comforted. Do not give way to sorrow. There is no doubt that your son has gone to the highest region. He was one of the celestial Vasus, who had to assume human form because of a curse. He has happily gone to Heaven of his own will. All the gods could not have killed him in battle. Do not, therefore, grieve for him, O goddess. Let the fever of your heart be dispelled."

Thus consoled by Kṛṣṇa and also by Vyāsa, that queen of all rivers Gaṅgā cast off her grief, and reverted to her nature as a river. All those present, headed by Kṛṣṇa, honoured the river-goddess and received her permission to depart.

Aśvamedha Parva

LXXVI

After Bhīṣma had passed away, Kṛṣṇa prepared to return to Dvārakā. The Pāṇḍavas embraced him in farewell and then let him depart. As he proceeded toward Dvārakā, he came upon a sandy desert, where he saw that foremost of ascetics, the sage Utañka. After mutual salutations, Utañka asked, "O Kṛṣṇa, by your mediation between the Pāṇḍavas and the Kauravas, did you succeed in establishing a durable understanding, such as should exist between brothers?"

Kṛṣṇa replied, "I tried my best to bring about peace with the Kauravas. But in spite of all my efforts, I could not succeed in averting war. And it happened that all the Kauravas with their relatives and kinsmen died." "It seems to me, O Kṛṣṇa," said Utānka, "that you could have saved the Kauravas who have all met with destruction, if you had not been indifferent to their fate."

"O best of Brāhmaṇas," answered Kṛṣṇa, "know that Dharma whose essence is mercy for all creatures is my eldest offspring, born from my mind. I take birth in various forms, constantly changing myself, in order to protect Virtue and to establish it. In this task, I seek the help of men both living and departed. I am the creator of all objects that exist. Knowing no change myself, I am also the destroyer of all creatures that live in sinfulness.

"In every cycle," he continued, "I have to repair the causeway of Virtue, and I am born in diverse forms, out of my desire to do good to my creatures. When I am born among the celestials, I act like a celestial. When I am born among the Gaṅdharvas, I act in every respect like a Gaṅdharva. Since I am now born in the order of men,

I appealed to the Kauravas as a human being. But stupefied as they were and deprived of their senses, they refused to accept my counsel and ignored my piteous entreaties. I then became angry, and tried to frighten them. But once more I had to revert to my human form. Those unrighteous men, assailed by fate, were righteously killed in battle, and have no doubt gone to the celestial region. The Pāṇḍavas too have acquired great fame. O best of Brāhmaṇas, this is my answer to your accusation."

LXXXVII

Even before his departure for Dvārakā, Kṛṣṇa had promised Yudhiṣṭhira that he would return to Hāstinapura when the time fixed for the horse sacrifice had come. Accordingly Kṛṣṇa returned to Hāstinapura some time later and was met by Kuntī, who said to him in a voice choking with sobs, "O hero, this child of your sister's son was killed by Aśvatthāmā and is stillborn. Please revive him, as you promised to do. In this child is contained the life breath of the Pāṇḍavas and myself! On him depends the obsequial cake[1] of Pāṇḍu, as well as that of my father-in-law, and of Abhimanyu too, that favourite nephew of yours who was so like you!"

Thereupon Kṛṣṇa, who had promised to revive the child, said these words, in the hearing of the whole universe, to the princess Uttarā, "O Uttarā, I never utter a falsehood. My words will prove true. I shall revive this child in the presence of all. As virtue is dear to me, let Abhimanyu's son, who was born dead, live!" After these words were pronounced by Kṛṣṇa, the child began gradually to show signs

[1] "Obsequial cake" or piṇḍa is a ball or cake of cooked rice or flour offered to one's deceased ancestors at a Srāddha ceremony. Monier-Williams observes that a Srāddha is "not a funeral ceremony but a supplement" to it: it is "an act of reverential homage to a deceased person performed by relatives, and is moreover supposed to supply the dead with strengthening nutriment after the performance of the previous funeral ceremonies has endowed them with ethereal bodies." Until the first Srāddha has been celebrated, the dead ancestor is believed to exist as a preta or restless, wandering ghost. Thereafter he attains a position as a Pitṛ or Divine Father. The Srāddha is supposed to be most efficacious when performed by a son or direct male descendant, hence Kuntī's anxiety.

of life. Soon he began to move with energy and spirit. On seeing this, the Bhārata ladies were all filled with joy.

After the revival of Parikṣit, the Pāṇḍavas and the Vṛṣṇis together entered the city of Hāstinapura. Then Yudhiṣṭhira said to Vyāsa, "O holy one, this treasure has been obtained through your favour. I desire to devote it to the performance of the great horse sacrifice."

Vyāsa replied, "I give you permission, O king. Perform the horse sacrifice according to rites with profuse gifts. The horse sacrifice is the purifier of all sins. When you have performed it you will surely be purged of every evil deed."

With the holy Vyāsa's permission Yudhiṣṭhira began to make the necessary preparations for the horse sacrifice. In accordance with the scriptures, priests who were well versed in ritual performed every day all the rites necessary to complete the great sacrifice.

When King Yudhiṣṭhira had duly performed the sacrifice, the illustrious Vyāsa with his disciples showered eulogies on him. The king poured forth a veritable torrent of gifts of jewellery and every other desirable object. Purged of all his sins, and with the sacrifice completed, the king then reentered the city.

Āśramavāsika Parva

LXXXVIII

Having regained their kingdom, and killed all their enemies, the Pāṇḍavas ruled the earth. To the old king, Dhṛtaraṣṭra, upon whom Vidura, Sañjaya, and Yuyutsu used to wait, they showed every respect, consulting him in all matters. In this way fifteen years rolled by.

Then, one day, Dhṛtarāṣṭra said to Yudhiṣṭhira, "O son, I have acquired merit to the best of my ability. Though her sons have been killed, Gāndhārī has looked after me with great fortitude. You should now let me do what is for my own good and that of Gāndhārī. With your leave, we shall retire to the forest, clad in rags and bark." Reluctantly, Yudhiṣṭhira agreed to the old king's request.

Having settled the hour of his departure for the forest, Dhṛtarāṣṭra summoned the Pāṇḍavas at dawn one day. It was the day of the full moon in the month of Kārtika. The old king first had the minor rites performed by Brāhmaṇas, and then he caused the daily ritual fire to be taken up. Wearing deerskins and bark, and accompanied by his daughters-in-law, he then left the palace.

Kuntī walked first, leading Gāndhārī, who followed with bandaged eyes. King Dhṛtarāṣṭra walked confidently behind Gāndhārī, with his hand on her shoulder. At his departure, all the citizens of Hāstinapura were deeply distressed, as they had been at the departure of the Pāṇḍavas many years earlier, after their defeat in the game of dice. They followed the old king to the outskirts of the city.

When the citizens had stopped, King Dhṛtarāṣṭra requested Yudhiṣṭhira and the ladies of the royal household also to stop. Seeing that his mother Kuntī was desirous of retiring to the forest, Yudhiṣṭhira said to her, "Let me follow the old king. Please return to the city, with your daughters-in-law!" Though Yudhiṣṭhira, with his eyes bathed in tears, entreated her thus, Kuntī went on with Gāndhārī. She said, "I shall live in the forest with Gāndhārī, engaging in penance, and devoting myself to the service of these two venerable persons."

LXXXIX

Some time later, Yudhiṣṭhira, accompanied by his brothers, Draupadī, Subhadrā, Vidura, and the sage Vyāsa, visited the old king in the forest. Queen Gāndhārī, with bandaged eyes, joined her hands in supplication and saluted the holy Vyāsa. Deeply afflicted as she was with grief over the destruction of her sons, she pleaded, "O foremost of ascetics, this king has passed sixteen years without peace of mind, and grieving for the death of his sons. He spends all his time sighing heavily, and never sleeps at night. O holy one, I know that you have the capacity to create new worlds through the power of your penances. Can you not show the king his dead children?"

"This Kṛṣṇā," Gāndhārī continued, "the daughter of Drupada, has lost all her kinsmen and children. She is the dearest of my daughters-in-law, and she too grieves greatly. Subhadrā of sweet words, burning with grief for the loss of her son, is similarly affected. Alas, my hundred sons, who were all heroes and who never retreated in battle, have been killed on the battlefield. Their widows are all grieving, and adding to our sorrows. Through your grace, O holy one, liberate us all from our grief."

Vyāsa replied, "Blessings be on you, O Gāndhārī! You shall see all your sons and brothers and friends and kinsmen, like men risen from sleep, this very night. Kuntī shall see Karṇa, and Subhadrā too shall see her son Abhimanyu. Draupadī shall see her five sons, her father, and her brothers also. Today I shall dispel that sorrow which has long existed in all your hearts, because of your anxiety about the fate of those who have passed to the other world. Proceed tonight to the river Gaṅgā, and there you shall see all those who were killed on the field of battle."

That day passed slowly. To them who were waiting for the night to see the dead princes, it seemed as long as a whole year. When night came at last, they all finished their evening rites, and approached Vyāsa together. Dhṛtarāṣṭra, with purified body and concentrated mind, sat there with the Pāṇḍavas, while the royal ladies sat with Gāndhārī in a secluded spot.

Then the holy Vyāsa entered the sacred waters of the Gaṅgā, and summoned all the deceased warriors who had fought on the side of the Pāṇḍavas, as well as those who had fought for the Kauravas. Immediately there was a deafening uproar from within the waters and the kings, headed by Bhīṣma and Droṇa, with all their armies, arose in their thousands from the waters of the Gaṅgā.

There were Virāṭa and Drupada, with their sons and forces. There were the sons of Draupadī, and Abhimanyu and the rakṣasa Ghaṭotkaca. There were Karṇa, Duryodhana, Śakuni, and the other sons of Dhṛtarāṣṭra, headed by Duḥśāsana. There were also the son of Jarāsaṅdha, Bhagadatta, Jalasaṅdha, Bhūriśravas, Śāla, Śalya, Vṛṣasena with his younger brother, Prince Lakṣmaṇa, the son of Dhṛṣṭadyumna, and all the children of Śikhaṇḍī, and Dhṛṣṭaketu with his younger brother.

These and many others appeared, emerging from the waters of the Bhāgīrathī, with shining bodies. All of them were dressed in celestial vestments and wore brilliant earrings. They were free from all animosity and pride, anger and jealousy. Through the power of his penances, the great Vyāsa gave Dhṛtarāṣṭra celestial vision. The illustrious Gāndhārī too saw all her children as well as all the others who had been killed in battle. Seeing all those heroes with the celestial vision obtained by Vyāsa's grace, Dhṛtarāṣṭra was overjoyed.

Shorn of anger and jealousy, and purged of every sin, the heroes met with each other. All of them were happy of heart. Son met with father or mother, wife with husband, brother with brother, and friend with friend. Full of joy, the Pāṇḍavas greeted Karṇa as well as Abhimanyu, and the children of Draupadī.

At long last, the Pāṇḍavas were reconciled with Karṇa. All the other warriors, meeting by the grace of the great ascetic, also were reconciled with one another, renouncing enmity and becoming established in friendship. Thus they passed that night in great happiness.

When day dawned, they embraced each other and took their respective places. Thereupon Vyāsa, foremost of ascetics, dismissed them. Within the twinkling of an eye they disappeared in the very sight of all. Plunging into the sacred river Gaṅgā, they proceeded to their respective abodes. Some went to the regions of the gods, some to that of Brahmā, Varuṇa, Kubera, or Sūrya.

King Dhṛtarāṣṭra had never seen his own sons. Getting vision through Vyāsa's grace, he had now looked for the first time on those children of his who were so like himself. After beholding that wonderful spectacle, the reappearance of his children, the royal sage Dhṛtarāṣṭra renounced his grief and returned to his hermitage.

XC

When two more years had passed, the celestial sage Nārada happened to visit Yudhiṣṭhira, who said to him, "People living on the banks of the Gaṅgā report that the great Dhṛtarāṣṭra is practising the most austere of penances. Have you seen him there? Is he well? Are Gāṅdhārī and Kuṅtī and Sañjaya well? How, indeed, is my royal sire? O holy one, please tell me if you have seen the king."

Nārada replied, "Listen calmly to me, O king, as I tell you what I heard and saw in that hermitage. After your return from the visit to the forest, Dhṛtarāṣṭra proceeded from Kurukṣetra towards Gaṅgādvāra. He took with him his sacred fire, and was accompanied by Gāṅdhārī and Kuṅtī, as well as Sañjaya and all the yājakas. The king had no fixed dwelling. He wandered through those forests, while the two queens, and Sañjaya, followed him.

"One day," continued Nārada, "the king went to a spot on the bank of the Gaṅgā. He bathed in the sacred river and after finishing his ablutions prepared to return to his hermitage. The wind rose high. A fierce wild fire set in, which began to burn the forest all around. The king, who had taken no food, could move only slowly, as the forest fire raged thus, endangering all the creatures living there, nor could your two mothers, who were exceedingly emaciated, move.

"Seeing the fire surrounding him on all sides, the king said to Sañjaya, 'O Sañjaya, escape from the fire.' Sañjaya succeeded in doing so, but not the king or the two queens. Thus did the great Kuru meet with his death, along with Gāṅdhārī and Kuṅtī, your two mothers."

The Pāṇḍavas were overcome by grief on hearing of the departure of Dhṛtarāṣṭra from this world. King Yudhiṣṭhira wept in great agony thinking of his mother, and all his brothers did likewise. When the news spread to the royal ladies' quarters, a great wailing sound arose. All the people were grieved upon hearing that the old king, who had become childless, had been burnt to death and that the helpless Gāṅdhārī had shared his fate.

Mausāla Parva

XCI

Thirty-six years after the great battle at Kurukṣetra, Yudhiṣṭhira saw many unusual portents. One day the Vṛṣṇi heroes, including Balarāma, saw the sages Viśvāmitra, Kaṇva, and Nārada, who had arrived at Dvārakā. As fate would have it, they decided to play a prank on the holy men. Disguising Sāṁba as a woman, the heroes approached the ascetics and said, "This is the wife of the illustrious Vabhru who wishes to have a son. Do you know for certain whether she will bear a boy or a girl?"

The ascetics, who knew that this was an attempt to impose on them, said, "This kinsman of Kṛṣṇa, by name Sāṁba, will produce a dreadful iron bolt for the destruction of the Vṛṣṇis and the Aṅdhakas. You are wicked and cruel and intoxicated with pride. Through that iron bolt you will become the exterminators of your family, with the exception of Balarāma and Kṛṣṇa. The blessed Balarāma will enter the ocean, renouncing his body, while a hunter of the name of Jarā will strike the great Kṛṣṇa when he is lying on the ground." The holy men then departed.

Day by day strong winds blew, and many evil omens foretold the destruction of the Vṛṣṇis and the Aṅdhakas. Pondering these omens, Kṛṣṇa understood that the thirty-sixth year had come and that the curse of Gāṅdhārī, burning with grief because of the death of her sons, was about to work itself out.

He observed, "The present omens are exactly like the dreadful omens which appeared when the two armies were arrayed in battle order." He then asked the Vṛṣṇis to undertake a pilgrimage to some sacred water. Messengers proclaimed, at the command of Kṛṣṇa, that the Vṛṣṇis would go on a pilgrimage to the seacoast and bathe in the sacred waters of the ocean.

XCII

The Vṛṣṇis and the Aṅdhakas set out, with their whole families, on the pilgrimage, after preparing various kinds of viands and drinks for the journey, and proceeded first to Prabhāsa, where they took up their residence, each in the place assigned to him. Those heroes then began to indulge in an orgy of drinking. The entire field echoed with the blare of hundreds of trumpets, while actors and dancers amused the revellers. In the very sight of Kṛṣṇa, Balarāma began to drink, along with Kṛtavarmā, Sātyaki, Gada, and Vabhru.

Then Sātyaki, who was inebriated with wine, derisively laughed at Kṛtavarmā and insulted him in the midst of that assembly. He said, "What Kṣatriya is there who, himself armed, will kill unarmed men locked in the embrace of sleep? The Yādavas will never tolerate what you have done." When Sātyaki said these words, Pradyumna, foremost of car-warriors, applauded, showing his contempt for Kṛtavarmā.

Greatly enraged at this, Kṛtavarmā contemptuously pointed to Sātyaki with his left hand, and said, "Professing yourself to be a hero, how could you be so cruel as to kill the armless Bhūriśravas as he sat in Prāya on the field of battle?" Rising up in anger, Sātyaki said, "I swear that I shall soon cause this Kṛtavarmā to follow the five sons of Draupadī and Dhṛṣṭdyumna and Śikhaṇḍī, who, with the help of Aśvatthāmā, were killed while they were asleep. Kṛtavarmā's span of life and fame has come to an end." Saying this, Sātyaki rushed at Kṛtavarmā and cut off his head with a sword even as Kṛṣṇa looked on.

Thereupon, moved by the perversity of fate, the Bhojas and the Aṅdhakas as one man surrounded Sātyaki. Inebriated, they began to strike him with the pots out of which they had been eating. When

Sātyaki was being thus assailed, Rukmiṇī's son Pradyumna became greatly enraged. He rushed forward to rescue Sātyaki from the Bhojas and the Aṅdhakas. The two mighty heroes fought with great courage. But the odds were overwhelming, and both of them were killed before Kṛṣṇa's very eyes.

Seeing his own son and Sātyaki killed, Kṛṣṇa took up, in anger, a handful of the eraka grass which grew there, transforming it into a terrible bolt of iron infused with the energy of the thunderbolt, with which he destroyed all those who were before him. Thus was the curse of Gāṅdhārī, as well as that of the three holy sages, fulfilled.

XCIII

Then Dāruka, Kṛṣṇa, and Vabhru left that place, along with Balarāma. Balarāma retired to a solitary place, and sat thoughtfully, reclining against a tree. Going to the forest, Kṛṣṇa saw Balarāma rapt in yoga, while out of his mouth issued a powerful snake. Leaving the human body, that white snake, which had a thousand heads, a body as large as a mountain, and a red visage, proceeded towards the big ocean.

After his brother had thus left the human world, Kṛṣṇa, absorbed in thought, wandered for a while in the solitary forest. After some time he sat down on the bare earth. Having controlled all his senses, his speech, and his mind, he laid himself down in yoga.

A fierce hunter of the name of Jarā came, looking for game, mistook Kṛṣṇa, who was lying on the earth in yoga, for a deer, and struck him in the heel with an arrow and ran to capture his quarry. But he saw a man dressed in yellow robes and rapt in yoga. Considering himself an offender, and filled with fear, he touched Kṛṣṇa's feet. The high-souled Kṛṣṇa comforted him and then ascended upwards, filling the entire sky with splendour.

Dāruka went to the Pāṇḍavas and informed them of how the Vṛṣṇis had killed one another. After hearing this, Arjuna, dear friend of Kṛṣṇa, bade his brothers farewell, and started to see his uncle.[1] On the way he stopped to see the holy Vyāsa.

[1] Presumably Vasudeva, Kṛṣṇa's father and Kuṅtī's brother.

When Arjuna entered the hermitage of the truthful sage, he saw Vyāsa seated alone. Vyāsa asked, "Have you been defeated in battle? Why do you look like one shorn of prosperity? I am not aware that you have been defeated by any one. O Arjuna, if indeed you can confide in me, tell me everything, with no delay."

Arjuna said, "He whose complexion was like that of a cloud, and whose eyes were like a pair of large lotus petals, the lord Kṛṣṇa, has renounced his body and ascended to heaven, along with Balarāma. By his energy he scorched all the hostile troops whom I afterwards killed with arrows shot from Gāṇḍīva. Now that I see him no more, I am filled with grief and my head swims. Cheerless and in despair, I can find no peace of mind. O best of men, tell me what is good for me now, for I am a wanderer with an empty heart, with all my kinsmen killed and my prowess gone."

"The powerful car-warriors of the Vṛṣṇi and the Aṅdhaka race have all been consumed by the curse of the Brāhmaṇas," replied Vyāsa. "Therefore do not grieve over their destruction. What has taken place had been ordained. It was their destiny. Kṛṣṇa allowed it to take place although he could have counteracted the curse of even the great Brāhmaṇas, since he was able to alter the very course of the universe."

He continued, "That ancient sage, the four-armed Vāsudeva, used to sit in front of your car, armed with cakra and mace, through affection for you. Having lightened the burden of the earth and cast off his human body, he has returned to his own high station. O foremost of men, with the help of Bhīma and of the twins you too have done the great work of the gods. The time has come, however, for all of you to follow the principal path of virtue. I consider this would be highly beneficial for you all, O Bhārata!"

After Vyāsa had said these words, Arjuna took leave of him and returned to the city of Hāstinapura. He then went straight to Yudhiṣṭhira, whom he informed of the fate of the Vṛṣṇis and the Aṅdhakas.

Mahāprasthānika Parva

XCIV

After hearing the details of the destruction of the Vṛṣṇis, Yudhiṣṭhira decided to leave the world. He said to Arjuna, "Time cooks every creature in its cauldron and binds us all with its cords. You can see that what has taken place is due to Fate." Thus addressed, Arjuna repeated the word—"Fate, Fate"—endorsing the view of his eldest brother, the wise Yudhiṣṭhira.

Bhīma and the twins fully supported Arjuna's views. Yudhiṣṭhira, determined to retire from the world and acquire merit, made over the kingdom to his regent Yuyutsu. Installing Parikṣit on the throne and anointing him as king, Yudhiṣṭhira sadly said to Subhadrā, "This son of your son will be the king of the Kurus. The survivor of the Yadus, Vajra, has also been made a king. Parikṣit will rule in Hāstinapura, while the Yādava prince, Vajra, will rule in Iṅdraprastha. You should protect him."

Renouncing his ornaments, Yudhiṣṭhira wore the bark of trees. Bhīma and Arjuna and the twins and the illustrious Draupadī clad themselves likewise. Seeing the princes in that guise the royal ladies wept aloud. Having performed the preliminary religious rites, they consigned their sacred fire to the water.

The five brothers, with Draupadī forming the sixth, and a dog forming the seventh member of the party, then started on their journey from the city to Hāstinapura followed for some distance by the citizens and the royal ladies. Setting their minds on yoga, and resolved to observe the vow of renunciation, those great souls passed through various countries and crossed many rivers and seas.

Then they beheld in the northern direction the great Himālayan mountain. Crossing the Himālayan range, they saw a vast sea of sand. Next appeared the towering mountain Meru, highest of peaks. As they were proceeding quickly, rapt in yoga, Draupadī fell from yoga, and dropped on the earth. Seeing her fall, Bhīma said to Yudhiṣṭhira, "O king, this princess never did anything sinful. Why did she fall by the wayside?" Yudhiṣṭhira replied, "She was partial to Arjuna."

The wise Sahadeva now dropped down. Thereupon Bhīma said to the king, "This son of Mādrī used to serve us all with great humility. Why has he fallen?" Yudhiṣṭhira replied, "He thought nobody was his equal in wisdom. That sin is the reason for the prince's fall."

Seeing both Draupadī and Sahadeva fall, the brave Nakula, whose love for his brothers was very great, fell next. Upon the fall of the heroic and handsome Nakula, Bhīma once more spoke to the king. "This brother of ours was righteous and always obeyed our commands. He was also of peerless beauty. Why has he fallen?" Yudhiṣṭhira replied, "He thought that there was nobody who equalled him in personal beauty. It is for this vanity that Nakula has fallen."

Seeing Nakula and the others fall, Arjuna, the hero of white horses, destroyer of hostile heroes, fell down in great grief. When that foremost of men, Arjuna, who was gifted with the energy of Indra, fell, Bhīma said to the king, "I do not recollect a single untruth uttered by the great Arjuna. Indeed, not even in jest did he say anything false. What is the sin whose evil consequence has made him fall?" Yudhiṣṭhira replied, "Proud of his heroism, Arjuna had said that he would conquer all our enemies in a single day. This, however, he did not do. Hence he has fallen down."

Having answered thus, the king went on. Then Bhīma fell. As he was falling, Bhīma said to King Yudhiṣṭhira the just, "O king! I who am dear to you have fallen! Why have I dropped down? Tell me." "You were a gluttonous eater," said Yudhiṣṭhira, "and you ate without regard to the wants of others. You also used to boast of your strength. It is for that, O Bhīma, that you have fallen." Having spoken these words Yudhiṣṭhira went on, without looking back. He had only one companion left, the dog, which continued to follow him.

XCV

Causing heaven and earth to reverberate, Indra came to Yudhiṣṭhira on a chariot and asked him to ascend it. Seeing his brothers fallen on the earth, and burning with grief, Yudhiṣṭhira said to Indra, "My brothers have all fallen here! They must go with me. Without them I do not wish to go to the celestial region, O lord! The delicate princess Draupadī, deserving of every comfort, should also go with us! Please permit this."

"You will behold your brothers in the celestial region." Indra replied. "They have reached there before you. You will see them all there, along with Draupadī. Do not give way to grief, O chief of the Bhāratas! They renounced their human bodies before going there, O king! As for you, it has been ordained that you shall go there in this very body."

Yudhiṣṭhira said, "This dog, O lord, is highly devoted to me. He should go with me. My heart is full of compassion for him." "Today you have acquired immortality and a status equal to mine," replied Indra. "Prosperity and high success attend you, and all the felicities of heaven are open to you. Cast off this dog. There will be no cruelty in doing so."

"O lord of a thousand eyes!" answered Yudhiṣṭhira. "It is extremely difficult for one of virtuous conduct to commit an unrighteous act. I do not wish for prosperity if I have to abandon a creature who is devoted to me." Hearing these words of King Yudhiṣṭhira the just, the dog was transformed into Dharma, the god of Virtue. Well pleased with Yudhiṣṭhira, the deity praised him in a sweet voice. He said, "You are well born, O king of kings, and endued with the intelligence and good conduct of your fathers! You have mercy for all creatures. Just now, out of consideration for the dog which was devoted to you, you renounced the very car of the celestials. Hence, O king, there is no one in heaven to equal you."

Then Dharma, Indra, the maruts, the Aśvins, and other deities, as well as the celestial sages, made Yudhiṣṭhira ascend Indra's car, bound for heaven. Amidst that concourse of celestials, Nārada, foremost of all speakers, and conversant with all the worlds, said these words, "Yudhiṣṭhira has transcended the achievements of all the royal sages who are here. Covering the universe by his fame and splendour and by the nobility of his conduct, he has reached heaven in his own human body! No one else has been known to achieve this."

Hearing these words of Nārada, the righteous King Yudhiṣṭhira saluted the celestials and all the royal sages present, and said, "Happy or miserable, whatever be the region where my brothers are now, I wish to go there. I do not wish to stay anywhere else."

Iṅdra addressed Yudhiṣṭhira, "O king of kings, live in this place, which you have earned by your meritorious deeds. Why do you still cherish human affections?" Yudhiṣṭhira replied, "O conquerer of Daityas, I do not wish to live anywhere, separated from my brothers. I wish to go where they have gone, and where that foremost of women, Draupadī, has gone!"

Svarga-Ārohaṇika Parva

XCVI

Though he could not see Draupadī and his brothers anywhere in heaven, Yudhiṣṭhira saw Duryodhana radiant with prosperity and seated on an excellent seat. Thereupon he was suddenly overcome by anger and turned away from the sight. He said, "O you gods, I have no wish to see Duryodhana! I wish to go where my brothers are."

Nārada smilingly told him, "O king of kings! Meet Duryodhana politely now. This is heaven, O king! There can be no enmities here!" Despite Nārada's words, Yudhiṣṭhira persisted in asking about his brothers, saying, "If these eternal regions are reserved for heroes like Duryodhana, that unrighteous and sinful wretch, that man who was the destroyer of friends and of the whole world, that man for whose sake the entire earth was devastated, then I wish to see what regions have been attained by those great heroes, my brothers of high vows, performers of promises, truthful in speech, and distinguished for courage, and by the great Karṇa, by Dhṛṣṭadyumna, by Śātyaki, by the sons of Dhṛṣṭadyumna and those other Kṣatriyas who met with death in the observance of their duties. Where are those kings, O Nārada? I do not see them here, nor Virāṭa nor Drupada nor the other great Kṣatriyas headed by Dhṛṣṭaketu. I wish to see them all, as well as Śikhaṇḍī, the Pāñcāla prince, the sons of Draupadī, and Abhimanyu, who was irresistible in battle."

Addressing the celestials, Yudhiṣṭhira continued, "O foremost of gods! What is heaven to me if I am separated from my brothers? To me, heaven is where those brothers of mine are. This, in my opinion, is not heaven." "If you wish to go there, O son," replied the gods, "go forthwith. If the king of the celestials permits, we are ready to do what you like." Then they told their messenger, "Show Yudhiṣṭhira his friends and kinsmen."

The royal son of Kuntī and the celestial messenger went together to where the other Pāṇḍavas were. The heavenly messenger went first, followed by the king. The path was difficult, trodden by men of sinful deeds, and foetid with the stench of corpses. Along that inauspicious path the righteous king went, filled with various thoughts.

Seeing that foul region, Yudhiṣṭhira asked the celestial messenger, "How far must we go along a path like this?" When Yudhiṣṭhira the just spoke to him, the messenger of heaven stopped in his course and replied, "Thus far I have come with you. The dwellers of the celestial region ordered me to stop at this point. If you are tired, O king of kings, you may return with me!"

Yudhiṣṭhira was disconsolate and stupefied by the foul stench. Resolved to return, he retraced his steps. But as the righteous king turned back stricken with sorrow, he heard piteous cries all around: "O son of Dharma, O royal sage, O you of holy birth, O Pāṇḍava, stay a while as a favour to us! At your approach a delightful breeze has begun to blow, bearing the sweet smell of your body. We have been greatly refreshed by this. Remain here, O Bhārata, for some time! As long as you are here tortures cease to afflict us."

From all sides, the king heard these and many other piteous appeals, uttered by persons in distress. The voices of those woebegone and afflicted persons seemed to him to be familiar, although he could not place them. Unable to recognize the voices, Yudhiṣṭhira inquired, "Who are you? Why do you stay here?" In reply, they answered him from all sides, saying, "I am Karṇa!" "I am Bhīma!" "I am Arjuna!" "I am Nakula!" "I am Sahadeva!" "I am Dhṛṣṭadyumna!" "I am Draupadī!" "We are the sons of Draupadī!"

Hearing those painful cries, the royal Yudhiṣṭhira asked himself, "What perverse destiny is this? What are the sins which were committed by those great beings, Karṇa and the sons of Draupadī and the slender-waisted princess of Pāñcāla, that they have been compelled to live in this region of foul smell and great distress? I am not aware of any sin that can be attributed to these persons. By what act of merit has Dhṛtarāṣṭra's son, King Duryodhana, with all his wicked followers, acquired such prosperity?"

Musing thus, Yudhiṣṭhira was filled with righteous indignation, and censured the celestials as well as Dharma himself. Though almost overcome by the foul smell, he told the celestial messenger, "Go back to those whose messenger you are. Tell them that I shall not return to them, but shall stay here since my companionship has brought comfort to these suffering brothers of mine."

XCVII

King Yudhiṣṭhira had not waited for more than a moment when all the celestials, headed by Iṅdra, appeared. The God of Righteousness, in his embodied form, also came to see Yudhiṣṭhira.

Upon the arrival of those celestials of radiant bodies and noble deeds, the darkness that had enveloped that region immediately disappeared. The tortures afflicting those of sinful deeds were no longer to be seen. The river Vaitaraṇī, the thorny Śalmali, the iron jars, and the terrible boulders of rock also vanished from sight, as did the repulsive corpses which the Kuru king had seen. Then, because of the presence of the celestials, a gentle breeze, bringing with it a pleasant and fragrant odour, pure and delightfully cool, began to blow on that spot.

Iṅdra, the lord of the celestials, consoled Yudhiṣṭhira, saying, "O mighty Yudhiṣṭhira! Join the ranks of the celestials who are pleased with you. These illusions have ended. Hell, O son, should be seen by all kings. There is some good and bad in all things. You once deceived Droṇa concerning his son, and have therefore been shown hell by an act of deception. Like yourself, Bhīma, Arjuna, and Draupadī have reached hell by an act of deception. Your brothers and the other kings who fought on your side have all attained to their respective places. Let the fever of your heart be dispelled! Here is the celestial river, sacred and sanctifying the three worlds. It is called the celestial Gaṅgā. Plunging into it, you will attain your proper place."

Then Dharma the god of virtue said, "O king, your brothers were not such as to deserve hell. All this has been an illusion created by the king of the celestials. O son, all kings must see hell at least once. Hence you have for a little while been subjected to this great sorrow. Neither Arjuna, nor Bhīma, nor the twins, nor Karṇa, ever truthful in speech and endued with great courage, could be deserving of hell for a long time. Nor could the princess Draupadī be deserving of that place of sinners. Come, come, O Bhārata, and see Gaṅgā, who flows over the three worlds."

The royal sage then proceeded with Dharma and all the other celestials. Having bathed in the celestial river Gaṅgā, sacred and purifying, he renounced his human body. Assuming a celestial form, Yudhiṣṭhira the just, through that bath, became divested of all his enmities and his grief. Surrounded by the celestials, he then went away from there, accompanied by Dharma, as the great sages praised him. Finally he reached the place where those heroes, the Pāṇḍavas and the Dhārtarāṣṭras, freed from human wrath, were enjoying each his respective position.

XCVIII

Thus honoured by the celestials, the maruts, and the sages, Yudhiṣṭhira joined his kinsmen. He saw Kṛṣṇa in his Brahmā-form, being worshipped by the heroic and radiant Arjuna. In another place, he saw Karṇa, foremost of warriors, resembling a dozen suns in splendour. Elsewhere he saw the mighty Bhīma sitting in the midst of the maruts.

In the place belonging to the Aśvins, Yudhiṣṭhira saw Nakula and Sahadeva blazing with splendour. He also saw Draupadī, the princess of Pāñcāla, decked in garlands of lotuses. Having reached the celestial region, she was sitting there, radiant as the Sun. King Yudhiṣṭhira suddenly wished to question her. The illustrious Indra, king of the celestials, anticipating this, said, "This one is the goddess of prosperity herself. It was for your sake that she took human form, without being born of any mother, O Yudhiṣṭhira! For your pleasure she was created by the wielder of the trident. She was born in the race of

Drupada and was the wife of you all. These five blessed Gandharvas, bright like fire, are the sons of Draupadī and yourselves."

"Look at Dhṛtarāṣṭra, the king of the Gandharvas, who was the eldest brother of your father," continued Indra. 'This one, Karṇa, is the son of Kuntī and of the Sun-god. He is your eldest brother, though he was known as the son of Rādhā. Look at the son of Subhadrā, invincible in battle, now staying with the Moon-god. He is the powerful bowman Abhimanyu, now shining with the gentle effulgence of the Moon. Here is the mighty archer Pāṇḍu, now united with Kuntī and Mādrī. Look at the royal Bhīṣma, the son of Śantanu, now in the midst of the Vasus.[1] Know this one by the side of Bṛhaspati to be your preceptor Droṇa."

Indra concluded by saying, "These and other kings, O son of Pāṇḍu, who fought on your behalf, now walk with the Gandharvas or yakṣas or other superhuman beings. Some have attained to the dignity of guhyakas, O king. Having renounced their bodies, they have conquered the celestial region by the merit they acquired through word, thought, and deed."

XCIX

Hearing this history from Vaiśampāyana in the intervals of the sacrificial rites, King Janamejaya was filled with wonder. The sacrificial priests then completed the remaining rites. Having rescued the snakes from a fiery death, Āstīka was filled with joy. King Janamejaya pleased, with profuse gifts, all the Brāhmaṇas, who, thus honoured by the king, returned to their respective abodes. After the learned Brāhmaṇas had left, King Janamejaya returned from Takṣaśila to Hāstinapura.

Sauti[2] said to the sages assembled in the forest of Naimiśa, "I have now recounted everything that Vaiśampāyana narrated, at the command of Vyāsa, to King Janamejaya at his snake sacrifice. This great

[1] The Vasus, whose number is usually eight, were originally personifications of natural phenomena—Āpa (water), Dhruva (the Pole-Star), Soma (the moon), Dhava or Dhara, Anila (the wind), Anala (fire), Pratyuṣa (the dawn), and Prabhāsa (light). Bhīṣma, as explained on p. 7, above, was one of the eight Vasus.

[2] He is called Sūta in the Poona edition.

history, which is sacred and excellent, was composed by the sage Vyāsa of truthful speech, whose desire was to spread the fame of the great Pāṇḍavas and that of the other Kṣatriyas throughout the world. As the sacred ocean and the snow-clad mountain are both regarded as mines of precious gems, so is this *Mahābhārata*."

Genealogical Tables

I. The Line of Śaṅtanu

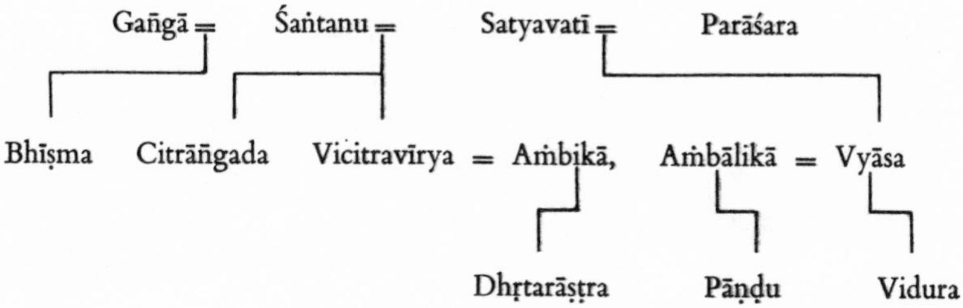

II. The Kauravas

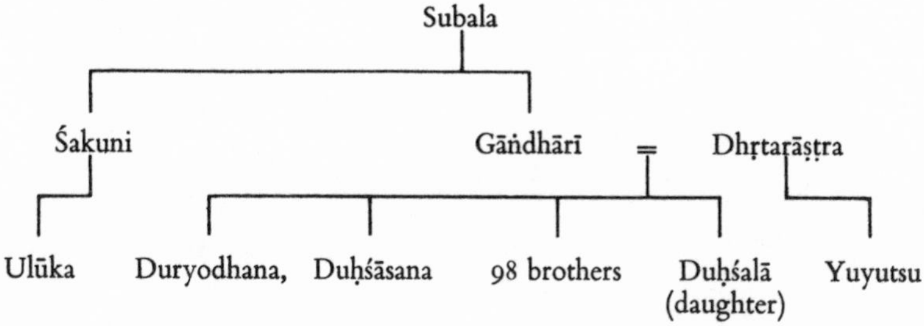

III. The Pāṇḍavas

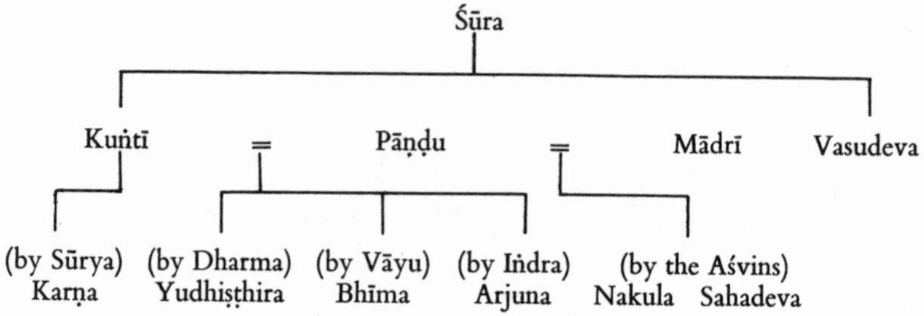

IV. The Line of Drupada

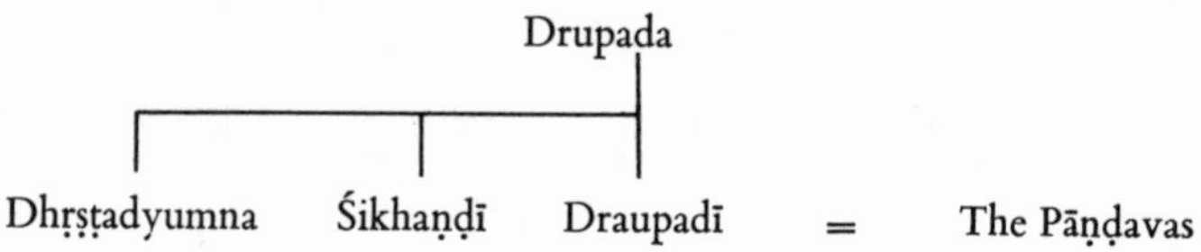

V. The Ancestry of Janamejaya

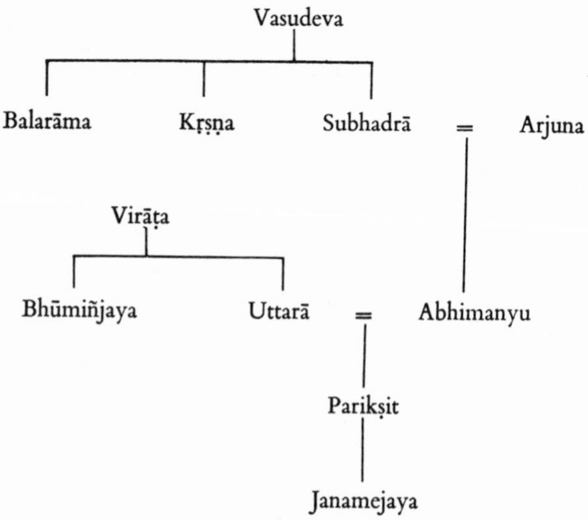

Glossary

A

Abhimanyu	Son of Arjuna and Subhadrā.
Acyuta	Another name for Kṛṣṇa.
Adhiratha	A charioteer, who brought up Karṇa.
Ādhirathi	Another name for Karṇa.
Ādi Parva	The book of the beginning, the first book of the epic.
Āditya	Another name for Sūrya.
Āgneya	Fiery, born of fire, a missile.
Agni	The fire-god, deity of a missile (see also Astra).
Airāvata	A mythical serpent.
Ajātaśatru	Another name for Yudhiṣṭhira.
Akṛtavarṇa	Name of a sage.
Akṣauhiṇi	Division of an army.
Alolupa	A son of Dhṛtarāṣṭra.
Amarāvatī	Capital city of Indra.
Aṁbā	The first of three daughters of the king of Kāśī.
Aṁbālikā	The third of three daughters of the king of Kāśī.
Aṁbikā	The second of three daughters of the king of Kāśī.
Anādhṛṣṭi	An ally of the Pāṇḍavas.
Ānarta	Name of a kingdom.
Aṅdhaka	A clan, closely allied to the Vṛṣṇis; also the name of a demon who was killed by Śiva.
Aṅga	The kingdom which Duryodhana bestowed on Karṇa.
Aṅgiras	Name of a sage.
Anuśāsana Parva	The book of precepts, the thirteenth book of the epic.
Apsaras	The celestial nymphs.
Āraṇyaka Parva	The book of the forest, the third book of the epic.
Ariṣṭanemi	Name assumed by Sahadeva in Virāṭa Parva.
Arjuna	The third of the Pāṇḍavas, born of Kuṅtī by Iṅdra.
Arka	Another name for Sūrya.

Āśramavāsika Parva	The book of residence in a hermitage, the fifteenth book of the epic.
Asta	The western mountain behind which the sun sets.
Āstīka	Name of a sage.
Astra	A missile, requiring the invocation of a deity before discharge.
Asura	A demon, traditionally the enemy of the celestials.
Aśvamedha	The horse sacrifice.
Aśvamedha Parva	The book of the horse sacrifice, the fourteenth book of the epic.
Aśvasena	The serpent which Karṇa discharged as a missile against Arjuna.
Aśvatthāmā	Son of Droṇa and Kṛpī.
Aśvin	The twin physicians of heaven.
Atharva	The fourth of the four Vedas.
Atiratha	A champion among car warriors.
Avaṅti	Name of a city and of its inhabitants.
Avasthāna	A manoeuvre in single combat.

B

Bāhlika	An ally of Duryodhana.
Balarāma (Baladeva)	Elder brother of Kṛṣṇa.
Ballava	Name assumed by Bhīma in Virāta-parva.
Bhadrā	Sister of Kṛṣṇa, also known as Subhadrā.
Bhagadatta	An ally of Duryodhana.
Bhagavān	Another name for Kṛṣṇa.
Bhāgīrathī	The river Gaṅgā.
Bhānu	Another name for Sūrya.
Bharadvāja	Name of a sage, father of Droṇa.
Bharata	The common ancestor of the Kauravas and Pāṇḍavas.
Bhārata	Literally, descendant of Bharata, commonly applied to both Kauravas and Pāṇḍavas.
Bhārgava	Another name for Paraśurāma.
Bhāskara	Another name for Sūrya.
Bhava	Another name for Śiva.
Bhīma	Son of Dhṛtarāṣṭra.
Bhīmabāhu	Son of Dhṛtarāṣṭra.
Bhīmaratha	Son of Dhṛtarāṣṭra.
Bhīma(sena)	The second of the Pāṇḍavas, born of Kuṅtī by Vāyu.
Bhīṣma	The son of Śaṅtanu and Gaṅgā.
Bhīṣma Parva	The book of Bhīṣma, the sixth book of the epic.

Bhoja	Name of a king.
Bhūmiñjaya	The son of Virāṭa, also called Uttara.
Bhūriśravas	Son of Somadatta, and an ally of Duryodhana.
Bībhatsu	Another name for Arjuna.
Brahmā	The Creator, an aspect of the Hindu triad.
Brāhmaṇa	The priestly caste.
Brahmarākṣasa	A demon, supposedly the ghost of a Brāhmaṇa who had led an evil life.
Brahmaśiras	Name of a missile.
Bṛhadaśva	Name of a sage.
Bṛhadbala	An ally of Duryodhana.
Bṛhannaḍā	Name assumed by Arjuna in Virāṭa Parva.
Bṛhaspati	The preceptor of the celestials.

C

Cakra	A sharp, circular missile of Kṛṣṇa.
Cedi	A kingdom.
Cekitāna	An ally of the Pāṇḍavas.
Citrāñgada	Elder son of Satyavatī; also the name of a Gaṅdharva king.
Citrasena	King of the Gaṅdharvas, and a friend of Arjuna.

D

Daitya	Literally, born of Diti, an asura.
Dakṣiṇā	A fee or gift.
Dāmagraṅthi	Name assumed by Nakula in Virāṭa Parva.
Dānava	Literally, born of Danu, an asura.
Dāruka	The charioteer of Kṛṣṇa.
Dāśārha	The clan to which Kṛṣṇa belonged.
Daśārṇa	Name of a clan, of which Hiraṇyavarma was king.
Deva	A celestial.
Devadatta	The conch of Arjuna.
Devakī	Mother of Kṛṣṇa.
Devakīputra (Devakīsuta)	Son of Devakī; another name for Kṛṣṇa.
Devala	Name of a sage.
Devarāja	Another name for Iṅdra.
Devasthāna	Name of a sage.
Devavrata	Bhīṣma's name at birth.
Dhanada	Another name for Kubera.
Dhanañjaya	Another name for Arjuna, literally, winner of wealth; also the name of a Brāhmana sect.

Dhaneśvara	Another name for Kubera.
Dharma	The god of virtue; also usage, right, justice, virtue, morality.
Dharmaputra (Dharmarāja)	Another name for Yudhiṣṭhira.
Dhārtarāṣṭra	Any of the sons of Dhṛtarāṣṭra.
Dhātā	Deity of a missile (see also Astra).
Dhaumya	Name of a sage.
Dhṛṣṭadyumna	Son of Drupada.
Dhṛṣṭaketu	An ally of the Pāṇḍavas.
Dhṛtācī	Name of a celestial nymph.
Dhṛtarāṣṭra	Son of Ambikā; father of the Kauravas.
Divākara	Another name for Sūrya.
Drauṇi	Son of Droṇa; another name for Aśvatthāmā.
Draupadī	Daughter of Drupada; wife of the Pāṇḍavas.
Droṇa	The preceptor of the Kauravas and Pāṇḍavas.
Droṇa Parva	The book of Droṇa, the seventh book of the epic.
Drupada	The king of Pāñcāla, son of Pṛṣata.
Duḥsaha	Son of Dhṛtarāṣṭra.
Duḥśalā	Daughter of Dhṛtarāṣṭra.
Duḥśāsana	Son of Dhṛtarāṣṭra.
Durdhara	Son of Dhṛtarāṣṭra.
Durmada	Son of Dhṛtarāṣṭra
Durmarṣaṇa	Son of Dhṛtarāṣṭra.
Durmukha	Son of Dhṛtarāṣṭra.
Durvāsa	Name of a sage who was notoriously irritable and short-tempered.
Duryodhana	Eldest son of Dhṛtarāṣṭra.
Duṣpradharṣa	Son of Dhṛtarāṣṭra.
Dvaipāyana	Literally, the island-born, another name for Vyāsa.
Dvaipāyana	The lake in which Duryodhana took refuge.
Dvaitavana	A forest where the Pāṇḍavas encamped during their exile.
Dvārakā	The capital city of Kṛṣṇa.

E

Ekacakra	Name of a town.
Eraka	A species of grass.

G

Gada	One of the Vṛṣṇi princes.
Gājasahvayanagara (Gājasahvayapura)	Literally, the city of the elephant; another name for Hāstinapura.

Gaṅdhamādana	Name of a mountain.
Gāṅdhāra	Name of a kingdom.
Gāṅdhārī	Daughter of Subala; wife of Dhṛtarāṣṭra.
Gaṅdharva	Celestial musician.
Gāṅdharvaveda	The science of music.
Gāṇḍīva	The bow of Arjuna.
Gaṅgā	Name of a river, who in human form became the wife of Saṅtanu and the mother of Bhīṣma.
Gaṅgādatta	Literally, given by Gaṅgā; Bhīṣma.
Gaṅgādvāra	Name of a place.
Gāṅgeya	Literally, born of Gaṅgā; Bhīṣma.
Garuḍa	The Indian eagle, supposed to be Viṣṇu's vehicle.
Gauramukha	A disciple of Śamīka.
Gautamī	Another name for Kṛpī.
Gāvalgaṇi	Son of Gavalgaṇa; Sañjaya.
Ghaṭotkaca	A demon, son of Bhīma and Hiḍimbā.
Ghī	Clarified and melted butter.
Gomati	Name of a river.
Gopa	Literally, a cowherd; a soldier in Kṛṣṇa's army.
Gopāla	Name assumed by Sahadeva in Virāṭa Parva.
Goviṅda	Another name for Kṛṣṇā.
Graṅthika	Name assumed by Nakula in Virāṭa Parva.
Gudākeśa	Another name for Arjuna.
Guhyaka	A class of demigods.

H

Halāyudha	Another name for Balarāma.
Hārdikya	Another name for Kṛtavarma, son of Hṛdīka.
Hari	Another name for Kṛṣṇa.
Hāstinapura	Literally, the city of the elephant; the capital of Dhṛtarāṣṭra.
Hiḍiṁba	A man-eating demon.
Hiḍiṁbā	Sister of Hiḍiṁba, who married Bhīma and bore Ghaṭotkaca.
Himālaya	The snowy mountains of the north.
Hiraṇvatī	Name of a river.
Hiraṇyavarma	A king, who gave his daughter in marriage to Śikhaṇḍi.
Hotravāhana	Grandfather of Ambā.
Hṛdīka	Father of Kṛtavarma.
Hṛsikeśa	Another name for Kṛṣṇa.

I

Iṅdra	King of the celestials.
Iṅdrakīla	Name of a mountain.
Iṅdraprastha	Name given to their capital city by the Pāṇḍavas (see also Khāṇḍavaprastha).
Iṅdrasena	Name of a servant of the Pāṇḍavas.
Īsvara	Another name for Śiva.

J

Jahnu	Name of a sage.
Jāhnavi	Daughter of Jahnu; another name for Gaṅgā.
Jalasaṅdha	Son of Dhṛtarāṣṭra.
Jāmadagni	Another name for Paraśurāma.
Janamejaya	A descendant of the Pāṇḍavas, son of Parikṣit.
Janārdhana	Another name for Kṛṣṇa.
Jara	The name of a hunter.
Jarāsaṅdha	The tyrannical king of Magadha.
Jaya	Son of Dhṛtarāṣṭra.
Jayadratha	Son-in-law of Dhṛtarāṣṭra, king of the Siṅdhus; and an ally of Duryodhana.
Jiṣṇu	Another name for Arjuna.

K

Kaikeyī	Daughter of Kekaya; another name for Sudeṣṇā.
Kaliṅga	Name of a kingdom.
Kāmapāla	Another name for Balarāma.
Kāṁboja	Name of a kingdom.
Kamsa	Brother of Devakī.
Kāmyaka	Name of a forest, where the Pāṇḍavas encamped during their exile.
Kānīna	An illegitimate issue.
Kaṅka	Name assumed by Yudhiṣṭhira in Virāṭa Parva.
Kaṇva	Name of a sage.
Karṇa	Eldest son of Kuṅtī, by Sūrya.
Karṇa Parva	The book of Karṇa, the eighth book of the epic.
Karṇikāra	A species of tree, an emblem on Abhimanyu's flag.
Kārtavīrya	Name of a hero who opposed, and was killed by, Paraśurāma.
Kārtika	Name of a month.
Kārtikeya	Another name for Skaṅda.
Kāśī	Name of a city.

Kauṅteya	Literally, son of Kuṅtī; another name for Yudhiṣṭhira.
Kaurava	Literally, descendant of Kuru, generically applied to the sons of both Dhṛtarāṣṭra and Pāṇḍu, specifically to the former.
Kausalyā	Another name for Aṁbikā.
Kekaya	Father of Sudeṣṇā.
Keśava	Another name for Kṛṣṇa.
Keśiniṣūdhana	Another name for Kṛṣṇa.
Khāṇḍavaprastha	The name of the city bestowed by Dhṛtarāṣṭra on the Pāṇḍavas, which they rebuilt and renamed Iṅdraprastha.
Kīcaka	Virāṭa's commander in chief, brother of Sudeṣṇā.
Kiṅdama	Name of a sage.
Kirāta	A hunter; a member of a mountain tribe living by hunting.
Kirīṭi	Another name for Arjuna.
Krauñcāruṇa	A battle array named after the bird called krauñca or curlew.
Kṛpa	Son of Śaradvata; brother-in-law of Droṇa.
Kṛpī	Daughter of Śaradvata; wife of Droṇa.
Kṛśa	Friend of Śṛṅgī.
Kṛṣṇa	Son of Vasudeva and Devakī, steadfast ally of the Pāṇḍavas, and one of the ten incarnations of Viṣṇu; also, another name for Arjuna.
Kṛṣṇā	Literally, dark, another name for Draupadī.
Kṛṣṇa Dvaipāyana	Another name for Vyāsa.
Kṛtavarma	An ally of Duryodhana.
Kṣatta	Another name for Vidura.
Kṣatriya	The kingly or warrior caste.
Kubera	The god of wealth.
Kuṇiṅda	Name of a clan.
Kuṅtī	Mother of Karṇa, Yudhiṣṭhira, Bhīma, and Arjuna.
Kuṅtibhoja	Adopted father of Kuṅtī.
Kuru	The forefather of the Kauravas and the Pāṇḍavas; also used as a generic term for his descendants
Kurukṣetra	The battlefield where the eighteen-day battle between the Kauravas and Pāṇḍavas was fought.

L

Lakṣmaṇa	Son of Duhśāsana.
Lakṣmī	The goddess of wealth; consort of Viṣṇu.

Lokapāla	One of the guardian deities of the four cardinal and the four intermediate points of the world: Iṅdra (East), Agni (Southeast), Yama (South), Sūrya (Southwest), Varuṇa (West), Vāyu (Northwest), Kubera (North), and Soma (Northeast).
Lomaśa	Name of a sage.

M

Madra	Name of a kingdom.
Madrarāja	Another name for Śalya, king of Madra.
Mādrī	Princess of Madra, who married Pāṇḍu; mother of Nakula and Sahadeva; sister of Śalya.
Mādhava	Another name for Kṛṣṇa.
Madhusūdhana	Another name for Kṛṣṇa.
Magadha	Name of a kingdom.
Maghavān	Another name for Iṅdra.
Mahābhiṣa	Another name for Śantanu.
Mahādeva	Another name for Siva.
Mahāprasthānika Parva	The book of the great or final journey, the seventeenth book of the epic.
Mahāratha	Great car-warrior; champion.
Maheṅdra	Another name for Iṅdra.
Makara	A fabulous aquatic monster; also the name of a battle array.
Mālava	Name of a kingdom and of its inhabitants.
Mālinī	Name assumed by Draupadī in Virāta Parva.
Maṇḍala	A circular array.
Maṅtra	An incantation, charm, or spell.
Marut	The storm-gods.
Mātali	Charioteer of Iṅdra.
Matsya	Literally, fish; the kingdom of Virāṭa.
Mausāla Parva	The book of the club fight, the sixteenth book of the epic.
Maya	The chief architect of the Dānavas.
Māyā	Illusion; spell; wizardry.
Meru	Name of a mountain.
Mleccha	Generic term for foreigner or barbarian.
Mūka	An asura.

N

Nāga	A species of serpent-demon.

Nāgasāhvayanagara (Nāgasāhvayapura)	Literally, the city of the elephant; another name for Hāstinapura.
Naimiśa	Name of a forest.
Nakula	The fourth of the Pāṇḍavas, born of Mādrī by the Aśvins.
Nala	Name of a king.
Naṅdana	Literally, delighter; descendant or scion.
Nara	Literally, man; Arjuna.
Nārada	Name of a sage.
Nārāyaṇa	Another name for Viṣṇu; Kṛṣṇa. In the plural, the warriors of Kṛṣṇa's army.
Niṣāda	The tribe of hunters.
Niṣka	A gold coin or ornament.
Nivātakavaca	A class of Dānavas or Daityas.

P

Pākaśāsana	Another name for Iṅdra.
Pākaśāsani	Another name for Arjuna.
Pāñcajanya	The conch of Kṛṣṇa.
Pāñcāla	The kingdom of Drupada.
Pāñcālī	Another name for Draupadī.
Pāṇḍavas	The sons of Paṇḍu.
Pāṇḍu	Son of Ambālikā; father of the Pāṇḍavas.
Parameṣṭhi	Deity of a missile (see also Astra).
Parāśara	Name of a sage; father of Vyāsa.
Paraśurāma	Name of a sage, who was also a warrior and exterminator of the Kṣatriyas.
Parikṣit	Son of Abhimanyu and Uttarā; father of Janamejaya.
Pārikṣita	Another name for Janamejaya.
Parjanya	Name of a missile.
Pārṣata	Another name for Drupada.
Pārtha	Literally, son of Pṛthā or Kuṅtī; usually applied to Arjuna.
Parva	A book; a section of the epic.
Pāśupata	Literally, of Paśupati; name of a missile.
Paśupati	Another name for Śiva.
Paulomī	Daughter of Puloma; wife of Iṅdra.
Paurava	Descendant of Puru.
Phalguna	Name of a month; also a name for Arjuna.
Piśāca	An evil spirit; a ghost.
Prabhāsa	Name of a holy place.

Prabhadraka	Name of a clan which fought for the Pāṇḍavas.
Pradyumna	Son of Kṛṣṇa by Rukmiṇī.
Prajāpati	Deity of a missile (see also Astra).
Prajña	Name of a missile capable of reviving unconscious people; antidote to the Pramohana missile.
Pramohana	Name of a missile causing unconsciousness.
Prāṇāyāma	A breath exercise; one of the processes of yoga.
Prasvapa	Name of a weapon.
Prātikāmī	Duryodhana's servant.
Pratīpa	Father of Śaṅtanu.
Pratismṛti	Literally, recollection; name of a particular kind of magic.
Prativiṅdhya	Son of Yudhiṣṭhira and Draupadī.
Prāya	Fasting unto death; renunciation of life.
Pṛṣata	Father of Drupada.
Pṛthā	Another name for Kuṅtī.
Puraṅdara	Another name for Iṅdra.
Purocana	A counsellor of Duryodhana.
Puru	Name of a king of the lunar race.
Puṣkara	A place of pilgrimage.

R

Rādhā	Adhiratha's wife, who brought up Karṇa.
Rādheya	Another name for Karṇa.
Raivataka	A hill near Dvāraka.
Rājasūya	A great sacrifice performed at the coronation of a king.
Rākṣasa	A male demon.
Rākṣasī	A female demon.
Rāma	A shorter form of Paraśurāma, and also of Balarāma.
Rauhiṇeya	Son of Rohiṇī; another name for Balarāma.
Rohiṇī	Name of a star; also the name of Balarāma's mother.
Ṛṣi	A sage; a hermit.
Rudra	Another name for Śiva.
Rukmiṇī	Wife of Kṛṣṇa; mother of Pradyumna.

S

Sabhā Parva	The book of the assembly, the second book of the epic.
Sahadeva	The fifth of the Pāṇḍavas, born of Mādrī by the Aśvins.
Sahasrākṣa (Sahasranetra)	Literally, endowed with a thousand eyes; another name for Iṅdra.
Sahoḍha	An illegitimate issue.

Sairaṅdhrī	A maid servant in the women's apartments.
Śakaṭavyūha	A battle array in the shape of a waggon.
Śakra	Another name for Iṅdra
Śakrapura	Another name for Iṅdraprastha.
Śakti	Literally, power;. name of a missile.
Śakuni	Son of Subala; brother of Gāndhārī.
Śāla	A species of tree.
Śalmali	A species of tree.
Śālva	Name of a king, with whom Ambā was in love.
Śalya	King of Madra; brother of Mādrī.
Śalya Parva	The book of Śalya, the ninth book of the epic.
Sāma	Son of Dhṛtarāṣṭra.
Sāmaveda	The third of the four Vedas.
Samaṅga	Name of a shepherd.
Samaṅtapañcaka	Name of a holy place near Kurukṣetra.
Sāṁba	A kinsman of Kṛṣṇa.
Śaṁbara	Name of a demon killed by Iṅdra.
Śamī	A species of tree.
Śamīka	Name of a sage, whom Parīkṣit treated with disrespect.
Samśaptaka	Band of soldiers, who had sworn to kill Arjuna.
Sañjaya	Dhṛtarāṣṭra's companion and counsellor; son of Gavalgana.
Śaṅkara	Another name for Śiva.
Saṅkarṣaṇa	Another name for Balarāma.
Śānti Parva	The book of tranquillity, the twelfth book of the epic.
Śāṅtanava	Son of Śantanu; Bhīṣma.
Śaṅtanu	Father of Bhīṣma.
Śaradvata	Father of Kṛpa and Kṛpī.
Śāradvata	Another name for Kṛpa.
Śāradvatī	Another name for Kṛpī.
Sāraṇa	Another name for Balarāma.
Sarasvatī	Name of a river.
Sarvatobhadra	A battle array in the form of a square.
Śatakratu	Another name for Iṅdra.
Śatānīka	Son of Nakula and Draupadī.
Śatānīka	Brother of Virāṭa.
Śataśṛṅga	Name of a mountain.
Sātvata	Name of a clan.
Satyabhāmā	Wife of Kṛṣṇa.
Sātyaki	A kinsman of Kṛṣṇa, and one of the principal allies of the Pāṇḍavas.

Satyavatī	Wife of Śantanu; mother of Citrāṅgada, Vicitravīrya, and Vyāsa.
Satyavatīsuta	Son of Satyavatī; another name for Vyāsa.
Saubala	Another name for Śakuni.
Saubha	Name of a town, Śālva's capital.
Sauptika Parva	The book of nocturnal combat, the tenth book of the epic.
Śauri	Another name for Kṛṣṇa.
Sauti	Name of a sage; also called Sūta.
Savitā	Deity of a missile (see also Astra); also another name for Sūrya.
Sāvitra	Another name for Karṇa.
Savyasacī	Literally, capable of drawing a bow with the left hand, ambidextrous; another name for Arjuna.
Senāpati	Son of Dhṛtarāṣṭra.
Śibi	Name of a king renowned for his liberality and unselfishness.
Siddha	A semidivine being of great purity and perfection.
Śikhaṇḍī (Śikhaṇḍinī)	Amba reborn as the daughter of Drupada. She obtained manhood temporarily from Sthūṇakarṇa.
Simhasena	An ally of the Pāṇḍavas.
Siṅdhu	Name of a kingdom, and of its people.
Śini	Father of Sātyaki.
Sitāśva	Another name for Arjuna.
Śiva	The destroyer, an aspect of the Hindu triad.
Śiva	Name of the palace at Varāṇāvata.
Skaṅda	Son of Śiva and Umā.
Soma	The Moon-god, deity of a missile (see also Astra).
Somadatta	Father of Bhūriśravas; an ally of Duryodhana.
Somaka	Name of a clan who fought on the side of the Pāṇḍavas.
Śṛṅgāṭaka	Name of a battle array.
Śṛṅgī	Son of Śamīka.
Sṛñjaya	Name of a clan who fought on the side of the Pāṇḍavas.
Śrutakarmā	Son of Arjuna and Draupadī.
Śrutakīrti	Son of Arjuna.
Śrutasena	Son of Sahadeva and Draupadī.
Śrutāyus	An ally of Duryodhana.
Sthūṇakarṇa	Name of a yakṣa, who temporarily bestowed his manhood on Śikhaṇḍinī.

Strī Parva	The book of women, the eleventh book of the epic.
Subāhu	King of the Kuṇiṅdas.
Subala	Father of Śakuni and Gāṅdhārī.
Subhadrā	Sister of Kṛṣṇa; wife of Arjuna; mother of Abhimanyu.
Sudakṣiṇa	King of Kāṁboja; an ally of Duryodhana.
Sudeṣṇā	Queen of Virāta.
Śūlapāṅi	Another name for Śiva.
Sulocana	Son of Dhṛtarāṣṭra.
Śūra	Father of Vasudeva and Kuṅtī.
Sūrya	The Sun-god
Susāma	Name of a priest.
Suśarmā	King of the Trigarta clan.
Suṣeṇa	Son of Dhṛtarāṣṭra.
Sūta	Another name for Sauti.
Sūta	Charioteer.
Sūtaja	Another name for Karṇa.
Sutasoma	Son of Bhīma and Draupadī.
Suyodhana	Another name for Duryodhana.
Svarga-Ārohaṇika Parva	The book of the ascent to heaven, the eighteenth book of the epic.
Svayaṁvara	Literally, self-choice; the choice of a spouse by a princess at an assembly where all the suitors are present.
Śvetavāhana	Another name for Arjuna.
Śyenavyūha	A battle array in the form of a hawk.

T

Takṣaka	A serpent; a Nāga.
Takṣaśilā	Name of a city.
Taṅtripāla	Name assumed by Sahadeva in Virāta Parva.
Tapana	Another name for Surya.
Tīrtha	Any place of pilgrimage on the banks of sacred waters.
Trigarta	Name of a clan.
Tvaṣṭā	Deity of a missile (see also Astra); another name for Surya.

U

Udyoga Parva	The book of endeavour; the fifth book of the epic.
Ugra	Son of Dhṛtarāṣṭra.
Ulūka	Son of Śakuni.
Umā	Consort of Śiva.

Umāpati	Another name for Śiva.
Upaniṣad	Sacred books containing the exposition of the Vedas.
Upaplavya	The Pāṇḍava camp close to Kurukṣetra.
Upayaja	Name of a sage.
Upeṅdra	Younger brother of Iṅdra.
Utaṅka	Name of a sage.
Uttamaujas	Son of Drupada.
Uttara	Son of Virāta; also called Bhūmiṅjaya.
Uttarā	Daughter of Virāṭa; wife of Abhimanyu and mother of Parikṣit.
Urvaśī	A celestial nymph.

V

Vabhru	One of the Vṛṣṇis.
Vaiḍūrya	A gem, the cat's-eye.
Vaikartana	Another name for Karṇa.
Vaiśampāyana	Name of a sage.
Vaiśravaṇa	Another name for Kubera.
Vaiśya	The third of the four castes, usually engaged in trade.
Vaitaraṇī	Name of a river in hell.
Vaiyāghrapadya	A Brāhmaṇa clan.
Vajra	Name of the Yādava prince who survived the club fight described in Mausāla Parva.
Vajra	The thunderbolt of Iṅdra.
Vajravyūha	A battle array, probably in the form of a column or pillar.
Vālī	Name of a Daitya.
Vāraṇāsāhvayanagara (Vāraṇāsāhvayapura)	Literally, the city of the elephant; another name for Hāstinapura.
Vārāṇasī	Another name for Kāśī.
Vāraṇāvata	Name of a city.
Vārṣṇeya	Another name for Kṛṣṇa.
Varuṇa	The ocean god; also the deity of a missile (see also Astra).
Vāsava	Another name for Iṅdra.
Vasiṣṭha	Name of a sage.
Vasu	A particular class of gods, whose number is usually eight.
Vasudeva	Father of Kṛṣṇa, Balarāma, and Subhadrā.
Vāsudeva	Another name for Kṛṣṇa.
Vāsuki	A serpent, a Nāga.

Vasuṣeṇa	Another name for Karṇa.
Vāyu	The Wind-god.
Vāyuputra	Son of Vayu; another name for Bhīma.
Veda	Literally, knowledge; name of four celebrated works which constitute the basis of the Hindu religion.
Vedāñga	Literally, a limb of the Veda; name of six works regarded as auxiliary to the Veda.
Vibhāvasu	Another name for Surya.
Vicitravīrya	Younger son of Śaṅtanu and Satyavati.
Vidura	Son of Vyāsa and half brother of Dhṛtarāṣṭra and Pāṇḍu.
Vijaya	Name of Karṇa's bow; also, another name for Arjuna.
Vikarṇa	Son of Dhṛtarāṣṭra.
Vikartana	Another name for Surya.
Vikaṭa	Son of Dhṛtarāṣṭra.
Virāta	King of the Matsyas, in whose court the Pāṇḍavas spent the thirteenth year of their exile.
Virocana	Another name for Surya.
Virāṭa Parva	The book of Virāṭa; the fourth book of the epic.
Viṣṇu	The preserver, an aspect of the Hindu triad.
Viśvakarmā	The celestial architect who designed Karṇa's bow.
Viśvāmitra	Name of a sage.
Viśvāvasu	A gaṅdharva; father of Citrasena.
Vivimśati	An ally of Duryodhana.
Vivitsu	Son of Dhṛtarāṣṭra.
Vṛddhakṣatra	Father of Jayadratha.
Vṛkodara	Another name for Bhīma.
Vṛṣasena	An ally of Duryodhana.
Vṛṣni	The clan to which Kṛṣṇa belonged.
Vṛṣṇipravīra	Another name for Kṛṣṇa.
Vṛtra	A demon who was slain by Iṅdra.
Vyāghradatta	An ally of the Pāṇḍavas.
Vyāsa	Name of the sage who was the son of Satyavatī and the sage Parāśara; the progenitor of Dhṛtarāṣṭra, Pāndu, and Vidura.
Vyūha	A military array.

Y

Yādava (Yadu)	Two names for Kṛṣṇa's clan.
Yadukulanaṅdana	Another name for Kṛṣṇa.

Yaja	Name of a sage.
Yājaka	One who offers sacrifices.
Yajñasena	Another name for Drupada.
Yājñaseni	Another name for Draupadī.
Yakṣa	A class of semidivine beings, subservient to Kubera.
Yama	The god of Death.
Yamunā	A river, tributary of the Gaṅgā.
Yoga	Self-concentration; abstract meditation.
Yudhāmanyu	An ally of the Pāṇḍavas.
Yudhiṣṭhira	The eldest of the Pāṇḍavas, born of Kuṅtī by Dharma.
Yuga	An age or eon.
Yuvarāja	Literally, young prince; heir apparent.
Yuyudhāna	Another name for Sātyaki.
Yuyutsu	Younger son of Dhṛtarāṣṭra by a Vaiśya wife.

List of Alternative Names

While the Glossary contains only those names which are used in the translation, many of the principal figures (and even places) are referred to by a variety of other names in the original Sanskrit text. A complete list is given below.

Arjuna, also referred to as:
- Bībhatsu
- Dhanañjaya
- Gudākeśa
- Jiṣṇu
- Kirīṭī
- Kṛṣṇa
- Nara
- Pākaśāsani
- Pārtha
- Phalguna
- Savyasācī
- Sitāśva
- Śvetavāhana
- Vijaya

Aśvatthāmā, also referred to as:
- Drauṇi

Balarāma, also referred to as:
- Baladeva
- Halāyudha
- Kāmapāla
- Rauhiṇeya
- Sañkarṣana
- Sāraṇa

Bhīma, also referred to as:
- Vāyuputra
- Vṛkodara

Bhīṣma, also referred to as:
- Devavrata
- Gaṅgādatta
- Gāṅgeya
- Śāntanava

Draupadī, also referred to as:
- Kṛṣṇā
- Pāñcālī
- Yājñasenī

Droṇa, also referred to as:
- Bhāradvāja

Drupada, also referred to as:
- Pārṣata
- Yajñasena

Duryodhana, also referred to as:
- Gāndhārī
- Suyodhana

Gaṅgā, also referred to as:
- Bhāgīrathī
- Jāhnavī
- Jahnusutā

Iṅdra, also referred to as:
- Devarāja
- Maghavān
- Maheṅdra
- Pākaśāsana
- Puraṅdara
- Sahasrākṣa
- Sahasranetra
- Śakra
- Śatakratu
- Vajrī
- Vāsava

Iṅdraprastha, also referred to as:
- Śakrapura

Janamejaya, also referred to as:
- Pārikṣita

Karṇa, also referred to as:
- Ādhirathi
- Rādheya
- Sāvitra
- Sūtaja
- Vaikartana
- Vasuṣeṇa

Kṛpa, also referred to as:
- Śāradvata

Kṛpī, also referred to as:
- Gautamī
- Śāradvatī

Kṛṣṇa, also referred to as:
- Acyuta
- Bhagavān
- Devakīputra
- Devakīsuta
- Goviṅda
- Hari
- Hṛṣīkeśa
- Janārdana
- Keśava

Krsna (cont.)
- Keśiniṣūdhana
- Mādhava
- Madhusūdana
- Nārāyaṇa
- Śauri
- Vārṣṇeya
- Vāsudeva
- Vṛṣṇipravīra
- Yadukulanandana

Kubera, also referred to as:
- Dhanada
- Dhaneśvara
- Vaiśravaṇa

Paraśurama, also referred to as:
- Bhārgava
- Jāmadagni

Śakuni, also referred to as:
- Saubala

Śalya, also referred to as:
- Madrarāja

Śiva, also referred to as:
- Bhava
- Iśvara
- Paśupati
- Rudra
- Śaṅkara
- Śūlapāṇi
- Umāpati

Sūrya, also referred to as:
- Āditya
- Arka
- Bhānu
- Bhāskara
- Divākara
- Savitā
- Tapana

Sūrya (cont.)
- Tvaṣṭā
- Vibhāvasu
- Vikartana
- Virocana

Uttara, also referred to as:
- Bhūmiñjaya

Vidura, also referred to as:
- Kṣattā

Vyāsa, also referred to as:
- Kṛṣṇadvaipāyana
- Satyavatīsuta

Yudhiṣṭhira, also referred to as:
- Ajātaśatru
- Dharmaputra
- Dharmarāja
- Kauṅteya

Index of Verses on Which English Version Is Based

ĀDI PARVA

POONA EDITION

Chapter	*Book*	*Chapter*	*Verses*
I	1	36	8–23
	1	37	1, 12–21
	1	38	11–30
	1	39	21–32
	1	40	5–7
II	1	45	3–5
	1	46	34–36
	1	47	1, 17–20
	1	51	16–23
	1	53	9–10
	1	54	1–8, 17–24
III	1	92	1, 17–55
	1	93	43–44
	1	94	19–20
IV	1	94	21–94
V	1	95	1–12
	1	96	1–25, 38–58
VI	1	97	1–2, 8–13, 25
	1	98	3–4
	1	99	2–49
	1	100	4–27
VII	1	102	15–20
	1	103	9–16
	1	107	7–34

Chapter	*Book*	*Chapter*	*Verses*
XVI	1	179	1, 14–20
	1	180	1, 11–13
	1	181	5, 32, 36–40
	1	182	1–2
XVII	1	183	2, 6–9
	1	186	1–3, 13
	1	187	1–2, 9–12, 21–28, 32
	1	188	4
	1	189	41–49
	1	190	3, 6, 13, 18
XVIII	1	192	16–17, 21, 25, 29
	1	193	4
	1	194	1, 11, 24–25
	1	195	1–4
	1	196	2
	1	197	23
	1	198	1, 4, 7
	1	199	10–11, 23–27, 36
	1	200	6
XIX	1	210	1–5, 15–21
	1	211	1, 13–23
	1	212	6–9, 25–31
	1	213	2, 6–7, 11–13, 58–73, 82

SABHĀ PARVA

POONA EDITION

Chapter	*Book*	*Chapter*	*Verses*
XX	2	1	5, 10–12, 19
	2	3	19–20, 27–28, 34
	2	5	1–2
	2	11	62, 68–73
	2	12	5, 25, 31–37
	2	13	60–61
	2	18	2, 7, 20
	2	19	25–27

Chapter	Book	Chapter	Verses
XX	2	20	24–28
	2	21	2–3, 17–18
	2	22	6, 29–30, 41–45
	2	23	3, 7–10
	2	30	23–26, 34, 53–54
	2	32	15
	2	42	34, 59–60
XXI	2	43	1–12, 18–21
	2	44	1, 12–21
	2	45	4–6, 23, 35–47
	2	51	20–26
	2	52	1, 5–9, 14–17, 37
XXII	2	53	1, 13–16, 22–25
	2	54	1–3
	2	58	1, 7–31, 37–43
	2	59	1–2
	2	60	1–7, 18
XXIII	2	60	19–24, 28, 33–39
	2	61	2–4, 40–48
	2	62	4, 7, 11
	2	63	9, 12–14, 27–36
	2	65	1–2, 16–17
XXIV	2	66	4, 11, 17–24
	2	67	2–4, 8–21
	2	68	1, 23–29
	2	69	5–6
	2	70	1–7, 21–23

ĀRAṆYAKA PARVA

POONA EDITION

Chapter	Book	Chapter	Verses
XXV	3	3	2–4, 9–14
	3	4	1–3, 10
	3	13	1–6
	3	23	42, 46–50

Chapter	Book	Chapter	Verses
XXV	3	37	20, 26–30
	3	38	12–16
XXVI	3	38	29–38, 43–44
	3	40	2–30, 49–52
	3	41	13, 25
	3	43	38
	3	44	19–20
	3	45	4
	3	78	14–17
	3	89	1, 4–6, 10–18
	3	90	1–3, 9, 14, 17
XXVII	3	93	1–6
	3	141	26–30
	3	161	13, 16–28
	3	171	11, 16
	3	172	17–22
XXVIII	3	226	2, 11, 18
	3	227	2–3, 18–20
	3	228	1–7, 21–22, 29
	3	229	16, 19–20, 29
	3	230	1–12, 26–27
	3	231	1–2, 6–11
	3	232	15–17
	3	233	2, 9–16
	3	234	1–2, 7–9, 20–21, 25–28
	3	235	1–4, 11–22
XXIX	3	284	5–6, 13–15, 20, 25–27, 31, 35
	3	286	10, 14
	3	294	1–4, 14–15, 21–36
	3	299	1, 28–29

VIRĀTA PARVA

POONA EDITION

Chapter	Book	Chapter	Verses
XXX	4	1	4–5, 13–14, 19–22
	4	2	1, 7, 21, 24–26
	4	3	2–3, 6–7, 13–18

Chapter	Book	Chapter	Verses
XXXIV	4	66	1–11, 15–16, 21, 28–29
	4	67	1–5, 9–12, 15, 19

UDYOGA PARVA

POONA EDITION

Chapter	Book	Chapter	Verses
XXXV	5	1	1–6, 10–11, 23–24
	5	2	3, 4
	5	3	21–23
	5	4	1–7
	5	5	1–2, 8–9, 13–18
	5	6	18
XXXVI	5	7	2–35
XXXVII	5	8	1, 5–7, 10–15, 24–27, 32
	5	18	25
XXXVIII	5	20	1–4, 14, 21
	5	21	3, 8, 13, 18–20
	5	22	35–39
	5	23	1, 6
	5	24	1
	5	25	4
	5	26	1, 27–28
	5	27	20–24
	5	28	10
	5	29	1–2, 16, 29–31, 35, 40–41, 43
	5	30	1–3, 46–47
	5	31	23
	5	32	1, 9–10, 16, 30
XXXIX	5	46	2–3
	5	47	1–3, 6–8
	5	48	1, 19–20, 26–28
	5	50	57–59
	5	53	1, 19
	5	54	1
	5	56	37–38, 43
	5	57	6, 9–12, 15–20, 27

Chapter	*Book*	*Chapter*	*Verses*
XLVI	5	170	1–3
	5	172	1–10, 16–17
	5	173	1, 7–10
	5	174	1, 14, 17, 20–22
	5	175	10, 13
	5	176	16, 21–23, 41–42
	5	177	23–24
	5	178	1–2, 5–7, 11–14
	5	185	2, 15–18, 22–23
	5	186	1, 7–8
	5	187	1–4, 6–9
XLVII	5	187	18
	5	188	7–13
	5	189	2–5, 8–15
	5	190	1–2, 8–10, 14, 19
	5	192	17–20, 23–26, 29
	5	193	1–2, 5–7, 30, 34, 36, 41, 44, 46, 60, 64, 66

BHĪṢMA PARVA

POONA EDITION

Chapter	*Book*	*Chapter*	*Verses*
XLVIII	6	1	26, 29–32
	6	2	1–9
	6	4	5–9
	6	5	1
	6	16	11–13, 24, 39, 44–45
	6	20	3–5
XLIX	6	23	20–31, 37, 47
	6	24	1–4, 9–11, 19, 22, 30–32, 37–38, 47
	6	25	3, 8, 19, 30
	6	33	1, 32–34
	6	40	1–2, 7, 9, 43, 61–62, 73
L	6	41	6–8, 32, 34, 36, 38, 89–91, 95
	6	43	1–2, 77–78

Chapter	*Book*	*Chapter*	*Verses*
L	6	45	1–3, 60–63
LI	6	46	39–40
	6	47	10–11
	6	51	33–38, 43
	6	52	1–3, 10
	6	55	3–4, 21–25, 32, 40–41, 51–53, 59, 63, 86–87, 93–101, 110–111
LII	6	56	1
	6	58	29
	6	59	16–18
	6	60	24–28, 32–33, 37, 45–46, 48–49, 65–71
	6	61	24–33
	6	64	12–18
LIII	6	65	1, 4, 7
	6	66	1
	6	70	1, 7–8, 11–12, 18, 23–29, 34–36
	6	71	1, 4–5, 14
	6	73	8, 16, 32, 35, 42, 47, 49
	6	75	59
LIV	6	77	11–12, 21
	6	82	23–24, 41–42
	6	83	1, 5, 15–17
	6	84	1–4
	6	87	9–12
	6	89	1
	6	90	39–40, 46
	6	93	1–2, 7–10, 33–39
	6	94	1, 6–14, 18–19
LV	6	95	26, 34
	6	99	1–2, 4, 7
	6	102	9–10, 72–74
	6	103	1–2, 10, 44–45, 53–59, 70–71, 75–80, 83
LVI	6	104	2–3
	6	105	9–10
	6	106	1–3
	6	112	78–80

Chapter	Book	Chapter	Verses
LVI	6	114	1, 23–37, 43, 46–49, 54–55, 61, 73, 80–82, 109, 112
LVII	6	115	8, 24–27, 30–36, 41–44, 47–49
	6	116	10–12, 14, 17–25, 37–39, 47–48
LVIII	6	117	4–5, 9–13, 19–22, 27–34

DROṆA PARVA

POONA EDITION

Chapter	Book	Chapter	Verses
LIX	7	1	23, 30
	7	2	8
	7	5	5, 7, 12, 14, 16, 36
	7	11	5–6
	7	15	37–39, 44–50
	7	32	1–2, 12–15
	7	33	12, 15–20
LX	7	34	11–14, 18–21
	7	35	12–15, 40
	7	39	25–28
	7	41	5–6, 18
	7	46	4
	7	47	34, 37
	7	48	9–14
LXI	7	49	1–2
	7	50	1–4, 17–22, 61–65
	7	51	1–12, 20–21, 37
	7	53	1–3, 25–33
	7	54	9–11
LXII	7	56	7
	7	64	9–10, 29, 32
	7	65	3–5, 12, 31–32
	7	66	1, 35–36
	7	67	1–2
	7	68	31–32, 52–54
	7	72	1–3
	7	81	2

Chapter	Book	Chapter	Verses
LXII	7	85	2–3, 35–39, 44–47
	7	87	53, 66–67
	7	103	9–11, 22–30
LXIII	7	104	9–11, 29–30
	7	110	28–31, 35–36
	7	116	1–2
	7	117	1, 21, 46–55, 61–62
	7	118	3–4, 16–18, 31–36
LXIV	7	120	2–3
	7	121	9–11, 15–40
	7	129	5, 12–13, 34–35
LXV	7	131	24–26, 29–30, 33
	7	133	2, 5, 12–14, 46–47
	7	137	5–6, 31–33
	7	148	31–35, 53–60
	7	150	20, 22, 30
	7	154	51–58
	7	155	1–2, 11–14, 27–28
LXVI	7	159	2–3
	7	161	28–37
	7	164	58, 66–73, 97–99, 103–114, 127
	7	165	27–29, 32–38, 51–53, 67–68

KARṆA PARVA

POONA EDITION

Chapter	Book	Chapter	Verses
LXVII	8	2	1, 6–7, 9–10, 13
	8	6	36
	8	7	14–15, 27
	8	21	34–37
	8	22	30, 34, 36, 46–51
	8	23	1–6, 21–22, 29, 41–42, 48–54
LXVIII	8	29	3–6, 31–37
	8	42	2–5
	8	60	29–30
	8	61	1–7, 10–11, 15–17

Chapter	Book	Chapter	Verses
LXIX	8	66	1–12, 20–24, 42–43, 60, 64–65
	8	67	1–6, 16, 19–21, 24–27, 35–36

ŚALYA PARVA

P. C. ROY EDITION

Chapter	Chapter	Verses
LXX	6	19–26
	16	1, 9, 14, 21, 28
	17	38, 46, 49, 55
	28	1–2, 16, 27–30, 32, 56–58, 63–64
LXXI	29	1, 6–11, 14, 16–18, 25, 33–34, 49, 52, 63–64
	30	3–7, 35–36, 42–43, 45, 51–52
LXXII	31	2–3, 6, 15–17, 38, 42, 46, 50, 54, 61, 65
	32	10–13, 25–28, 47
	33	1, 4, 6, 11, 14, 17–22, 27
	34	1–4
LXXIII	57	1–2, 6–7
	58	1–4, 7–8, 19–21, 42–47
	59	3–5
	60	3–5, 24–25, 30–34
LXXIV	61	26–28, 30–37, 51–64, 66–68
LXXV	65	1–5, 22–23, 28, 32–42
LXXVI	63	32–39, 42–43, 45, 48–50, 50, 52, 54, 58–59, 62–76

SAUPTIKA PARVA

P. C. ROY EDITION

Chapter	Chapter	Verses
LXXVII	1	26, 29–32, 34, 36, 39, 43–47, 51–56
LXXVIII	8	10, 12, 14, 16, 33–34, 39, 45, 49, 51–62, 102, 105, 127
	9	1, 46–56

Chapter	Chapter	Verses
LXXIX	10	1, 7
	11	4–6, 13–15, 20–22, 31
	13	6–7, 11–22
LXXX	14	1–6, 11–13
	15	1, 10–11, 19–20, 25–27, 31–35
	16	1–4, 8–10, 20–22, 26–27, 34–35

STRĪ PARVA

P. C. ROY EDITION

Chapter	Chapter	Verses
LXXXI	1	4–5, 8, 10, 14, 18, 20
	12	2–4, 11–17, 21–23
LXXXII	14	1–3, 7, 16, 19–21
	15	1–3, 13–21
LXXXIII	15	24–41
	25	39–44

ŚĀṄTI PARVA

POONA EDITION

Chapter	Book	Chapter	Verses
LXXXIV	12	1	1–4
	12	27	1–3, 22, 27, 32
	12	34	2, 36
	12	39	1, 14
	12	40	1–4, 12–15, 22
	12	41	1–2, 4, 7–14

ANUŚĀSANA PARVA

P. C. ROY EDITION

AŚVAMEDHA PARVA

P. C. ROY EDITION

ĀŚRAMAVĀSIKA PARVA

P. C. ROY EDITION

MAUSĀLA PARVA

P. C. ROY EDITION

Chapter	Chapter	Verses
XCI	1	1, 15–21, 25
	2	4, 20–24
XCII	3	7–10, 15–21, 25–28, 30–36
XCIII	4	1, 12–13, 17, 21–24
	5	1–3
	8	1, 6–7, 21–30, 36–38

MAHĀPRASTHĀNIKA PARVA

P. C. ROY EDITION

Chapter	Chapter	Verses
XCIV	1	2–9, 19–25, 30
	2	2–26
XCV	3	1–9, 17–18, 21–37

SVARGA-ĀROHAṆIKA PARVA

P. C. ROY EDITION

Chapter	Chapter	Verses
XCVI	1	4, 6, 10–11, 18–26
	2	12–16, 22, 26–45, 50–52
XCVII	3	1–6, 9–10, 12, 15–16, 21, 28, 36–44
XCVIII	4	1–23
XCIX	5	30–35, 38, 62